ON INFORMATION TECHNOLOGY

Video education courses are available on these topics through
National Education Training Group, 1751 West Diehl Road,
Naperville, IL 60563-9099 (tel: 800-526-0452 or 708-369-3000).

Database	Telecommunications	Networks and Data Communications	Society
AN END USER'S GUIDE TO DATABASE	TELECOMMUNICATIONS AND THE COMPUTER (third edition)	PRINCIPLES OF DATA COMMUNICATION	THE COMPUTERIZED SOCIETY
PRINCIPLES OF DATABASE MANAGEMENT (second edition)	COMMUNICATIONS SATELLITE SYSTEMS	TELEPROCESSING NETWORK ORGANIZATION	TELEMATIC SOCIETY: A CHALLENGE FOR TOMORROW
COMPUTER DATABASE ORGANIZATION (third edition)	**Distributed Processing**	SYSTEMS ANALYSIS FOR DATA TRANSMISSION	TECHNOLOGY'S CRUCIBLE
MANAGING THE DATABASE ENVIRONMENT (second edition)	COMPUTER NETWORKS AND DISTRIBUTED PROCESSING	DATA COMMUNICATION TECHNOLOGY	VIEWDATA AND THE INFORMATION SOCIETY
DATABASE ANALYSIS AND DESIGN	DESIGN AND STRATEGY FOR DISTRIBUTED DATA PROCESSING	DATA COMMUNICATION DESIGN TECHNIQUES	**SAA: Systems Application Architecture**
VSAM: ACCESS METHOD SERVICES AND PROGRAMMING TECHNIQUES	**Client/Server**	SNA: IBM's NETWORKING SOLUTION	SAA: COMMON USER ACCESS
DB2: CONCEPTS, DESIGN, AND PROGRAMMING	CLIENT/SERVER DATABASES	LOCAL AREA NETWORKS: ARCHITECTURES AND IMPLEMENTATIONS (second edition)	SAA: COMMON COMMUNICATIONS SUPPORT: DISTRIBUTED APPLICATIONS
IDMS/R: CONCEPTS, DESIGN, AND PROGRAMMING	ENTERPRISE NETWORKING	DATA COMMUNICATION STANDARDS	SAA: COMMON COMMUNICATIONS SUPPORT: NETWORK INFRASTRUCTURE
Security		COMPUTER NETWORKS AND DISTRIBUTED PROCESSING: SOFTWARE, TECHNIQUES, AND ARCHITECTURE	SAA: COMMON PROGRAMMING INTERFACE
SECURITY, ACCURACY, AND PRIVACY IN COMPUTER SYSTEMS		TCP/IP NETWORKING: ARCHITECTURE, ADMINISTRATION, AND PROGRAMMING	

CLIENT/SERVER DATABASES

A *[signature: James Martin]* **BOOK**

Contents

Preface *xiii*

WHO SHOULD READ THIS BOOK

This book is intended for a broad range of readers, including the following:

- Information systems and data administration managers and technical staff members in professional information systems organizations who maintain and administer distributed databases and who need a thorough understanding of client/server database technology.
- Information systems and database administration technical staff members who select, install, and support client/server database hardware and software products and who deal with the complexities of a multivendor distributed database environment.
- Executives and technical staff members in user departments that employ database management systems and who desire an understanding of the technology behind the client/server database tools that are used in their work environments.
- End users who will be developing their own database applications or will be helping professionals determine their requirements.
- Students who are studying database technology.

PLAN OF THE BOOK

The chapters of this book are divided into six parts. Part I presents the fundamentals of modern database technology. The chapters in Part I describe the environment in which database software operates, describe different views of data that are important in the database environment, and discuss the data modeling that must be done correctly to derive the most benefits from database software.

Part II describes the general capabilities of modern database software. The chapters in Part II discuss the evolution of database technology, describe the functions that database software provides for accessing and manipulating data, and examine the capabilities that database software has for enhancing the integrity of an organization's data.

Part III examines the distributed, client/server environment in which many of today's database applications run. The chapters in Part III examine the wide variety of application configurations that can be created when processing can be spread across multiple computers, show how database software can be used in the client/server environment, and examine the major architectural models that permit databases to be distributed among multiple computing systems in a network.

Part IV concentrates on the relational data model on which all major client/server database software systems are based. The chapters in Part IV introduce the characteristics of the relational data model, examine the various types of relational operations that can be performed on relational data, describe the two integrity constraints—entity integrity and referential integrity—that are defined by the relational data model, and describe the data normalization process that is used during logical database design to produce stable data structures.

Part V introduces the capabilities of the Structured Query Language (SQL) that is used by almost all client/server database software for accessing the data stored in relational databases.

In Part VI, three appendices examine the characteristics of the Query by Example language on which many modern relational database end user query facilities are based, list Codd's twelve "relational rules" that can be used in evaluating the capabilities of client/server relational database software, and introduce the technology behind object-oriented database software currently representing the leading edge of database technology. A glossary concludes the book.

James Martin
Joe Leben

THE DATABASE ENVIRONMENT

It eventually became clear that it would be desirable to isolate application programs not only from changes in file hardware but also from additions to the data elements stored in the file's records. Database software attempts to insulate end users and application developers from changes that need to be made to the stored data.

Appropriate database software makes it possible to add new data elements to records without requiring rewriting application programs that access those records. Database software typically relates to the data at the level of individual data elements rather than at the level of entire records. One programmer's logical description of the data stored in a database may contain data elements different from another programmer's description of data obtained from the same database.

Database technology allows many different logical files to be derived from the same stored data. Database technology also allows the same data to be accessed in different ways by applications with different requirements. This often leads to a need for complex data structures. Good database software, however, protects users and application developers from the complexities of the data structure. Regardless of how the database is organized in the computer, users and application developers should be able to view the data they need in a simple structure that meets the needs of a particular application.

As database software has evolved, functions have been added that go far beyond the simple data management functions performed by file-oriented data management software. Much of today's database software provides sophisticated facilities for allowing end users to formulate queries directly without requiring conventional application programming. Many database software packages also include report generators and fourth-generation languages that allow database applications to be built quickly and easily. Most database software also allows programs to be created using conventional programming languages, like C and Visual Basic, and provides an easy-to-use interface to those languages. Many database software packages also include functions related to recovery, reliability, and data integrity, such as two-phase commit protocols for transaction management and data distribution and replication facilities.

DATABASE ADVANTAGES

There are many advantages to maintaining in a database all of the data used by an individual, or for an organization as a whole, so it can be shared by a number of application programs. We have alluded to some of these in the preceding section. These issues have been discussed at length elsewhere (see James Martin's other general database books listed in the front matter of this book), and it is not our intent to examine these advantages at length.

In general, we can place the advantages of the database approach to data management into two broad categories:

- Enhancing data integrity
- Improving application development productivity

The following sections briefly describe each of these major categories of database advantages.

ENHANCING DATA INTEGRITY

Effective use of database software can enhance the integrity of the data stored in database form in a number of ways. These include:

- Reducing data redundancy
- Increasing data independence
- Enhancing security
- Handling recovery and restart operations
- Providing for concurrent data access

The following sections discuss each of these objectives.

Reducing Data Redundancy

As we have already discussed, in the traditional file environment, application programmers design their own data files and establish their own record formats. This makes their programs dependent on the format of those records, and it tends to create a high degree of data redundancy. Through effective use of database techniques, this redundancy can be better controlled. Ideally, each piece of information is stored only once in the central pool, and all end users and application programs that require the information gain access to it via the database software. Data redundancy often leads to problems with the *consistency* of data, since it is difficult to ensure that the same changes are made to all the copies of a particular piece of data. By controlling redundancy, it is much easier for the installation to ensure that multiple copies of the same data element do not have different values, at least not for very long.

Database software provides for the consistent storage and management of data. Data managed by database software can be accessed by a variety of applications without requiring multiple copies of the data to be maintained. Thus, the use of database software has the effect of reducing data redundancy. When a change is made to the database, all applications that use the shared database will access the changed data.

When discussing the minimization of data redundancy, it is important to note that the database software itself may use *replication* facilities to allow the organization to maintain multiple copies of certain data if that is required for performance or availability reasons. The database software has functions that cause the various replicas of a given data element to be brought into synchronization.

Increasing Data Independence

A major problem associated with file systems is that of *data dependence* in application programs. A particular file might be used by many application programs. Each program

Personnel roles in the database environment are specialized in the database environment. The data administrator is an individual who is responsible for the overall centralized control of the organization's data. The database administrator (DBA) is responsible for designing, controlling, and coordinating the data that is stored in databases and has overall control over the database software. The database designer is responsible for designing, controlling, and coordinating the data in an individual database and typically performs both logical database design and physical database implementation, Application developers are responsible for analyzing and documenting the needs of end users and then developing the application programs that will access the database. End users are those who access the database in order to perform useful work.

Effective data administration is the foundation stone for building a computerized organization. Senior management must fully understand the financial importance of successful data administration, and information technology practitioners must employ sound methods in implementing distributed computer applications, which includes the use of good database software tools.

Chapter 2 begins an investigation of the nature of computerized information and discusses the different views that we can have of the information stored in a database.

Chapter 2

Views of Data

As we described in Chapter 1, database software provides for the centralized definition and description of the data stored in a database. Many database software packages allow for a separation between different levels of data description. In talking about the data stored in a database, it is common to look at the data in at least three different ways, depending on who is viewing the data. These three views of data, shown graphically in Fig. 2.1, are summarized below:

- **User View.** A user view is a set of data elements and defined relationships among them as they are perceived by one or more end users, by an individual application program, or by a group of related application programs. A user view generally encompasses only a subset of the data elements stored in a database.

- **Logical Data Model.** This is the entire collection of data elements, and the relationships among them, that will be stored in database form. It documents the organization's overall view of a database and is a logical map that identifies all the data stored in a database. This logical map combines all the individual user views into one integrated structure.

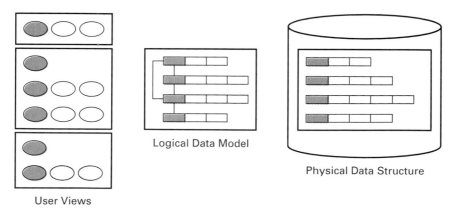

Logical Data Model

Physical Data Structure

User Views

Figure 2.1   Three views of the data stored in a computer database.

schemas in ANSI/SPARC terminology, correspond generally with the three views of data we just described, and the term schema is used in much database literature to refer to various views of data. Figure 2.2 illustrates the relationship between the three ANSI/SPARC schemas and the terms we have been using to refer to the three views of data.

The following sections briefly describe the three ANSI/SPARC schemas.

External Schema

A given database will generally have many *external schemas*, each of which corresponds to the way in which a specific application program views the database. An external schema corresponds directly to a user view. An external schema is a computerized representation of a user view. A user view may exist in the form of a chart drawn on paper. An external schema exists in the form of statements coded in a computer language.

Conceptual Schema

The *conceptual schema* describes all the different types of data elements that are stored in the database and the relationships among them. All the external schemas must be derivable from the conceptual schema. In effect, the conceptual schema is a computerized representation of a logical data model.

An individual database software package may require that the data in a logical data model be structured in certain ways. A translation may then be required to convert an abstract logical data model into a conceptual schema. Like a user view, a logical data model typically exists in the form of a chart drawn on paper. A conceptual schema takes the form of statements coded in a computer language.

Most of today's full-function database software is capable of representing any conceivable logical data model. However, each database software package supports its own computer language that the database administration staff must use in defining the conceptual schema.

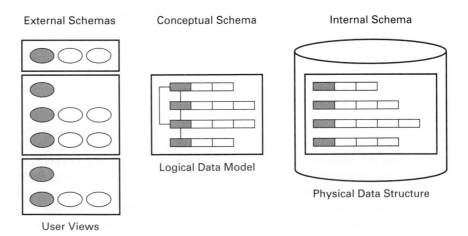

Figure 2.2   ANSI/SPARC three-schema architecture.

With very complex logical data models, a single conceptual schema might be used to represent only a portion of the logical data model, and multiple conceptual schemas may be required to represent the entire logical data model. But the collection of conceptual schemas still typically represents all the information in the logical data model.

Internal Schema

The *internal schema* defines the actual data that is stored in the database. In effect, the internal schema is a computerized representation of the physical data structures that are used to implement a conceptual schema. Computerized descriptions of the physical data structures define the data files that make up the database to both the database software and to the operating system software.

Most of today's database software implements a three-schema architecture that is conceptually similar to the ANSI/SPARC architecture. Software that implements a three-schema approach to database management generally provides a *data description language* (DDL) that allows each of the three types of schemas to be described independently. The database software then performs the transformations that are necessary to convert from one schema to the others.

SUMMARY

Data stored in a database can be viewed in one of three different ways, depending on who is viewing the database and for what purpose. The three data views are the user view, the logical data model, and the physical data structures. A user view is a set of data elements and defined relationships among them as they are perceived by one or more end users, by an individual application program, or by a group of related application programs. A logical data model describes the entire collection of data elements, and their relationships, that are stored in the database. The logical data model is a logical map that describes all the data stored in a database. Physical data structures are the data files, data element occurrences, indices, pointers, and other data structures used to physically implement the logical data model in a computer system.

The ANSI/Systems Planning and Requirements Committee (ANSI/SPARC) was a study group of ANSI that published a report documenting a three-schema architecture for database technology. An external schema describes the way in which a specific application program views the database and is a computerized representation of a user view. A conceptual schema describes all the data elements that are stored in the database and the relationships among them and makes up a computerized representation of a logical data model. An internal schema defines the actual data that is stored in the database and comprises a computerized representation of the physical data structures that are used to implement a database.

Chapter 3 introduces the logical data modeling task that must be performed in order to identify the data elements making up a database and to describe their inherent relationships.

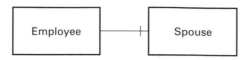

Figure 3.2   One-with-one association.

second entity. For example, one and only one instance of the Spouse entity is associated with any given instance of the Employee entity. This is shown in Fig. 3.2.

With a one-with-one association between the Employee entity and the Spouse entity, suppose we have the data stored for a particular occurrence of the Employee entity. We can then use that data to access the data stored for the associated instance of the Spouse entity.

One-with-Many Associations

A one-with-many association from entity A to entity B means that one instance of entity A has zero, one, or multiple instances of entity B associated with it at any point in time. While a married employee can only have one spouse at a given time, he or she might have zero, one, or multiple dependents, as shown in Fig. 3.3.

Showing Cardinalities in Both Directions

In an entity-relationship diagram, cardinalities are generally shown in both directions for most associations. Figure 3.4 shows the complete entity-relationship diagram for the Employee, Spouse, and Dependent entities with cardinalities for mappings in both directions on each link.

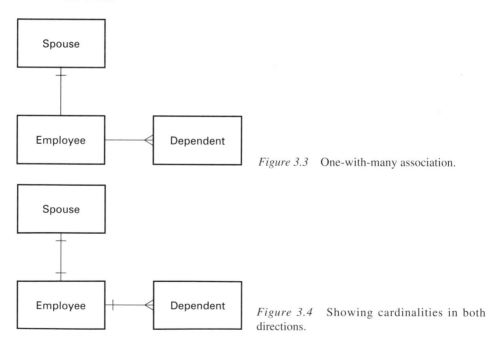

Figure 3.3   One-with-many association.

Figure 3.4   Showing cardinalities in both directions.

Many-with-Many Associations

In some cases, we may need to represent a many-with-many association in an entity-relationship diagram. For example, Fig. 3.5 shows how an employee may be associated with zero, one, or multiple projects, and a project may be associated with zero, one, or multiple employees.

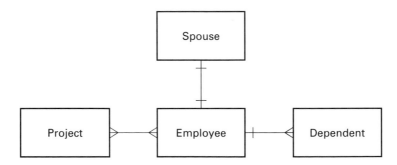

Figure 3.5   Many-with-many association.

Showing Zero and One Possibilities

A "many" cardinality symbol by itself indicates zero, one, or multiple. Sometimes, in an entity-relationship diagram, we may want to explicitly show that some "many" cardinalities really mean one or more, and others mean zero, one, or more. For example a married employee might have zero dependents, and we might require each project to have at least one employee assigned to it. We might also want to show that a one-with-one association allows zero as a possibility in one or both directions.

We can explicitly show the possibility of a zero value on the "one" or "many" side of an association by including a "zero" cardinality symbol with the "one" or "crow's-foot" cardinality symbol. We can also explicitly show the possibility of a one value in the "many" side of an association by including a "one" cardinality symbol along with the crow's foot symbol.

The cardinality symbols in the entity-relationship diagram shown in Fig. 3.6 explicitly documents the following facts:

- An employee can have zero or one spouse.
- An employee can have zero, one, or multiple dependents.
- An employee can work on zero, one, or multiple projects.
- A project must have at least one employee assigned to it.

The entity-relationship diagrams shown thus far are quite simple. It is important to realize that the entity-relationship diagrams an organization may develop may be much larger and may take considerable time to analyze and document.

one association leading from A to B. When A identifies B, then, if we have a value of A, we can find *a single value of B* that is associated with that value of A. To make the relationship more clear, we sometimes say that A *uniquely identifies* B.

In Fig. 3.9, only one value of Salary is associated with a particular value of Employee_# at any instant in time. Therefore, we draw a one-with-one link from the Employee_# data element to the Salary data element. This means that Employee_# identifies Salary. If we know a particular value of Employee_#, we can use it to find a single associated value of Salary.

Note that a one-with-one association in one direction does not always imply that there is also a one-with-one association in the opposite direction. The fact that Employee_# identifies Salary does *not* imply that Salary also identifies Employee_#. There is no one-with-one association between the Salary data element and the Employee data element because it is entirely possible for two or more employees to all be paid the same amount.

One-with-Many Associations

A one-with-many association from A to B means that for any single value of A there are zero, one, or multiple values of B associated with it. A one-with-many association is drawn using a crow's foot cardinality symbol, as shown in Fig. 3.10.

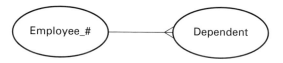

Figure 3.10   One-with-many association between Employee_# and Dependent.

Many-with-Many Associations

In some cases, we may identify the need for a many-with-many association in a logical data model. For example, an employee may be associated with zero, one, or multiple projects, and a project may be associated with zero, one, or multiple employees, as shown in Fig. 3.11.

Many-with-many associations occur less frequently in logical data models than one-with-one and one-with-many associations. While many-with-many associations are allowed to remain in entity-relationship diagrams, it is often best to remove them from logical data models. Techniques for resolving many-with-many associations are described later in this chapter.

Figure 3.11   Many-with-many association between Employee_# and Project_#.

Reverse Associations

Between any two data elements there can be a mapping in both directions. This gives four possibilities for forward and reverse associations. If the data elements are Man and

Woman, and the relationship between them represents "Marriage," then the four theoretical possibilities are shown in Fig. 3.12.

All the reverse associations are not necessarily of interest in a bubble chart. The reverse association from Department_# to Employee_# is shown in the bubble chart in Fig. 3.13 because users want to be able to determine what employees work in a given department.

The reverse associations between Salary and Employee_# and Spouse_Name and Employee_# are not of interest in Fig. 3.13. For example, there is no link from

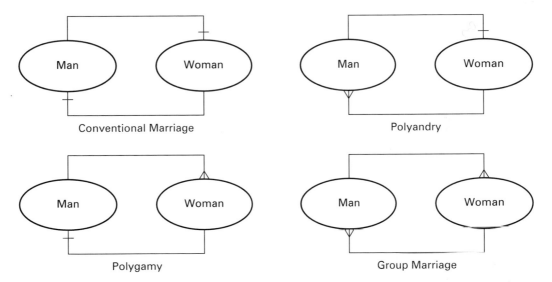

Figure 3.12   Four theoretical "marriage" associations.

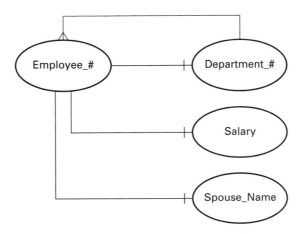

Figure 3.13   Reverse association from Department_# to Employee_#.

Spouse_Name back to Employee_# because no user wants to access the database with queries like: "Give me a list of all the employees who have a spouse named James." However, if it is important to be able to obtain a list of all the employees who have a salary greater than some specified value, the bubble chart should include a crow's-foot symbol on the Employee_# side of the Salary to Employee_# link, as shown in Fig. 3.14. Note that a reverse association can be shown on a separate line, or a single line can be used for the associations in both directions.

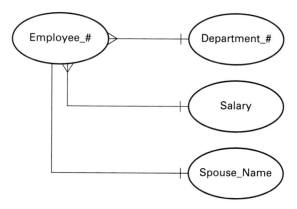

Figure 3.14   Reverse association from Salary to Employee_#.

TYPES AND OCCURRENCES

It is important to understand that the terms we use to describe data can refer to *types* of data or to individual *occurrences* of that data. Employee_Name refers to a data element type. Fred Smith is an occurrence of the Employee_Name data element type. Employee may refer to a type of record. There are many occurrences of the Employee record type, one for each person employed.

A logical data model shows the associations among *types* of data. For example, we may have many employees, each with a salary and with zero, one, or many children. The reader might imagine a third dimension to a bubble chart showing the many values of each data element type, as shown in Fig. 3.15.

When discussing data, it would be more precise to always explicitly state whether the term data element refers to a general category of data or to a specific data value, or occurrence. For brevity, database literature often does not do this. In most cases, the meaning is made clear by the context. In this book, a data element shown in a database diagram almost always refers to a general category or type of data, not to a specific value or occurrence of it.

KEYS AND ATTRIBUTES

Data elements in a bubble chart can play three different roles, based on the types of associations that are drawn among them.

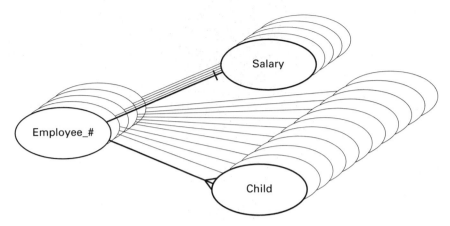

Figure 3.15   Types and occurrences.

- **Attributes.** An attribute is a data element whose bubble has no one-with-one links leading to any other bubble. Most of the data elements in a typical bubble chart are attributes.

- **Primary Keys.** A primary key is a data element whose bubble has one or more one-with-one links leading to other bubbles.

- **Secondary Keys.** A secondary key is a data element whose bubble has no one-with-one links leading to other bubbles but has one or more crow's-foot links leading to other bubbles.

The bubble chart in Fig. 3.16 shows examples of attributes, primary keys, and secondary keys. All the data elements not labeled as primary or secondary keys are

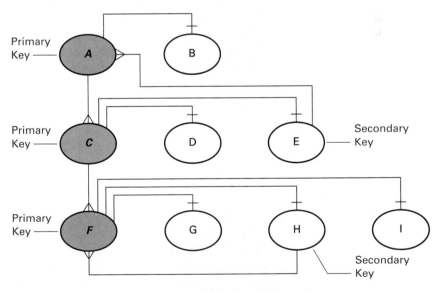

Figure 3.16   Attributes, primary keys, and secondary keys.

attributes. Each primary key *identifies* all the data elements to which it is connected with a one-with-one link. All the data elements that a primary key identifies are considered to be attributes associated with that primary key.

A data element that is a secondary key is also considered to be an attribute. All data elements, then, are either primary keys or attributes. For example, in the bubble chart in Fig. 3.16, data elements E and H are attributes and are also secondary keys. A secondary key has a link to another data element, but it does not identify that data element. One value of a secondary key may be associated with zero, one, or multiple values of the data element with which it is associated.

Concatenated Keys

It is possible to have a data element that cannot be identified by any other single data element in the bubble chart. However, this does not mean that it has no primary key. It may have a primary key made up of more than one data element in combination. Such a key is called a *concatenated key*. In Fig. 3.17, the primary key for Grade is made up of Teacher_# and Student_# joined together, or concatenated.

A teacher may have multiple students, a student may have multiple teachers, and each teacher gives each student a different grade. Therefore, neither Teacher_# nor Student_# alone identifies the Grade data element. Grade is identified by a combination of both Teacher_# and Student_#.

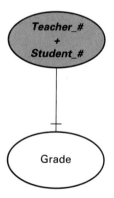

Figure 3.17   Teacher_# + Student_# concatenated key.

Exploding a Concatenated Key

After drawing a concatenated key in a bubble chart, the database designer should also immediately place each component part of the concatenated key in its own individual bubble. A one-with-many association is then used to connect individual bubbles with the complete concatenated key. This process is referred to as *exploding* the concatenated key and is shown in Fig. 3.18.

If Teacher_# and Student_# appeared alone in a bubble chart, a many-with-many relationship would have to be shown between them.   Exploding a concatenated key often avoids the necessity for having to show an explicit many-with-many association, such as

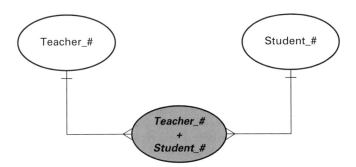

Figure 3.18 Exploding a concatenated key.

that between the Teacher_# and Student_# attributes. In the bubble chart in Fig. 3.18, the many-with-many association between Teacher_# and Student_# can be derived from the two one-with-many associations with the concatenated key. The role that concatenated keys play in resolving many-with-many associations is discussed further later in this chapter. Separating out the individual components of the concatenated keys also makes it easy later to depict the individual data elements as primary keys that themselves also identify other data elements, as shown in Fig. 3.19.

Analyzing Concatenated Key Associations

By introducing a concatenated key into the logical data model, each attribute bubble can always be made dependent on a single primary key bubble. However, whenever we introduce a concatenated key, we must carefully analyze each association with the concatenated

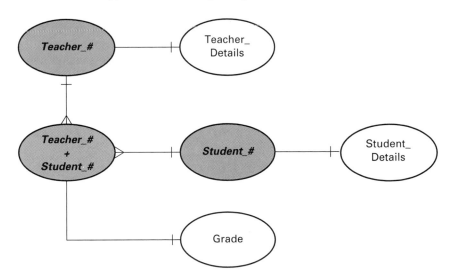

Figure 3.19 Using the individual primary key bubbles.

Many-with-Many Caution

It is necessary to be cautious when many-with-many associations appear in a bubble chart. Usually, a requirement for intersection data associated with the pair of data elements will arise as it becomes necessary to add more data elements to the bubble chart during logical data modeling. Even if there is no intersection data to start with, it is likely to be added later as the database evolves.

Data modeling is an attempt to find the most stable data model. Therefore, many-with-many associations that appear should immediately be resolved by creating and then exploding a concatenated key. In this manner it is easy to add intersection data later without changing the fundamental structure of the logical data model.

RECORD DIAGRAMS

Bubble charts clearly show the associations that exist among a set of data elements. However, when bubble charts grow in size, they often become difficult to read and interpret. A data structure containing many bubbles can often be made more clear by redrawing the bubble chart in the form of a record diagram. A record diagram can be used to document the data requirements for an individual user view or for a composite logical data model that combines multiple user views.

To create a record diagram from a bubble chart, we place each attribute and primary key in a box. We then group all the attributes associated with each primary key together with that primary key. Always show the primary key on the left in each group. The record diagram then explicitly shows only the associations that exist among primary keys and between secondary keys and the data elements to which they point.

Each data element group that is identified by a primary key is called a *record*. The term *logical record* is sometimes used to distinguish a record in a logical data model from whatever may be stored physically in computerized storage. The diagram in Fig. 3.25 shows a bubble chart describing a single logical record, with its equivalent record diagram.

Data Element Subgroupings

We can, if we like, show data element subgroupings in a record diagram. For example, it may be useful to split the Supplier_Address data element into component data elements. Figure 3.26 shows that Street, City, State, and Zip are collectively called Supplier_Address.

Supplier_Address does not in this case constitute a separate record with its own primary key. Such a data structure is useful only if the group name as well as the individual component names can all be individually referenced by users.

Secondary Keys

Secondary key associations can also be shown in record diagrams. Figure 3.27 shows a bubble chart we looked at earlier and how it can be redrawn in the form of a record diagram.

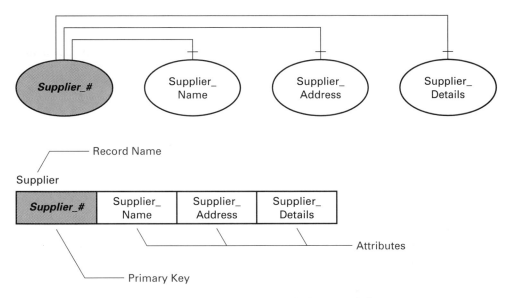

Figure 3.25   Bubble chart and an equivalent record diagram.

Supplier

Supplier_#	Supplier_ Name	Supplier_Address				Supplier_ Details
		Street	City	State	Zip	

Figure 3.26   Data element subgrouping.

BACHMAN NOTATION

Some database literature shows one-with-one and one-with-many associations in database diagrams using single-head and double-head arrows. This type of notation is sometimes called *Bachman notation*. Crow's-foot notation and Bachman notation are compared in Fig. 3.28.

The author has used single-head and double-head arrows in the database diagrams in some earlier books. These are avoided here because arrows tend to suggest a flow or time sequence and are used extensively for this in other types of information technology diagrams. The cardinality symbols used in this book are less ambiguous than Bachman notation and have been adopted for use with a variety of automated CASE design tools.

SHIPPING SYSTEM

Some of the early chapters in this book use a simple shipping system to illustrate database fundamentals and to show database examples. The shipping system is used by a hypothetical shipping company that uses a fleet of ships to carry cargo. This system uses

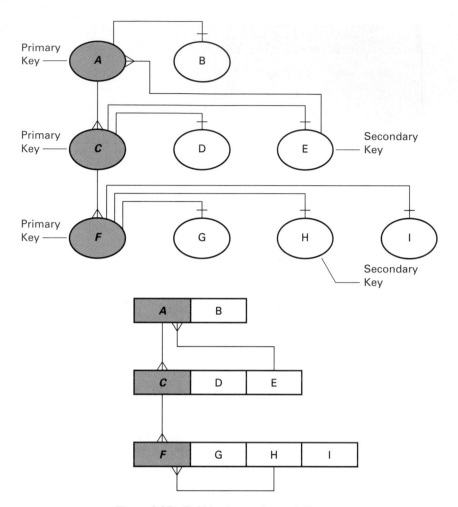

Figure 3.27   Bubble chart and record diagram.

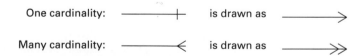

Figure 3.28   Comparing crow's-foot notation with Bachman notation.

a single database to manage the required information concerning cargo and the ships used to transport it.

Box 3.1 describes seven application programs that will access the information contained in the shipping database, and Box 3.2 lists the data elements that the seven application programs access and that will be stored in the shipping database.

BOX 3.1   Shipping system application programs.

- **Vessel Information Display.** The Vessel Information Display application displays a list of information about a particular vessel.

- **Itinerary Display.** Each vessel ordinarily stops at many ports on a particular journey. The Itinerary Display application displays a list of the stops that a vessel makes.

- **Consignee Container Display.** A *consignee* is a person or organization to whom a shipment will be delivered. The goods being shipped to a particular consignee are placed into a container that is identified by a unique container number. The Consignee Container Display application displays information about the containers that are being shipped to a particular consignee.

- **Shipper Container Display.** Shipments are sent by *shippers.* The Shipper Container Display application displays information about the containers that a given shipper is sending.

- **Waybill Display.** A *waybill* is a document containing information about a shipment of goods being carried between an origination port and a destination port on a particular vessel. The Waybill Display application displays waybill information for a particular shipment.

- **Container Offloading Display.** The Container Offloading Display application displays a list of the containers that are to be offloaded from a particular vessel at a particular port.

- **Container Loading Display.** The Container Loading Display application displays a list of the containers that are to be loaded onto a particular vessel at a particular port. For loading purposes, container details are needed.

BOX 3.2   Shipping system data element descriptions.

Vessel Record

- **Vessel_#.** A unique identification number assigned to each vessel.
- **Hold_Size.** Capacity of vessel's cargo hold in cubic feet.
- **Vessel_Details.** Other descriptive information about the vessel.

Port Record

- **Vessel_#.** A unique identification number assigned to each vessel.
- **Port_#.** A unique identification number assigned to each port at which a vessel stops on a journey.
- **Arrival_Date.** The date the vessel is scheduled to arrive at this particular port.
- **Departure_Date.** The date the vessel is scheduled to depart from this particular port.

(Continued)

BOX 3.2   *(Continued)*

Waybill Record

- **Waybill_#.** Unique identification number assigned to a waybill.
- **Consignee_#.** Unique identification number assigned to the individual or organization that is to receive a shipment.
- **Shipper_#.** Unique identification number assigned to the individual or organization that is the source of a shipment.
- **Delivery_Time.** Date and time the container is scheduled to be delivered to its intended recipient.

Container Record

- **Container_#.** Unique identification number assigned to a shipping container.
- **Contents_Description.** Description of the contents of this shipping container.
- **Handling_Instructions.** Special instructions concerning the handling of this shipping container.
- **Container_Size.** Volume in cubic feet of this shipping container.

Shipping System Logical Data Model Diagrams

Each of the individual application programs making up the shipping system has its own user view, which consists of a subset of the data elements that will be contained in the shipping database.

The logical data modeling for the shipping system is done by using an automated data modeling tool to describe the user view for each application program. The data modeling tool then combines all the user views and creates a single logical data model from which all the user views can be derived. Figure 3.29 shows a bubble chart representation of the logical data model for the shipping system. Figure 3.30 shows this bubble chart converted to an equivalent record diagram.

Shipping Database—Relational Representation

To convert a logical data model to a relational data representation, we start by making a table to represent each of the records in the logical data model. Redundant data elements must then sometimes be added to implement all the associations shown in the logical data model.

The diagram in Fig. 3.31 shows how the shipping system logical data model might be implemented using Microsoft Access relational database software. The primary key of each table is shown in white.

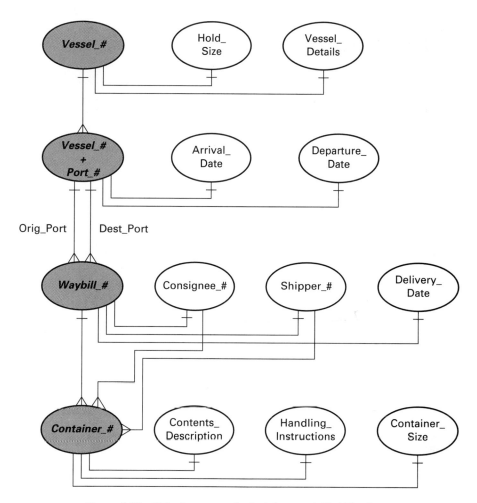

Figure 3.29   Shipping system logical data model bubble chart.

Details concerning relational data representation are discussed in Part IV, and these details need not concern us at this time.

SUMMARY

Top-down database planning takes the form of strategic information planning, which is usually led by the data administrator. Top-down planning is done for the organization as a whole using entity-relationship diagrams. Bottom-up database design takes the form of logical data modeling, which is done by the database administrator and database designers. Logical data modeling is done with one business area at a time, using bubble charts

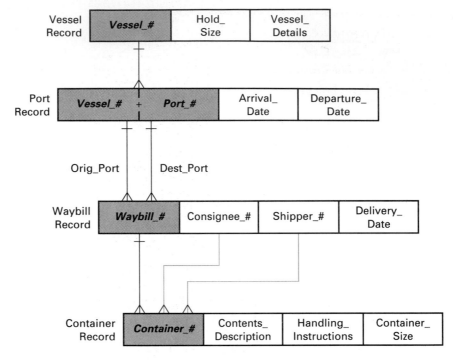

Figure 3.30   Shipping system logical data model record diagram.

and record diagrams. Logical data modeling should be done using automated data modeling and data dictionary software tools.

An entity-relationship diagram is a chart that shows what business entities are important to the enterprise and what are the relationships that exist among them. Entities are placed in boxes, and the associations among entities are drawn using lines that connect the boxes. Crow's-foot notation is used to show cardinalities at the ends of connecting lines. The cardinalities in the associations used in entity-relationship diagrams can be one-with-one, one-with-many, and many-with-many.

Bubble charts document individual data elements that will be stored in the database and the associations among them. As with entity relationship diagrams, associations are drawn using crow's foot notation. The cardinalities in associations used in bubble charts are one-with-one and one-with-many. Many-with-many associations that appear in bubble charts are usually converted to pairs of one-with-many associations by creating and then exploding concatenated keys.

Data elements in a bubble chart can play three different roles, based on the types of associations that are drawn among them. An attribute is a data element whose bubble has no one-with-one links leading to any other bubble. A primary key is a data element whose bubble has one or more one-with-one links leading to other bubbles. A secondary key is a data element whose bubble has no one-with-one links leading to other bubbles but has one or more crow's-foot links leading to other bubbles.

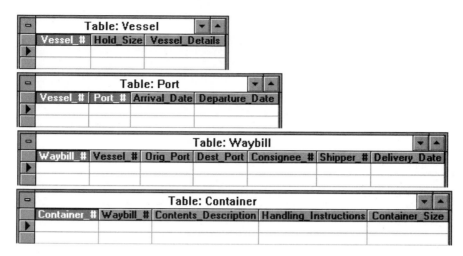

Figure 3.31   Relational implementation of the shipping system logical data model.

A record diagram shows the same set of data elements and associations contained in a bubble chart but uses connected boxes instead of bubbles. Connected boxes represent records that are each identified by a primary key. Associations between records are shown using crow's-foot notation.

Chapter 4 begins Part II of this book, where we describe the characteristics of the software that is used to store and manipulate computer databases.

REFERENCES

1. *Strategic Information Planning Methodologies, Second Edition.* James Martin and Joe Leben. Prentice Hall, Englewood Cliffs, NJ, 1989.

2. *Managing the Database Environment.* James Martin. Prentice Hall, Englewood Cliffs, NJ, 1983.

PART II

DATABASE SOFTWARE

Chapter **4**

Database Technology Evolution

Database technology, like information technology, has evolved over a period of many years. We can identify at least four separate waves of computing that are based on the predominant hardware in the computing environment (see Fig. 4.1).

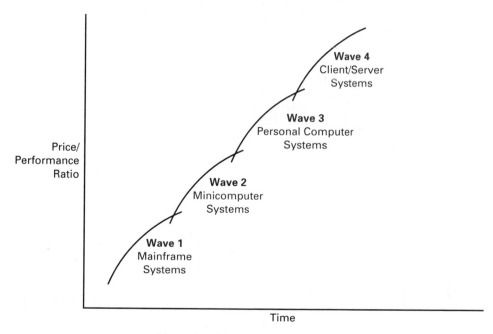

Figure 4.1 Four waves of computing.

THE MAINFRAME COMPUTING ENVIRONMENT

The first wave is based on the mainframe environment. Although differentiating between mainframes and other forms of computing equipment is becoming increasingly difficult and irrelevant, a mainframe is typically a system that costs in the millions of dollars and requires a specialized room with complex environmental controls and raised flooring to hide the interconnections between components.

The first database software packages were developed for the mainframe environment. Mainframe database software has been in use the longest and has had a long period of time to evolve. Many of the database packages available for mainframes are extremely sophisticated and implement a wide range of facilities; however, they are not particularly easy to use, nor are they oriented toward casual use by end users.

Examples of early mainframe database software packages are IBM's IMS family of database software systems and IDMS, marketed by Computer Associates.

THE MINICOMPUTER COMPUTING ENVIRONMENT

The second wave, which has coexisted with the mainframe wave in many organizations, is characterized by systems with a much lower cost than mainframes. A minicomputer is often a rack-mounted system that may or may not require special environmental controls and typically costs in the hundreds of thousands of dollars or less. A specialized form of minicomputer is the graphics workstation that resides on a user's desk and is typically used by an individual for a specialized purpose, such as engineering design or advanced computer graphics. Database software rivaling that developed for mainframes is available for the minicomputer environment.

Examples of minicomputer database software packages include the RDB family of database software products marketed by Digital Equipment Corporation, and the Oracle family of products marketed by Oracle Corporation. The Oracle product family also includes compatible database software versions that run in the mainframe and personal computer environments.

THE PERSONAL COMPUTER ENVIRONMENT

The third computing wave, in which many organizations find themselves today, is characterized by widespread use of inexpensive personal computers on the desktops of most knowledge workers. The first database software packages developed for the personal computer environment lacked power and flexibility and were little more than enhanced file management systems.

This has changed. Database software packages available for today's personal computers have many of the same features as mainframe and minicomputer database software. However, many of the personal computer database software packages are similar to the mainframe and minicomputer software in that they are designed to be run on a single machine. Thus, they cannot take full advantage of the ability to interconnect third-wave personal computers using various forms of networking technology.

THE CLIENT/SERVER COMPUTING ENVIRONMENT

The fourth computing wave, which organizations are just now beginning to adopt, is characterized by computing that takes full advantage of a network of interconnected processors. In the client/server environment, an application's processing load can be distributed among a variety of processors, with each machine being assigned the tasks for which it is best suited. Some processors operate in the role of clients and make requests for services; other processors operate in the role of servers and accept requests from clients and pass results back.

The fourth wave of computing is closely associated with the trend toward open-systems computing in which hardware and software from a variety of vendors work cooperatively on a single business problem.

GENERATIONS OF DATABASE TECHNOLOGY

As we have passed through the four major hardware waves, we have also seen at least six generations of software systems that were specifically designed for the purpose of managing the external storage of computer data. These six generations are compared in Fig. 4.2 and are briefly described in the following sections.

EARLY FILE MANAGEMENT SOFTWARE

In the very earliest days of information processing, programming languages were similar to the instructions actually executed by the computer. This resulted in a process-oriented model of information technology. For example, programs for addition were organized around the machine process of addition—loading registers with numbers, executing the add instruction, and making decisions based on the results. Few results were stored for any amount of time for later use, and the earliest programming systems provided no special support for the management of data stored on external storage devices.

However, programmers soon realized the value of recording results for later use. The need for recording program results greatly increased with the advent of rotating magnetic disk storage, which provided random-access capability for large amounts of storage.

When rotating disk storage devices were first used for information processing, the data on rotating magnetic media quickly became difficult to organize and manage. This situation led developers to create software subsystems, sometimes called *file management systems*, that were designed to make it easier for programmers to manipulate the disk storage devices.

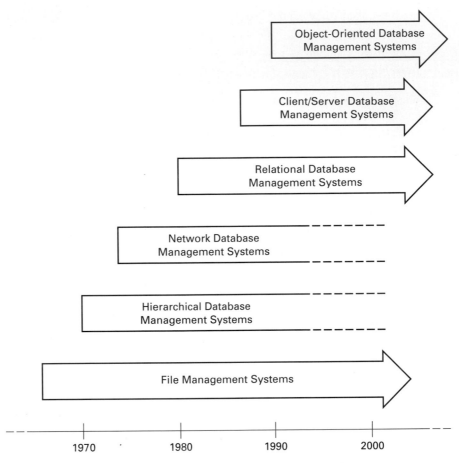

Figure 4.2   Six generations of data management software.

With the early file management systems, programmers could create files, store them, read them back later for analysis or presentation, and update existing files. Programs were still generally organized around the process-oriented model, and availability of higher-level languages, especially COBOL, led to the development of large business programs. These programs viewed the data in files according to their business purposes, and the files were typically sorted by categories or indexed by some logical key, for example, order number.

The notions of a *record* and of a *file* as a group of records was developed. Each record represented an instance of some business entity, such as a line item in an order. While the early file management systems aided the programmer, the data access methods were still primitive. Random access required the application program to know the physical placement of data on the rotating disk. Computing these unique addresses required hashing algorithms. Developing algorithms with a good, even distribution was an important skill—especially when different disk drives needed different algorithms.

This prompted the first major implementation-independent file management aid—the *indexed file*. Instead of requiring an application to furnish the exact location of a piece of recorded data, only a symbolic key was needed. The index-enhanced file system was necessary in order to compute and assign the data's physical location.

Hierarchical Databases

The ever-increasing demand for more capability from computer applications continued, and researchers realized that even indexed file systems were crude tools. Order processing applications, in particular, tended to impose a hierarchical model on their data. This corresponded to the hierarchical nature of an order with many line items and to products described via hierarchical assembly structures. These pressures prompted the creation of the first database software subsystems that were layered on top of the early file systems.

The best known and most widely used hierarchical database software product in the IBM mainframe environment is IBM's *Information Management System* (IMS). Beginning with the early hierarchical systems, database software packages began to be based on a model of data that was independent of any particular application that accessed the data. This first step toward implementation independence gave application developers more time to concentrate on application design. It also gave database designers a wide range of implementation freedom.

When database software began to be widely used, data design became the most important information processing activity, causing a fundamental paradigm shift to a *data-oriented* model of information technology. This shift to a data-oriented model also led to the combination of groups of related applications into integrated business systems, all running against a common shared database.

From this phenomenon, other needs arose, such as having multiple applications interact simultaneously with the database software, and creating independent utility applications to manage the database. Thus were born the notions of concurrency control and most of the activities that today make up database administration—backup, recovery, resource allocation, security, and so on.

In a hierarchical database structure, data elements are arranged in the form of an inverted tree. Data often tends naturally to break down into hierarchical categories, where one category of data is a subset of another. For example, a wine merchant stocks wine from many regions, such as Bordeaux and Burgundy. For each region there are many wine types—St. Emilion, Pomerol, Medoc, etc. For each wine type there are many years, some better than others. For wine type and year there are several shippers—the 1971 St. Emilion shipped by Austin Nichols, by Dreyfus Ashby, and so on. The organization of this wine data might be represented as a hierarchical structure, as shown in Figure 4.3.

Traditional company organization charts are also often hierarchical in nature. A corporation can consist of a number of divisions. Each division can contain a number of departments. And each department employs a number of people.

Much of the data in database systems lends itself to a hierarchical representation. Several database software products are based on a hierarchical model, with IBM's IMS a prime example.

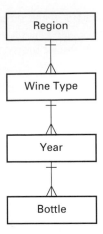

Figure 4.3   Hierarchical data structure.

Network Databases

The restrictions of the hierarchical data model imposed by IMS, and other systems like it, soon became apparent. Hierarchies provided a good model for many common business problems. However, developers began to realize that the world was not always inherently hierarchical, and that nonhierarchical data models were awkward to implement using a system like IMS.

Developers soon realized that database software could be more flexible if it allowed the storage of less restrictive *network* data structures. (The term network has nothing to do here with communication networks; it refers to the relationships that are permitted among the records that the database software stores.) For instance, an inventory control system needs to model the relationship between parts in an inventory and suppliers of those parts. This relationship cannot be modeled as a strict hierarchy, since most parts can be obtained from more than one supplier and most suppliers handle multiple parts. Database software is needed that allows data to be modeled as an arbitrary graph structure.

Network relationships occurred so commonly in business situations that new database software was developed that supported network-oriented data models as well as hierarchical models. Many network-oriented database systems are based on an architecture developed by the DataBase Task Group (DBTG) of the Conference on Data Systems Languages (CODASYL). (CODASYL is the same organization that produced the COBOL language.) In 1971 the CODASYL DBTG issued its final report documenting a network-oriented database model that was accepted as a standard by the American National Standards Institute (ANSI). Several database software packages were developed that implemented the CODASYL standard, the most widely known of which is *Integrated Database Management System* (IDMS), a version of which is still marketed by Computer Associates.

The CODASYL standard included a data description language (DDL) that was used to describe user views, logical data models, and physical database structures. It also defined a data manipulation language (DML) that was used to create and process the data stored in a CODASYL database. The CODASYL DDL and DML were typically used in conjunction with other programming languages, such as COBOL, to build database applications. CODASYL also eventually defined a set of ancillary functions for administering physical storage, implementing security and concurrency controls, and providing other database services not covered by the DDL or DML.

RELATIONAL DATABASE TECHNOLOGY

As computer systems built on top of database software grew, so did the problems, most of which came to be centered around reorganization and navigation.

Reorganization became a major problem, because with the early hierarchical and network database systems, the physical data structures were closely tied to the logical data model. Hierarchical and network data relationships were typically implemented through the use of pointers consisting of actual disk addresses that were stored in physical database records. The database software typically caused a data field for these pointers to be inserted into each application program that accessed the database. Unfortunately, this implied that any change to the record layout used by the database software required, at a minimum, recompilation of all programs. Worse yet, if the physical address of a record changed, all references to it in the database had to be found so that the correct new location could be inserted. As the size and complexity of databases grew, so grew the problems associated with physical reorganization. With the largest databases, database reorganizations could cause databases to be unavailable for days at a time.

Navigation, the second significant source of problems, refers to the way that applications are bound to the database software. Application programs use commands supported by the database software to find a particular logical record and then use other commands to access related records. For example, with a CODASYL database software implementation, a program might make an access request for a particular Order record. Subsequent requests might access all the Line Item records that are related to the Order record. In this way, application programs make explicit requests to navigate through the records stored in the database.

A requirement for explicit navigation means the application program has to have incorporated within it knowledge of the data relationships that are documented in the logical data model. However, since the logical description of the relationships and their physical implementation were close, the application also contained implicit knowledge of the implementation. This was potentially confusing. Major changes or extensions to the logical data model could make it necessary to navigate through the database differently, thus invalidating many application programs. In such a situation, recompilation alone would no longer cure the problem. Application programs often had to be rewritten to accommodate a new logical data model. In this environment, maintenance activities began to take precedence over new development, as systems became more and more expensive and time consuming to maintain.

The Relational Data Model

During this period, E. F. Codd, then of IBM, wrote a paper describing a *relational data model*, and several implementations of relational databases began to appear. Relational database systems had several important characteristics that solved many of the problems associated with the use of hierarchical and network databases.

The relational model has a formal mathematical foundation but at the same time defines a table-oriented view of data that is intuitive even to nontechnical end users. The relational data model also formally defines a set of operators that can be applied to the data in a relational database. An important aspect of the relational operations is that each operation uses tabular data as input and produces output that also consists of tables.

The relational data model moved the focal point of the system development process away from data structures and computer implementations toward modeling the business environment that the database system was supposed to support. This was its most important aspect. The entire process moved to a higher level as the important questions focused on the business model rather than on the most convenient implementation vehicle for a particular application. Relational database software packages finally made it possible for the database to be completely independent of the processes that accessed it.

Relational Data Structures

The relational data model defines three fundamental constructs: the *table*, the *column*, and the *row*. The model also specifies a number of *operators* that can be applied to the data. The relational data model provides several significant advantages over its predecessors, as seen in Box 4.1. All of these characteristics enable faster application development and easier application maintenance, which have led to the current popularity of relational database products. The relational data model is described in further detail in Part IV.

CLIENT/SERVER DATABASE TECHNOLOGY

The inherent data independence characteristic of the relational data model has an important side effect. Data independence makes it possible for database software to allow the location of the stored data to be hidden from the programs that access the database. An important step in the evolution of relational database software has been to implement the database software function so that the database can be stored on a different computing system from the application program needing access to the database.

In a simple client/server database scenario, an application program accesses *client* database software that runs in the local computing system. The local client database software communicates over a network with another computing system running complementary *server* database software. The remote server database software then accesses a database stored on the remote machine on behalf of the client database software.

In a typical system, a database application program issues a request to the client database software for a database service. The client database software sends the request

---

BOX 4.1   Characteristics of the relational data model.

- **Data Independence.** With the relational data model, the data representation in the computer is independent of the interface to the application. The most significant advantage over earlier systems is that the physical data representation can be modified without affecting applications. The database can be completely reorganized at the physical level without requiring the recompilation of programs. Performance facilities, such as indices, can be added or removed dynamically, tables can be partitioned across disk drives or compressed to reclaim unused space, and so on. None of this affects the application programs or the people who access the database.

- **Declarative Manipulation.** The relational data model defines a consistent set of operators that can be applied to relational data. An international-standard language, called *Structured Query Language* (SQL), has also been developed to express the relational model in a computer implementation. SQL is a declarative, nonprocedural language that is used to specify the kind of data desired—not the way to get it. SQL provides a simpler mechanism for manipulating a database than the data manipulation languages that preceded it. SQL embodies the philosophy of data independence. It allows the database system to choose from alternative mechanisms and to obtain the desired results from any physical realization of the database. The database software can dynamically optimize the way queries are executed, freeing the application programmer from this task.

- **Reduced Redundancy.** When a relational database is designed, a process called *normalization* can be applied to the data. Fully normalizing a data model produces a database in which data redundancy has been reduced to a minimum. The reduction of redundancy has two advantages over prior systems. First, it removes the possibility that portions of the database are out of synchronization due to redundant storage. This was a problem with both hierarchical and network databases, where redundant data elements were common. Second, it usually minimizes the amount of data stored, reducing the overall size of the database and saving disk space.

- **Simplicity of Data Representation.** The relational model has a limited number of data objects and a limited number of operators that can be applied to those objects—an improvement over the hierarchical and network database models. Most people, whether or not they are programmers, are already familiar with basic relational concepts, since they have worked with data organized in the form of tables, columns, and rows. The relational model is easy to learn and use.

- **Simplicity of Data Presentation.** The result of all relational operators is a new table, which often is the required application solution. Previous data models required extracting the appropriate information and then translating it into some desired result format—often a table of some kind. Relational database systems eliminate this last step, since the result is already in tabular form.

---

across the network to the database server. The database server software provides the requested service and returns the appropriate results to the client database software. It, in turn, relays the results to the application program. The local application program sees only the client database software. It appears to the local application program as if the database were stored locally, when in fact, it may be physically located a great distance away.

In a more complex client/server database software scenario, the database itself may be divided up and stored on a number of remote machines. Again, the local application program uses client database software to request access to the data as if it were all stored locally. Server database software running on a number of remote machines cooperate to access the required data on behalf of the local client database software and the application program.

There are substantial differences between database software that supports only a single-computer environment and database software that takes full advantage of the client/server environment. But almost any type of database software can be adapted to run in a client/server environment, given appropriate support software. Examples of database software useful in the client/server environment include many of the packages available for the mainframe and minicomputer environments as well as database products that are designed to run on personal computers.

Many database software subsystems for mainframes and minicomputers began as systems that supported terminal-oriented applications, in which a single computer performs all the application processing as well as all the database access processing. Examples of this type of database software are IMS, IDMS, and DB2 for mainframes. Some of these packages are now often used in a client/server environment in which the database is stored on the mainframe, while other computers attached to the mainframe via a network make requests for data that the mainframe satisfies.

Many personal computer database software packages are also designed primarily to run on individual end user systems and typically access databases stored on the same machine that runs the database software. Examples of these are Paradox and Access. But many of these end-user-oriented database packages have optional facilities that allow them to access databases maintained by database software running on other computers as well as their own local databases.

Other database software packages for small computers are specifically designed to be run in a client/server environment in which a single database application may involve multiple computers. Database packages like SQL Server and Oracle fall into this category.

It is interesting to note that the data independence provided by the relational data model is a prerequisite for many of the mechanisms that are used to implement a client/server database environment and to distribute a database among multiple machines. Today, most widely used client/server database software implements the relational data model. However, the type of database system we discuss next is beginning to come into the mainstream as well.

OBJECT-ORIENTED DATABASE TECHNOLOGY

As we mentioned in the foregoing section, today's client/server database software represents the mainstream in database technology. Most widely used database software implementations use some form of client/server technology with relational databases at their hearts. However, a new form of database, called an *object-oriented database*, is beginning to become important and will eventually coexist in many environments with today's client/server relational databases.

The relational data model that is at the heart of most relational databases, whether they are centralized or distributed, specifies that the database should store only data with no procedures. As we have seen, a major objective of conventional database technology is to make the data completely independent from the procedures. In contrast, an object-oriented database is used to store the objects that form the basis of object-oriented computing. An object-oriented database does not store data alone. It stores *objects*, which consist of *data* as well as *procedures* (called *methods*) that are used to perform operations on that data.

What is interesting about object-oriented database technology is that it will probably not replace relational database technology, but will build on it. Relational database technology will probably continue to coexist with object-oriented database systems, and conventional relational databases will be used with certain classes of computer applications while object-oriented databases will be used for others.

While object-oriented databases represent the future of advanced database technology, they have not yet made much penetration into the mainstream business information processing environment. Object-oriented database technology is described further in Appendix C.

EXTENSIONS TO THE RELATIONAL DATA MODEL

Object-oriented databases are not, at the time of writing, as widely used as relational databases. However, it is interesting to note that many modern relational database packages are beginning to adopt some of the characteristics of object-oriented technology. As database technology evolves, it may become difficult to decide whether a given database system uses a relational approach or an object-oriented approach. It may well implement many of the ideas of each.

Stored Procedures

Many of today's relational database systems, designed specifically for the client/server environment, allow *stored procedures* to be maintained in the database along with data. Such stored procedures can then be explicitly executed by application programs that access the database.

Database Triggers and Rules

Some database software also allows stored procedures to be executed automatically through a system of *database triggers*. A database trigger defines a set of *rules* that govern under what circumstances a stored procedure should be executed. The database software itself then executes the procedure whenever the rules specified in its associated database trigger are satisfied.

Encapsulation

Stored procedures and triggers allow database software systems to provide a limited form of the *encapsulation* mechanism used in object-oriented technology. The idea behind encapsulation is that an object should consist of procedures as well as all the data those procedures operate on. An object hides its data from other objects and allows access to the data only through the object's own procedures.

By storing procedural code in the database itself, the designer can create sets of procedures that database users can access instead of or in addition to the data in the database. An application program might be allowed to access a particular stored procedure but might be prevented from directly accessing the data elements the procedure manipulates. This provides a form of encapsulation, since an application program is then able to access certain data elements only through a specific stored procedure. Stored procedures and database triggers are examined further in Chapters 5 and 12.

DECISION SUPPORT SYSTEMS AND DATA WAREHOUSES

As we have seen, database technology is evolving to include extensions to conventional relational database systems and toward the newer object-oriented databases. At the same time, the applications for which organizations use database software is evolving as well. Our early books on database technology identified four different environments that organizations can implement for accessing computerized databases. These four environments are described in Box 4.2.

Decision Support Systems

Databases designed for a Class IV environment are often used to implement *decision support systems*. Managers and knowledge workers in the organization need timely access to the organization's data in order to make good decisions. In many cases, this data is available in the data files and databases accessed by the organization's production information processing systems. However, it is generally very difficult to allow access to production files and databases to satisfy ad hoc requests for information. This is why a Class III environment and a Class IV environment must often coexist.

The Data Warehouse

The need for a coexistence between the Class III environment and the Class IV environment has led to a requirement for the *data warehouse* concept. A data warehouse is an environment in which both production-oriented databases and databases optimized for end-user ad hoc queries are maintained by the organization.

A data warehouse can be characterized as a large repository of data objects that have been prepackaged and inventoried so they can be effectively distributed to managers and knowledge workers throughout the organization. In today's environment, the data objects generally consist of tables that are stored in relational databases. However, the data that a data warehouse makes available to end users is not the same as is stored in production databases. Warehouse data is often extracted from production databases and packaged in a form that is more useful for consumers of the data.

BOX 4.2   Four data environments.

- **Class I Environment—Files.** In this environment, database software is not used to control access to data. Programs use the simple access methods provided by the operating system to access the data in files. An advantage to this environment is simplicity. No complex software subsystems are used to manage access to data and applications are relatively easy to implement. But this environment is characterized by a proliferation of data files with high data redundancy and high maintenance costs.

- **Class II Environment—Application Databases.** In this environment, database software is used, but without much sharing of data between application areas. Separate databases are designed specifically for the needs of each computer application. This environment has many similarities to the Class I environment and is characterized by a proliferation of application databases with much of the same data redundancy that exists when database software is not used. This environment is also characterized by maintenance costs that can be higher than in the Class I environment

- **Class III Environment—Subject Databases.** In this environment, databases are created that are largely independent of any particular application. Databases are designed and stored independently of the specific functions for which they are used. Data for business subjects, such as customers, products, or personnel are associated and stored in shared databases. This environment requires thorough data analysis for success but can lead to much lower maintenance costs than the Class I and Class II environments. This environment can also lead to faster application development and direct user interaction with the databases. If this environment is not managed well, it can disintegrate into a Class II (or even Class I) environment.

- **Class IV Environment—Information Systems.** This environment is characterized by databases that are organized for fast information retrieval rather than for high-volume production runs. A variety of different languages and query facilities are often used to provide end users with direct access to the data they need to carry out their day-to-day work. New data elements are added to the databases as they are needed. In most organizations, a Class IV environment should coexist with a Class III environment, with the databases in each environment organized according to their intended purposes.

From a data warehouse perspective, users of data are not application programmers who write custom programs to access data for a particular purpose. Rather, they are end users who use the data to perform their day-to-day work. These users employ a wide variety of tools for accessing the data they need.

One of the functions of a data warehouse might be to serve as an integration tool to help organize and distribute the data used to run the organization's legacy information systems. Data warehouse functions might extract important data from the production files and databases that perform the day-to-day information processing and place it into databases optimized for a Class IV information-retrieval and decision-support environment.

IBM's Information Warehouse Framework

In 1991, IBM announced its *Information Warehouse Framework*. In the initial announcement, IBM defined the Information Warehouse Framework as:

a set of database management systems, interfaces, tools, and facilities that manage and deliver reliable, timely, accurate, and understandable business information to authorized individuals for business decision-making.

It is IBM's intention with the Information Warehouse Framework to provide decision makers with access to data wherever it is located in the enterprise. The Information Warehouse Framework consists of three major components, shown in Box 4.3.

At the time of writing, IBM has not yet announced specific products to implement its Data Warehouse Framework. Its mainframe orientation may also make it unsuitable for many organizations who are well along on the path toward a distributed computing environment in which mainframes play a reduced role. However, other vendors are also committed to the data warehouse concept and many advances are expected in this area over the next few years.

SUMMARY

Database technology has evolved as the information technology environment has passed through the four hardware waves of mainframes, minicomputers, personal computers, and client/server systems. As we have passed through these four major hardware waves, we have seen at least six generations of software systems that are specifically designed for the purpose of managing the external storage of computer data.

The earliest software for managing data on external storage devices were simple file systems that helped programmers manage the data on tape drives and early direct access storage devices. The file systems reflected the early process-oriented model of information processing.

BOX 4.3   IBM Information Warehouse components.

- **Enterprise Data.** IBM considers the enterprise data component to be the heart of the Information Warehouse Framework. It consists of databases maintained by the various database management systems that access the data used to run the enterprise. Not surprisingly, IBM's view is that the data managed by mainframe database software, such as IMS and DB2, makes up the bulk of the enterprise data used by an organization.

- **Data Delivery.** The data delivery component is the means by which business data is provided to managers and knowledge workers in the enterprise. Providing the data to authorized individuals may require copying, transforming, and enriching data using copy management tools and techniques. In this component, IBM makes a distinction between data extraction and data propagation. Extraction consists of making a copy of data for any purpose, including retrieval and updating. Propagation involves controlled copying between two databases such that the two databases implement a single logical copy of the database.

- **Decision Support.** In the decision support component are all of IBM's software tools for retrieving, manipulating, analyzing, and presenting information in the form required to support the decision-making process.

The first database systems were layered on top of the file systems and worked with databases that were hierarchical in nature. In a hierarchical database, information is logically arranged in an inverted tree structure. The earliest hierarchical database software began a shift to a data-oriented view of information processing in which data modeling became more important than process modeling.

The early hierarchical systems were soon joined by more flexible network-oriented database software that allowed arbitrary graph structures to be modeled in the database. Many of these database systems were based on the CODASYL specification for database management.

The hierarchical and network database architectures began to be replaced with a simpler relational data architecture in which data is viewed as a series of interrelated two-dimensional tables having rows and columns. The relational data model led the way toward converting the data-oriented view of computing to an orientation that concentrated on modeling the business environment that the information systems are designed to support.

The major advantages that the relational data model has over its predecessors helped to increase data independence, formalize the types of operations that could be performed on the database, reduce the redundancy of the data that had to be stored, and simplify the way in which the database software presents information to the user. All of the advantages of the relational approach enabled faster application development and reduced the maintenance that applications required.

The switch to the relational data model was a prerequisite for today's client/server database software that allows database processing to be performed by multiple computing systems interconnected in a network.

The newest type of database that is beginning to make an appearance is the object-oriented database that stores procedures as well as data in the database. Relational database systems are beginning to adopt some of the characteristics of object-oriented databases, and the distinction between them may begin to blur. Object-oriented databases and relational databases are likely to coexist, since each has a different set of goals and is designed for a different type of computer application.

Work is currently in progress on the idea of a data warehouse that can be used to implement decision-support systems. Data warehouse functions are designed to consolidate, manage, and transform an organization's production data in order to place the data into a form in which it can be presented to knowledge workers for use in the decision-making process.

Chapter 5 describes the capabilities of today's client/server database software and introduces the different database access functions that the database software performs.

Chapter 5

Database Access Software

A wide variety of database software packages is now available for mainframe, minicomputer, and personal computer platforms. This chapter describes the characteristics of the different types of database software that are available for accessing data stored in database form and discusses the general functions that database access software performs.

DATA DESCRIPTION FACILITIES

Any database software package must provide some facility for allowing the user or the database designer to define the data elements that will be stored in the database and to describe the relationships that exist among them. When using database software, we describe data elements and their relationships using a computer language, or other facility, that the database software understands.

Types of Database Languages

Early database software systems generally provided one or more specialized database languages that application developers, database designers, and database administrators used to interact with the database software for a variety of purposes. The sets of statements or other facilities that are used to control database software functions fall into the following three language categories:

- **Data Description Language.** The facilities making up a *data description language* (DDL) allow people to create, alter, and delete the various objects that implement the database, such as the tables, user views, domains, and indices of a relational database.

- **Data Manipulation Language.** The facilities making up a *data manipulation language* (DML) allow people to retrieve data from the database, to update and delete existing data, and to insert new data. Depending on the specific DML that the database software implements, these types of facilities can be employed either by an end user directly or by an application developer who is writing a program to access the database.

- **Data Control Language.** The facilities making up a *data control language* (DCL) allow people to perform administrative procedures relating to database objects, such as granting authorization to users for their access and requesting the execution of commitment or rollback functions.

Some database software packages implement DDL, DML, and DCL functions using a language, not unlike a programming language, that technical staff members employ to interact with the database software. Newer database software may provide more easy-to-use facilities, implemented through a graphical user interface (GUI), with which untrained users can interact directly to control at least some database software functions.

STRUCTURED QUERY LANGUAGE (SQL)

Most database software implements the relational data model that permits end users and programmers to employ a tabular view of the data that is stored in the database. The *Structured Query Language* (SQL) was developed specifically for use with relational databases, and SQL has now become an accepted standard that most relational database products implement in one form or another. This section introduces the characteristics of SQL, describes the environment in which SQL implementations are intended to operate, and introduces the types of data description language facilities that SQL provides.

When SQL was first defined, each vendor that implemented the language provided a few unique extensions to the language, and there were soon many dialects of SQL. In many cases, one vendor's SQL language definition was incompatible with all the others. SQL has now been standardized, and the statements making up the language are defined in an international standard. The various versions of SQL implemented by the different database software vendors are beginning to converge, and SQL has become a much more portable data access language than it has been in the past.

The SQL Environment

The SQL standard defines an SQL environment in which there exist different types of data objects used to implement a relational database on a storage system. The SQL data-related objects are illustrated in Fig. 5.1. The data making up a relational database consists of *SQL data* that is defined by an *SQL schema*. SQL schemas are defined in *catalogs* that may be grouped in *catalog clusters*. The following sections describe each of these categories of objects.

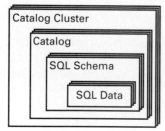

Figure 5.1   SQL data-related objects.

SQL Data

SQL data consists primarily of *tables* that are made up of *rows* and *columns*. The SQL standard also defines additional objects, such as *views*, *domains*, and *cursors*. Many relational database software systems also define objects not specifically referenced in the SQL standard, such as *indices*. Box 5.1 contains a summary of the types of SQL data objects that the standard defines.

BOX 5.1   SQL data objects.

- **Table.** A *table* is a set of data elements arranged in a two-dimensional array of columns and rows. A table is often called a *base table* to distinguish it from a view.
- **View.** A *view* is an alternative arrangement of the rows or columns from one or more base tables. It often defines a subset of the data contained in one or more base tables.
- **Domain.** A *domain* is a set of permissible values from which the values in one or more columns can be taken.
- **Cursor.** A *cursor* is an object that refers to a particular row in a table or view. A cursor is useful in application programs for processing the results of a relational operation one row at a time.

SQL Schemas

The data making up a particular collection of objects that defines one or more relational databases is defined by an object called an *SQL schema*. An SQL schema has a name that is unique within a particular catalog. It defines the owner of the SQL schema and contains descriptions of all the SQL data defined by the SQL schema. An SQL schema is essentially a computer-readable description of a relational database.

Catalogs and Catalog Clusters

One or more SQL schemas can be defined by a *catalog*. A catalog contains information about one or more SQL schemas. Catalogs can be grouped into collections of catalogs called *catalog clusters*. Catalog clusters are used to group schemas that are associated in some way.

SQL Data Description Language Statements

The SQL standard defines the following three SQL statements that can be used to perform data description language (DDL) functions:

- **CREATE.** Used to define a new SQL object, such as a table, view, or domain.
- **ALTER.** Used to modify the characteristics of an existing SQL object.
- **DROP.** Used to delete an existing SQL object from the SQL environment.

DATA DESCRIPTION USING SQL

The following shows what the SQL data description statements might look like to define the four tables that make up the shipping database introduced in Chapter 3:

```
CREATE TABLE Vessel
    (Vessel_#              CHAR (5),
    Hold_Size              SMALLINT,
    Vessel_Details         CHAR (20),
    PRIMARY KEY            (Vessel_#))
    IN DATABASE Shipping;

CREATE TABLE Port
    (Vessel_#              CHAR (5),
    Port                   CHAR (3),
    Arrival_Date           DATE,
    Departure_Date         DATE),
    PRIMARY KEY            (Vessel_#, Port))
    IN DATABASE Shipping;

CREATE TABLE Waybill
    (Waybill_#             CHAR (6),
    Vessel_#               CHAR (5),
    Orig_Port              CHAR (3),
    Dest_Port              CHAR (3),
    Consignee_#            CHAR (6),
    Shipper_#              CHAR (6),
    Delivery_Date          DATE,
    PRIMARY KEY            (Waybill_#))
    IN DATABASE Shipping;

CREATE TABLE Container
    (Container_#           CHAR (6),
    Waybill_#              CHAR (6),
    Contents_Description   CHAR (20),
    Handling_Instructions  CHAR (20),
    Container_Size         SMALLINT),
    PRIMARY KEY            (Container_#))
    IN DATABASE Shipping;
```

It is important to note that not all relational database software provides the same support for data description that the SQL standard defines. For example, the Microsoft Access implementation of SQL for personal computers uses SQL only as a data manipulation language (DML). Access handles data description language (DDL) functions through its own graphical user interface functions rather than through SQL. Many other database software products, such as IBM's DB2, make explicit use of the three SQL DDL statements for data description.

DATA DESCRIPTION USING MICROSOFT ACCESS

This section shows an example of how a database software product might implement data description functions without the use of SQL DDL statements. We show how the data description capabilities of Microsoft Access can be used to define a relational database that implements the shipping system logical data model that we introduced in Chapter 3.

Defining a Table

Figure 5.2 shows the windows that the Access software displays to allow us to begin defining one of the shipping system relational database tables.

Defining a Data Element

Access allows us to define the name of each of the data elements (which Access refers to as *fields*) in a table, specify the type of data to be represented by that data element, and provide a description of the data element. Access provides the user with online assistance in defining data element types and specifying their attributes through formatted windows, drop-down menus, and a comprehensive help system. Part of the definition dialog for one of the numeric data elements in the Vessel table is shown in Fig. 5.3.

　　　To define all the data elements for the shipping system database, the database designer calls up a separate window for each of the four tables and completes a dialog for each data element. Figure 5.4 shows the complete description of the Container table.

Defining Associations

After completing the table definitions, the database designer calls up a Relationships window to define the various associations that are needed between the tables. When complet-

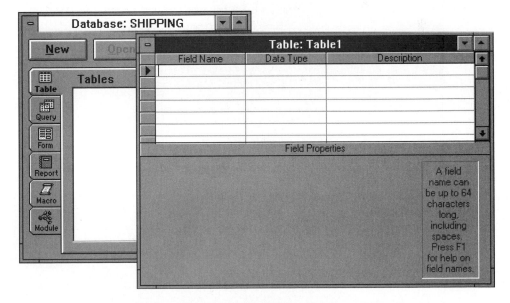

Figure 5.2　Microsoft Access database definition window.

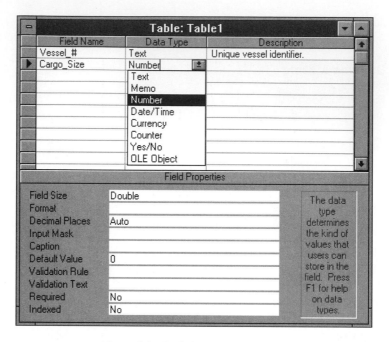

Figure 5.3 Defining a numeric field.

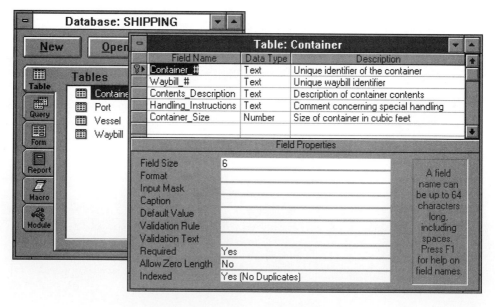

Figure 5.4 Container table definition.

ed, the Relationships window shows a graphical representation of how the tables making up the database are connected with one another. This is shown in Fig. 5.5.

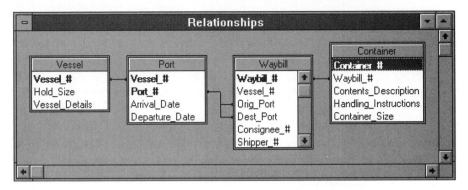

Figure 5.5   Microsoft Access Relationships window.

DATA ACCESS BY END USERS

A major purpose of database software is to impose an intermediary between the application program and the computer files that contain the stored data. The relationship between the application program, the database software, and the database is shown in Fig. 5.6.

Figure 5.6   Database software major functions.

The database software provides many application program facilities that previously needed to be coded into application programs when conventional file management systems were used. Data integrity can also be enhanced when a single software subsystem makes all data accesses. Many of these advantages were described in Chapter 1.

Early Database Software

The earliest database software provided facilities that could only be invoked by application programs written in conventional programming languages, such as COBOL. Some later database software products then began to provide specialized database languages that application developers could use to define database applications instead of using conventional programming languages. In the early days of database technology, a distinction was often made between two types of database software:

- **Host Language Database Software.** This term characterized a database software product that provided application programming support and required database applications to be written in a conventional programming language.

- **Self-Contained Database Software.** This term characterized a database software product that provided its own built-in language and other facilities for accessing the database and creating database applications.

Self-contained database software products evolved to the point where the database languages they supported were sometimes easy enough to use that end users could employ the database software directly to write applications without the help of professional application developers. Most host language database products also then began to include easy-to-use database languages in addition to support for conventional programming languages.

Today, the distinction between self-contained and host language database software is no longer useful. Most modern database products provide support for a variety of programming languages as well as support for easy-to-use query and reporting languages that can be employed by end users as well as by professional application developers.

End User Access with SQL

Many database products allow users to employ the user-interface device for directly entering data manipulation language (DML) statements that are part of SQL to query and manipulate the database. However, SQL is a powerful language and takes time to learn. Its primary use today is not as an end user language but rather as a language that professional application developers use in custom-written database applications. SQL is also often employed as an internal language used by the database software itself in exchanging information about database access requests among its various components. Therefore, while SQL can be employed by an end user, it is more often used by professional application developers and by the software itself.

Query by Example

Query by Example (QBE) is an easy-to-use database language that was introduced a number of years ago in the IBM mainframe environment. QBE allows the user to formulate queries and manipulate data using a tabular data format that is ideally suited to working with a relational database. QBE proved to be quite powerful and at the same time intuitive and easy to use. Now, many modern database software products provide an end-user-oriented query and data manipulation facility based on QBE.

Simple QBE Query

Although each implementation of QBE is different, all have similar characteristics. Here, we show an example of the Microsoft Access implementation of QBE. Appendix A contains a more comprehensive discussion of the QBE language.

Figure 5.7 shows how we might request a list of all the rows in the Vessel table using the graphical form of the *Query by Example* (QBE) query language supported by Microsoft Access. The upper part of the display shows the table or tables from which we are retrieving data, in this case the Vessel table. Access shows the column structure of the Vessel table. The column name in bold—Vessel_#—indicates the primary key of the

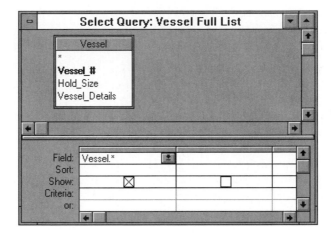

Figure 5.7 Microsoft Access QBE query to display Vessel Information.

table. We use the lower part of the display to describe the query we would like to make. In this example, the asterisk (*) character following the table name Vessel indicates that we want a list of the data in all the columns in the Vessel table.

Query Results

Figure 5.8 shows the results of running the above query.

Select Query: Vessel Full List

Vessel_#	Hold_Size	Vessel_Details
00165	12765	Tanker
00205	28775	Freighter
00276	12756	Tanker
00339	28775	Freighter
00463	12756	Tanker

Record: 1 of 5

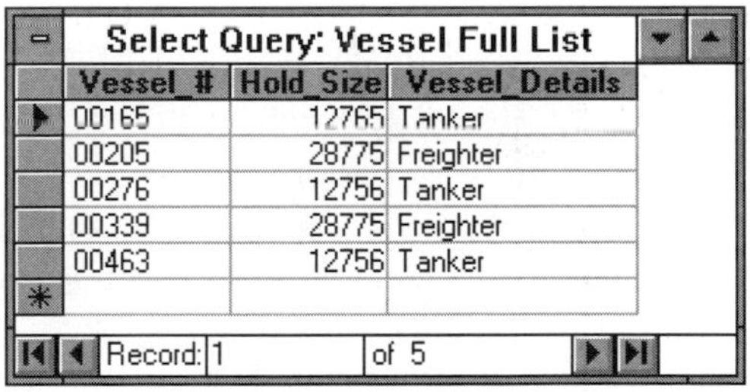

Figure 5.8 Vessel table query results.

Selecting Columns and Rows

Figure 5.9 shows a query that asks for only certain columns and rows from the Vessel table to be displayed. The QBE display indicates the following:

- We would like to see only the Vessel_# and Hold_Size columns.
- We would like the resulting table sorted by Vessel_# and then by Hold_Size.
- We would like to see only rows where the Hold_Size data element value is greater than 20,000.

Figure 5.10 shows the results of the query in Fig. 5.9.

Many database software products implement a variation of QBE, and it has been proven to be an easy-to-use, yet powerful, language for expressing database operations.

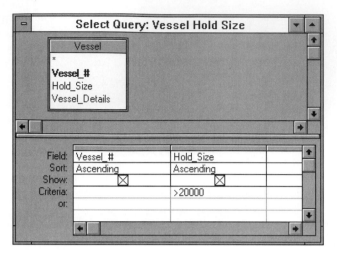

Figure 5.9   Selection query.

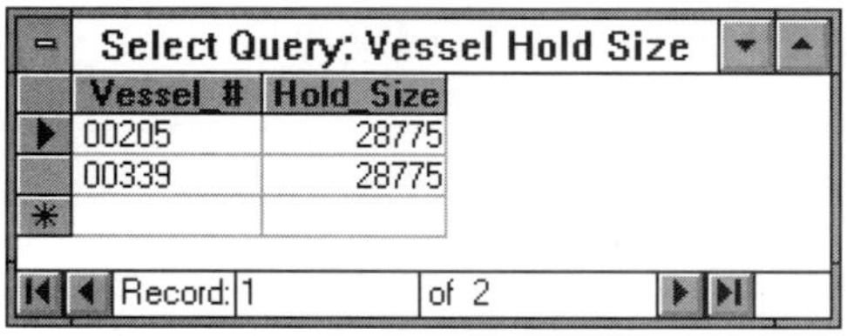

Figure 5.10   Selection query results.

However, many database software systems also implement a wide variety of fourth-generation languages and query and reporting facilities that have no relationship to QBE.

DATA ACCESS BY APPLICATION PROGRAMS

Most database software products implement facilities that professional application developers can employ in writing custom database applications. These facilities are generally provided in addition to more easy-to-use language facilities intended for end users, such as those based on Query by Example.

Over the years, a number of different data manipulation languages have been developed. In the early years of database technology, each database software vendor created a unique database language that programmers could use. This made it difficult to move an application from one database software package to another.

Application Program Access with SQL

Now that most modern database software products implement the relational data model, the Structured Query Language (SQL) has come to be almost universally supported as a data manipulation language for the database environment.

As we discussed earlier, SQL is not primarily intended for end users. It is a sophisticated data manipulation language that application developers can use in conjunction with a conventional programming language, or with a fourth-generation language, for creating custom database applications.

SQL Program-Related Objects

Earlier in this chapter, you saw the data-related objects that the SQL standard defines. The SQL standard also defines a set of *program-related objects*. These are objects in the SQL environment, shown in Fig. 5.11, that operate on the data-related objects that make up relational databases. The major program-related objects are SQL *statements* grouped to make up SQL *transactions*. The sequences of SQL statements making up SQL transactions are executed by entities called SQL *agents*, which operate within an *implementation* of the SQL language. Box 5.2 contains brief descriptions of the four types of program-related objects.

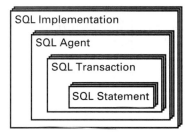

Figure 5.11   SQL program-related objects.

BOX 5.2   SQL program-related objects.

- **SQL Statements.** *SQL statements* are statements that conform to the rules of the SQL language. SQL statements operate directly on the data-related objects listed in Box 5.1. The functions of commonly used SQL statements that make up the SQL language are introduced later in this chapter.

- **SQL Transactions.** An *SQL transaction* is a sequence of SQL statements that are related with respect to recovery. The SQL statements making up a transaction must all be executed completely or they must not be executed at all. If the execution of any SQL statement making up a transaction fails, then the results of all the SQL statements that have already been executed as part of that transaction must be backed out. These are transaction management functions and are described more thoroughly in Chapter 6.

- **SQL Agents.** An *SQL agent* is defined by the SQL standard as an implementation-defined entity that causes the execution of the SQL statements in one or more transactions. In effect, SQL agents are the application programs that issue SQL statements.

- **SQL Implementation.** An *SQL implementation* consists of the database software that interprets the SQL statements on behalf of an SQL agent (application program) and carries out the computer processing that the SQL statements describe.

SQL Language Statements

The following is a list of the most commonly used SQL statements that make up the SQL data manipulation language (DML):

- **SELECT.** Used to specify database retrievals and to create alternative views of the data contained in one or more base tables.
- **UPDATE.** Used to change the values in existing rows in base tables or views.
- **INSERT.** Used to add new rows to tables or views.
- **DELETE.** Used to delete rows from tables or views.

SQL Queries

An easy way to become familiar with the data manipulation language capabilities of SQL is to work with a database software product that supports SQL as well as an easy-to-use end-user query facility. Microsoft Access is a good product for this purpose.

Figure 5.12 shows the query we looked at previously that asks for a display of the Vessel_# and Hold_Size data elements from the Vessel table for all those rows in which the Hold_Size value is greater than 20,000. Figure 5.13 shows the SQL SELECT statement that Access generates to implement the same retrieval. (The actual statement that Access generates has been simplified for clarity.) Figure 5.13 shows the general format of all SELECT statements. It begins with the keyword SELECT and then lists the columns that the resulting table should include. A FROM clause lists the table or tables containing the desired columns. A WHERE clause specifies selection criteria to be used to select rows to be displayed. Finally, an ORDER BY clause lists the columns on which the resulting table is to be sorted. Notice that the Access implementation of SQL allows the special character # to be used in a column name only if the name is enclosed in square brackets.

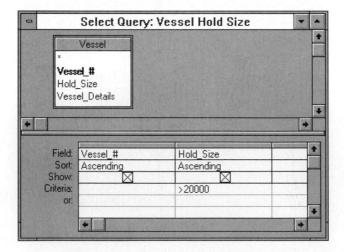

Figure 5.12   Selection query.

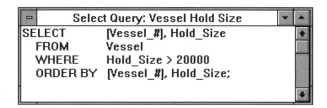

Figure 5.13   Generated SQL SELECT statement.

The SQL SELECT statement has many additional options that can be used to formulate almost any desired query. Structured Query Language is described in detail in Part VI.

INTELLIGENT DATABASES

As we introduced in Chapter 4, the relational database model has at its heart a database that stores only user data. The idea behind an object-oriented database is that the database should store not only data but also all the procedures that operate on that data.

Stored Procedures

Many vendors of client/server relational databases have expanded the role of the relational database model and allow the database to include stored procedures as well as user data. Database administrators and database designers can use such facilities to build a level of intelligence into the database.

Database software vendors often implement stored procedures through an extension to SQL. This extension often takes the form of procedural language statements that can be used in addition to the DML, DDL, and DCL statements that make up the SQL language.

For example, many Oracle database software products include a PL/SQL language component. PL/SQL defines procedural statements that can be used to define stored procedures that are placed into the database along with the tables of a relational database. An application program can access these procedures by name and cause predefined database processing to be performed whenever the procedure is executed. A stored procedure is different from a conventional subroutine because the procedure is executed by the database software in the machine on which the database software runs. Thus, in a distributed environment, a stored procedure may be run on a different machine from the machine with which the user is interacting.

Database Triggers and Rules

Some stored procedures can be designed to be executed on demand by application programs that access the database software. Other stored procedures might be designed to be executed automatically whenever some condition is met. A database trigger defines a set of rules under which a particular stored procedure executes. When a database trigger is used to invoke a stored procedure, the end user or the application program that is accessing the database may not be aware of stored procedures that are invoked through the use of triggers.

The language statements that a database software vendor makes available for defining stored procedures and database triggers determine the uses to which these facilities can be put. If the database software implements a full-function procedural language for these elements, then the database software can be made to perform almost any type of processing when a database trigger is activated.

As a simple example, suppose a database is accessed by a number of users concurrently using different application programs. Further suppose that you would like to write a special record to a log file after each 1000 new records have been added to the database. You could design a simple database trigger that is activated each time a program issues an INSERT SQL statement for the database in question. The database trigger would activate a stored procedure that simply counts the times it is activated and executes the procedural code necessary to write a log record after each 1000 activations.

Without a stored procedure facility, all the various application programs that add records to the database would need to cooperate to perform this simple function. With a stored procedure, it would be possible to add such a function to a set of database applications with requiring that any of the programs be modified in any way. The execution of the logging function would be hidden from the applications that access the database.

SUMMARY

The sets of statements or other facilities that are used to control database software functions fall into three language categories. The facilities making up a data description language (DDL) allow people to create, alter, and delete the various objects that implement the database, such as the tables, user views, domains, and indices of a relational database. The facilities making up a data manipulation language (DML) allow people to retrieve data from the database, to update and delete existing data, and to insert new data. The facilities making up a data control language (DCL) allow people to perform administrative procedures relating to database objects, such as granting authorization to users for their access and requesting the execution of commitment or rollback functions.

The Structured Query Language (SQL) is a standardized database language that can play the role of DDL, DML, and DCL. The SQL environment defines four types of data-related objects. SQL data consists primarily of tables that are made up of rows and columns. An SQL schema describes the SQL data defined for a database. A catalog contains information about one or more SQL schemas. Catalogs can be grouped into collections of catalogs called catalog clusters.

Database software generally provides one set of facilities that end users employ to access data and another that application programs use. While SQL statements can be issued directly by end users, most database software provides for end user access through simpler query and reporting facilities. Many end user query facilities are based on a language called Query by Example (QBE).

Most database software allows professional application programs to use SQL as a data manipulation language. The SQL standard defines four program-related objects that operate on the data-related objects. SQL statements are grouped to form an SQL transaction, a sequence of SQL statements that are related with respect to recovery. SQL transactions are executed by an SQL agent, which corresponds to an application program that issues SQL statements. An SQL implementation consists of the database software that interprets the SQL statements on behalf of an SQL agent. The most commonly used SQL DML statements are SELECT, UPDATE, INSERT, and DELETE.

Stored procedures and database triggers allow the database administrator or database designer to build intelligence into the database by storing procedural code in the database. A stored procedure can be executed by the database software on demand by application programs or automatically when database triggers are activated.

Chapter 6 describes facilities that database software provides to maintain the integrity of the data stored in the database.

Chapter **6**

Transaction Processing Software

Transaction processing software is often used in the enterprise computing environment to enhance the availability and accuracy of an organization's data and to protect it from unauthorized access. Transaction processing functions might be handled by the database software itself, by some software subsystem operating outside the scope of the database software, or by a combination of the two. The best known software for transaction processing in the enterprise computing environment is IBM's Customer Information Control System (CICS).

Some database software products implement minimal data integrity facilities. For example, a simple database package designed to be used on a single personal computer by a single user needs no special data integrity facilities. The user is responsible for data integrity and may provide it by physically limiting access to the computer on which the data resides and by implementing appropriate manual backup procedures. With more complex database software used to support enterprisewide functions, transaction processing facilities become more important.

Two factors complicate data integrity in an enterprise computing environment:

- **Concurrent Access.** The data stored in the database may be accessed concurrently by many users, many of whom need to update the data.
- **Data Distribution.** The data stored in the database may not all be located in a single central location. With distributed database software, the data may be stored on a number of different computing systems interconnected by a network.

TRANSACTION PROCESSING FUNCTIONS

The idea behind transaction processing is to allow application designers to bind together two or more operations on data so that an application can execute them as a single unit of work. The unit of work must either be executed in its entirety or not be executed at all. To bind together multiple operations in this manner, the developer constructs a single *transaction* that is made up of all the operations forming the unit of work.

Protected Resources and Synchronization

Transaction processing is based on the concept of *protected resources* and the *synchronization of updates* to those protected resources. Although the notion of a protected resource can be applied to any type of object in the computing environment, we will assume in this chapter that the protected resource comprises all the data files implementing the database.

When transaction management functions are used, an application program specifies at intervals during its execution either that changes made up to that point are to be considered *committed* (made permanent) or that the changes should be *rolled back* (undone). The specific point in an application's execution at which changes are either committed or rolled back is called a *synchronization point*.

At the time that an application declares a synchronization point, it must know that the different portions of the database affected by the changes the application has made up to that point are in synchronization with one another. In a distributed environment, the database might be spread over a number of different machines. Therefore, if a failure occurs in one machine, all the various portions of the database, on all the machines, must be restored to the condition in which they existed prior to the most recent synchronization point. After the protected database has been restored to its original condition, the application's execution can often be successfully restarted from that point.

An application's first synchronization point is established when the application begins execution. Another synchronization point is also established when the application terminates. If an application does not explicitly create other synchronization points, the entire processing of the application represents a single unit of work—a single transaction. If an application whose processing represents a single transaction terminates normally, all changes that the application has made to portions of the database under its control can be committed. If the application terminates abnormally, all changes that the application has made to the database must be rolled back. The single-transaction approach is often appropriate for an application that executes quickly, possibly processing a single short transaction each time it executes.

If an application executes for a longer period of time, it may be desirable to divide up that program's processing into a number of separate transactions. The database software must provide functions that the program can invoke to declare a synchronization point at intervals during its processing. The processing that the program does between any two synchronization points is considered a separate transaction. With this approach, the database software treats the processing associated with each transaction as a separate logical unit of work.

SQL Transaction Management Statements

The Structured Query Language (SQL) defines two statements, considered data control language (DCL) functions, that an application can issue to create synchronization points:

- **COMMIT.** Used to establish a synchronization point to indicate that all changes that have been made to the database up to that point are to be made permanent.

- **ROLLBACK.** Used to indicate that changes that have been made to the database since the most recent synchronization point are to be reversed, thus restoring the database to the condition in which it existed prior to the establishment of that synchronization point.

Database software that uses database languages other than sql may provide commands that provide equivalent functions for invoking the commit function and for requesting a rollback operation.

TWO-PHASE COMMIT PROTOCOL

Transaction management functions are complex, especially when the application program and the database management software are running in a distributed environment. In a distributed environment, transaction management functions are normally implemented through the use of a *two-phase commit protocol* that controls the processing necessary to commit the changes that an application's components have made.

The term *protocol* is often used in computer communications literature. A protocol is a specification that lays out the formats of a set of messages that are exchanged by two or more communicating processes, and specifies the rules that govern those exchanges.

A two-phase commit protocol consists of messages that are sent between the various components of a distributed system to control commit and rollback processing. The protocol is used to ensure that each transaction is either executed in its entirety as a complete unit of work or that changes to the database that have been made by a failed transaction are properly rolled back.

Resource Manager

In a distributed environment, commit and rollback operations must be coordinated by a software component that has a global view of the entire distributed environment. This component is sometimes called a *resource manager*. The resource manager must be capable of communicating with the database access software running in each machine in the distributed environment. To enhance availability, many machines in the distributed environment may be capable of running a resource manager component, but typically only one resource manager is active at any time for a particular protected resource.

Two-Phase Commit Operation

The following is a somewhat simplified description of the processing that must be carried out in executing each phase of the two-phase commit protocol.

Invoking the Commit Function

The application program begins the two-phase commit operation by invoking a commit function to establish a synchronization point. The local database software begins the commit operation by informing the resource manager that it is declaring a synchronization point and that the resource manager should begin commitment processing. If the local database software and the resource manager are running in different machines, this involves an exchange across the network of a commit message and an acknowledgment of the receipt of that commit message.

All of the subsequent processing involved in the execution of the two-phase commit protocol is then coordinated by the resource manager.

Phase One—Prepare to Commit

The resource manager begins phase one by sending a prepare to commit message to each of the database access components that is accessing any portion of the distributed database that may have been changed as a result of the processing of this transaction. These software components may be running on the same machine or on different machines from the resource manager and the application program that invoked the commit function.

Each database access software component that receives a prepare to commit message performs any processing that is required to be able to either commit changes that it has made to data under its control or to roll back any changes that it has made since the most recent synchronization point. This processing may include physically performing any updates that may be pending in buffers. If all the preparatory processing is successful, the database access software responds with a positive acknowledgment to the resource manager's prepare to commit message.

If the resource manager receives positive acknowledgments to *all* the prepare to commit messages it sent, it considers phase one of the protocol to be successful. It then begins phase two of the protocol. Figure 6.1 summarizes the steps involved in phase one of a successful commit operation with a distributed database.

If a database access component is not successful in completing the preparatory processing it started as a result of the prepare to commit message it received, the component responds to the resource manager with a negative acknowledgment. If the resource manager receives *any* negative acknowledgments to the prepare to commit messages it sent, it considers the entire commit operation to have failed. It is important to note that if one or more of the database access components does not respond within some time period to a prepare to commit message, possibly due to a hardware or software failure, the resource manager treats the time-out as a negative acknowledgment.

The resource manager handles a failure by initiating another exchange of messages to cause *all* the database software components to roll back the changes they have made since the most recent synchronization point. The resource manager also responds with a negative acknowledgment to the original commit message sent by the local database access software component on behalf of the application program. The application program is then notified that the commit operation it requested has failed.

Phase Two—Commit or Rollback

Phase two of the two-phase commit protocol begins only if *all* the database access software components respond with positive acknowledgments to the resource manager's prepare to commit messages.

The resource manager begins phase two of the protocol by sending a commit message to all relevant database access software components. When each database access

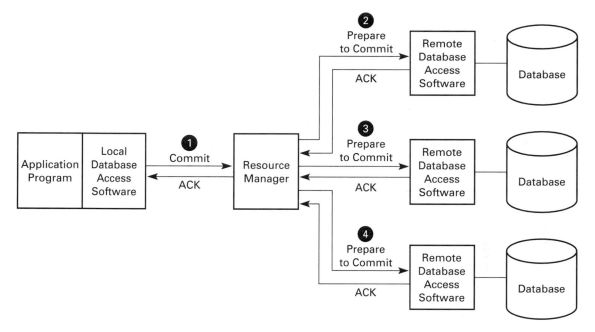

Figure 6.1 Phase one of a successful commit operation with a distributed database.

software component receives the commit message, that component commits the changes it has made to its portion of the database. Each database access software component then informs the resource manager that its portion of the commit operation is completed successfully by responding with a positive acknowledgment to the commit message.

If the resource manager receives positive acknowledgments to all the commit messages it sent, the resource manager considers the commit operation to have succeeded. The resource manager then responds with a positive acknowledgment to the original commit message sent by the local database access software on behalf of the application program. The application program is then informed that the commit operation has succeeded. Figure 6.2 summarizes the processing involved in phase two of a successful commit operation.

If any database access component is unable to successfully commit its changes, it responds to the resource manager with a negative acknowledgment to the commit message. If the resource manager receives *any* negative acknowledgments to the commit messages it sent, it considers the commit operation to have failed. Again, the resource manager treats the absence of a response to a commit message as a negative acknowledgment.

The resource manager handles a failure by causing all database changes to be rolled back. The application program is then notified that the commit operation it requested has failed. The application program may handle the failure by restarting itself and trying to execute the transaction again.

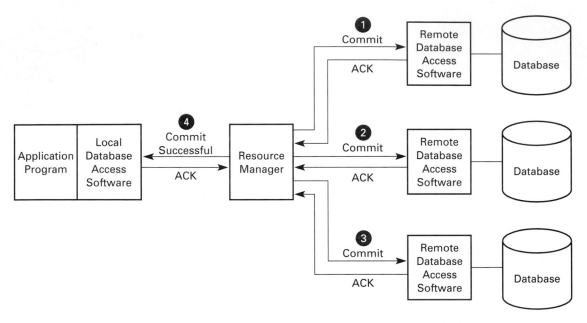

Figure 6.2   Phase two of a successful commit operation with a distributed database.

The processing steps involved in the two-phase commit operation have been simplified somewhat for clarity. However, the intent of the two-phase commit protocol is to ensure that either *all* the database changes associated with the transaction have been successfully made or that *all* the changes have been rolled back. A failure at any point in commitment processing causes the database to be restored to the condition in which it existed before the transaction began execution.

DATA INTEGRITY EXPOSURES

As we have already discussed, many database software packages are designed to allow multiple users to access a database at the same time. A number of data integrity exposures can result from allowing multiple users to have concurrent access to the same database. The following sections describe some of these.

Unrepeatable Reads

When a program reads a data element value from the database, it expects that data element value to remain constant during its execution, unless the program itself updates that value. If two programs are allowed to access the same data element value concurrently, a situation called an *unrepeatable read* can occur. The following shows an example of an unrepeatable read.

1. Program B retrieves a data element value from the database.

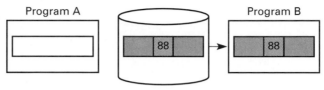

2. Program A retrieves the same value.

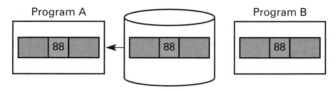

3. Program A updates the data element and writes the new value back into the database.

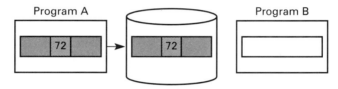

4. Program B now reads the same data element a second time. The data element value is now different from its value when Program B first accessed it.

An unrepeatable read is an example of a loss of read integrity in accessing the database. In many application situations, it is necessary that an application program is able to access a database as if that application program had exclusive control over the database, even though other users may be accessing it concurrently. Locking mechanisms can be used to prevent unrepeatable reads from occurring in a concurrent database access environment. We discuss locking mechanisms later in this chapter.

Access to Uncommitted Data

Another way in which loss of read integrity can occur is by allowing a program to access updated data that has not yet been committed. The following sequence shows an example of a situation that would permit access to uncommitted data.

1. Program A reads a data element value.

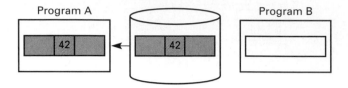

2. Program A updates the data element value and stores the new value into the database.

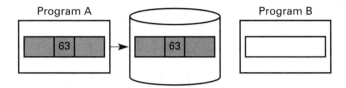

3. Program B reads the updated data element and uses it for its processing.

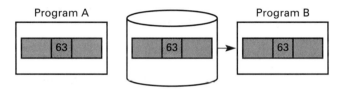

4. Program A then fails, and the database software rolls back the changes that program A made, thus restoring the data element to its original value.

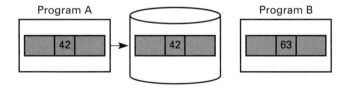

Program B's processing is now based on the wrong data. If program B reads the row a second time, the data element value will be different from its value when program B first accessed the table.

Lost Updates

Another potential problem with concurrency is that of *lost updates*. The following sequence shows how an update can be lost when two concurrently executing programs are both allowed to update the same data element.

1. Program A retrieves a data element that has the value 54.

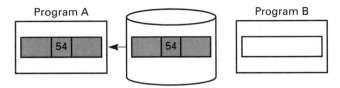

2. Program B retrieves the same data element.

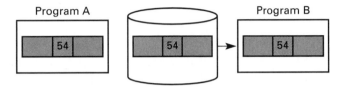

3. Program A updates the data element by deducting 10 from it and writing the new value into the database. At this point the value of the data element is 44.

4. Program B updates the same data element by deducting 5 from it and writing the new value into the database. The value of the data element in the database is now 49. The value for the data element should be 39, which reflects both updates.

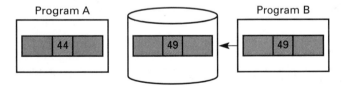

When two concurrently executing programs simultaneously update data element values, the results of the first program's update can be nullified by the second program, resulting in an incorrect value being stored in the database. A lost update is an example of a loss of write integrity in accessing the database.

LOCKING MECHANISMS

In order to avoid the problems associated with loss of either read or write integrity, a system of *locks* is often used. When the database software places a lock on database data, the lock controls whether some other user can access the database, and if so, in what way. The basic principle that database software generally follows is that no program should be allowed to access data that another program has changed but has not yet committed. The database software typically places a lock on data whenever a program performs an activity that potentially involves the updating of that data. The lock is released only after the program establishes a synchronization point and has either committed the changes or rolled them back.

In general, the database software automatically places locks on the appropriate data and removes the locks as required to protect the integrity of the data in the database. Generally, an application program is not concerned with acquiring and releasing of locks. However, many database software packages provide functions that allow programs to manually set and release locks for special purposes.

Lock Extent

Database software can potentially use locks that protect different portions of the database in controlling data integrity. The following are examples of some of the various lock extents that are possible:

- A lock might protect an entire relational database.
- A lock might protect one of the individual disk files that implements a portion of the database.
- A lock might protect an entire database table.
- A lock might protect some specified range of rows in a table.
- A lock might protect some arbitrary collection of data elements, such as all the data elements that are moved between disk and the computer's RAM in a single physical disk access.
- A lock might protect all the data elements in an individual table row.
- A lock might protect an individual data element in a table row.

Locks that protect large portions of a database tend to involve little software overhead in acquiring and releasing the locks, but they may cause large portions of the database to be unavailable to other users for significant periods of time. Locks that protect small portions of the database tend to involve more overhead because locks must be acquired and released more frequently. But a lock of small extent has less effect on other concurrent users who may also be requesting access to the database, because a larger portion of the database remains unaffected by the lock.

The database software may give the user or application program the option of specifying the extent of the locks that the software should acquire to protect the integrity of the database. Alternatively, the database software may itself determine the extent of lock that is appropriate, given the type of processing that is being performed.

Lock Types

The database software may implement various types of locks that indicate the type of access to the database being requested. The two types of locks that are the most commonly implemented are shared-access locks and exclusive-access locks:

- **Shared-Access Locks.** A *shared-access* lock allows the lock owner to read the locked data but not to change it. A user can acquire a shared-access lock on data after one or more other users has also acquired a shared access lock on it.

- **Exclusive-Access Locks.** An *exclusive-access* lock allows the lock owner to read and change the locked data in any desired way. No other user can access the locked data or acquire a lock on it while an exclusive-access lock is in effect. On the other hand, no user can acquire an exclusive-access lock on data that already has a shared-access lock on it.

The database software typically places a shared access lock on the appropriate data when an application program requests a database operation that retrieves data from the database. If the program then later declares its intention to update data that it has retrieved, the lock must be upgraded to an exclusive-access lock before the user will be allowed to perform the update operation. If other programs have also acquired shared-access locks on the same data, the program attempting to update the data must wait until all other users have released their shared-access locks before the update program's lock can be upgraded to an exclusive-access lock and the update operation permitted.

Deadlocks

A locking mechanism can allow *deadlocks* to occur. Suppose program A acquires a shared-access lock on data, and program B then also acquires a shared-access lock on the same data. Now suppose program A and program B both declare their intentions to update the data. An update requires that the lock be upgraded to an exclusive-access lock before the update will be permitted. Changing a lock to an exclusive-access lock requires that that there be no shared-access lock already on the data. Program A waits for program B to release its shared access lock. At the same time program B waits for program A to release its shared access lock. Therefore, both programs will wait indefinitely.

Database software uses various mechanisms to detect deadlock situations and to recover from them. Recovering from a deadlock situation generally requires that the database software abnormally terminate one of the programs to allow the other program to proceed.

AUTHENTICATION AND AUTHORIZATION

Authentication and authorization are two more facilities that many database software products implement that are related to data integrity.

Authentication

The term *authentication* refers to facilities in the computing environment that are used to determine the identity of a user or application program that is attempting to access a database. Authentication is handled sometimes by the database software and sometimes by facilities outside the scope of the database software. Systems of user IDs and passwords are most often used to implement authentication procedures.

Authorization

The term *authorization* refers to facilities designed to control the specific resources that a given user can access once that user has been authenticated. The SQL language provides two data control language (DCL) statements that can be used by an SQL implementation to handle authorization facilities:

- **GRANT.** Used to give users authorization to access an SQL object.
- **REVOKE.** Used to remove a user's authorization to access an SQL object.

SUMMARY

The two factors of concurrent database access and data distribution complicate data integrity in the client/server environment. Most database software designed for the enterprise computing environment use transaction processing functions to enhance data integrity. Transaction processing is based on the concept of protected resources and the synchronization of updates to those resources. An application program creates synchronization points at which changes made up to that point are to be considered committed (made permanent) or that the changes should be rolled back (undone). Application programs can control transaction processing by issuing the SQL COMMIT and ROLLBACK statements.

In a distributed environment, transaction management functions are normally implemented through the use of a two-phase commit protocol. In phase one of a two-phase commit, all the components in a distributed application prepare their protected resources for either a commit or a rollback. In phase two, the components all either commit their changes or all roll them back, depending on whether failures are detected.

Possible data integrity exposures in a concurrent processing environment include unrepeatable reads, allowing access to uncommitted data, and lost updates. Data integrity can be controlled through the use of locking mechanisms, including shared-access locks and exclusive-access locks.

Authentication refers to facilities in the computing environment that are used to determine the identity of a user or application program that is attempting to access a database. Authentication is often handled outside the scope of the database software. Authorization refers to facilities designed to control the specific resources that a given user can access. The SQL language provides the GRANT and REVOKE statements to support authorization operations.

Chapter 7 begins a discussion of the client/server approach to distributed computing and examines different possible configurations of client/server systems.

Chapter **7**

Client/Server Computing

Client/server computing is an overused buzzword. Marketers in the information technology industry have used it to describe almost every conceivable form of computing. In this chapter, we characterize client/server computing as a broad computing paradigm in which the centralized processors of an earlier era are being replaced by networks of smaller, less expensive computers. With client/server computing, the processing power of a collection of computer systems is brought to bear on a business problem.

The technology behind many of today's popular database software tools is based on a form of client/server computing. However, the use of client/server database software does not represent the only possible form of client/server computing.

This chapter examines a number of general application architectures that are based on the client/server paradigm. Then Chapter 8 looks at different ways in which client/server database applications can be configured. Finally, in Chapter 9, we look at various architectures that can be used when the database itself is distributed among a number of machines.

COMPUTING APPLICATION COMPONENTS

With client/server computing in its simplest form, an application component executing in one computing system, called the *client*, requests a service of an application component executing in another computing system, called the *server* (see Fig. 7.1). Both the application processes and the machines they run on are often referred to using the terms client and server.

Notice that the fundamental client/server application structure consists of three physical components:

- **Client Machine.** This is the computing system that runs the client component of the application. It makes one or more requests for services.

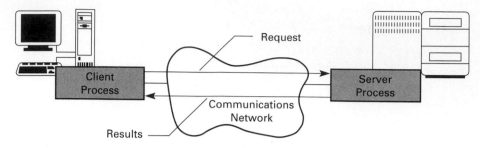

Figure 7.1   Client/server computing.

- **Server Machine.** This is the computing system that runs the server component of the application. It satisfies a client's request for a service and returns results to the client component.
- **Communications Network.** These are the communication facilities that allow one or more messages making up a request to be passed from the client to the server and that allow one or more messages containing results to be passed from the server back to the client.

The client/server computing paradigm allows many client components to access a common service that is provided by a shared server component. It also allows a client component to access many different servers. This broad paradigm can be adapted to create a variety of different forms of distributed computing. The different distributed computing variations allow client/server applications to be built using a variety of very different types of application development, database, and computer networking technologies.

As we will see in this chapter, there is great flexibility in configuring the three major components shown in Fig. 7.1. In the simplest case, the client and server components both run on the same machine and no communications network is necessary. In a very complex case, there may be many different client components, each running on its own machine, and many different server components, running on still other machines. The various machines might be tied together by an extensive, multivendor enterprise network that spans one or more continents.

The client component is generally considered to be the *active* component since it is the component that asks for a service to be performed. The server is generally the *passive* component and waits for a request to arrive from a client before it does its work. However, a server machine running database software might implement stored procedures and database triggers, and it is conceivable that the server component might play the active role when a trigger is activated and ask a user at a client machine to supply some needed data.

Machines operating in the roles of clients and servers can change their roles depending on the processing being performed. For example, client A might send a request for a service to server B. In order to satisfy client A's request, server B might have to play the role of client and make a service request of server C, and so on.

THREE-TIER MODEL OF CLIENT/SERVER COMPUTING

There are a number of possible architectural models that are useful in classifying client/server computing configurations. To help in discussing the types of configurations that are possible, we will begin by characterizing computing applications as consisting of a collection of individual components each of which falls into one of the following three categories:

- **User Interface Processing.** These are software components responsible for accepting input from users and for displaying or printing results.
- **Function Processing.** These are software components responsible for performing the processing necessary to solve a particular business problem.
- **Data-Access Processing.** These are software components responsible for accessing data stored on external storage devices, such as disk drives.

Any number of the three types of application components can be combined in various ways to create different configurations of client/server computing. Viewing computer applications as consisting of collections of components in the three categories listed above is sometimes called the *three-tier model* of client/server computing.

Four fundamental configurations are possible using the three-tier model:

- Single computing system model
- User interface distribution model
- Data access distribution model
- Function distribution model

The above configurations can be used in combination to produce configurations of any desired complexity. The following sections describe each of these client/server distribution models.

Single Computing System Model

Much of today's computing takes place in a single computing system, in which user interface processing, function processing, and data access processing are all executed in the same machine (see Fig. 7.2). In the configuration shown in Fig. 7.2, the personal computer on the left is used as a terminal, and the processing that implements the user interface is performed by the larger machine on the right.

In converting a single-computer application to a client/server configuration, decisions must be made regarding how software components will be distributed among two or more separate computing systems in a network. In a typical application that executes on a single computing system, components in all three categories are often intertwined in a way that makes it difficult to distinguish between the three components. In creating client/server computing applications it is important that components that fall into the three categories be clearly distinguished from one another. An

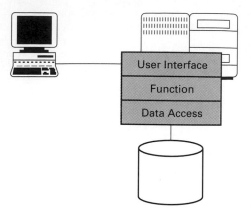

Figure 7.2   Single computing system model.

application consisting of undocumented spaghetti code will be difficult to convert to a client/server environment.

User Interface Distribution Model

The *user interface distribution* model represents a commonly used form of client/server computing. In this model, the application component that implements the user interface processing executes in one computing system, and the components that perform function processing and data access processing run in another computing system (see Fig. 7.3). In a common use of this configuration, a personal computer client system is used to handle user interface tasks, and a more powerful server system is used to handle all other application processing.

IBM has referred to a certain form of the user interface distribution model—in which the client machine is a personal computer and the server is a mainframe—as "cooperative processing." However, there is no agreement in the industry concerning definitions for such terms as "cooperative processing" or "distributed processing," so this book avoids using them.

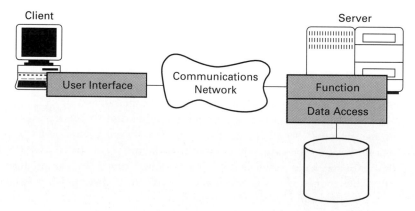

Figure 7.3   User interface distribution model.

Data Access Distribution Model

The data access distribution model is another widely used form of client/server computing. In this model, the application component that performs data access processing runs in a different computing system from application components that perform function processing and user interface processing. This is shown in Fig. 7.4.

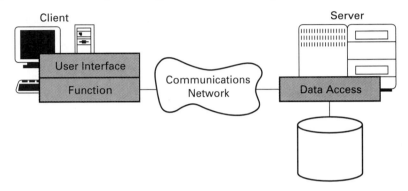

Figure 7.4   Data access distribution model.

Distributed applications that use client/server database software often conform to the data access distribution model. The database software may run on a computing system that plays the role of a *database server*. Application components that make requests for access to the database may run on other computing systems.

Function Distribution Model

In the function distribution model, the actual application functions are distributed among a number of different processors. The function processing components of the application might be distributed among one or more client components and one or more server components, each of which can be running in a different computing system.

Figure 7.5 shows a configuration that combines function distribution and data access distribution using three separate computing systems. With function distribution, a client component initiates a distributed activity. The target of that activity is a server. A particular service that a server provides is made up of a set of functions that the server performs on behalf of a client. Function distribution can be employed in conjunction with distributing the user interface and data access processing to create powerful applications having any number of components.

THE COMMUNICATIONS NETWORK

In all the previous examples in which an application's computer processing is spread over multiple machines, we have assumed that there is a communications network (shown as a blob) that allows one computer to exchange information with another.

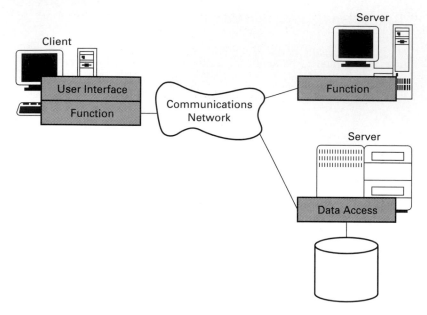

Figure 7.5   Function distribution and data access distribution.

In a client/server environment, the communications network might be very simple (or nonexistent in the case where the client and server components run on the same machine). In a simple example using two machines, the network might consist of a simple cable that is used to connect the client machine and the server machine. The client machine sends requests to the server machine over the cable, and the server machine sends results back to the client over the same cable. Since there are only two machines, the client machine has no difficulty finding an appropriate server. The server is simply the machine at the other end of the cable.

In a complex case, there may be many client machines and many server machines, all located in different places around the globe. The communications network might consist of a number of widely separated local area network (LAN) subnetworks interconnected using wide area network (WAN) transmission facilities. Connections between subnetworks may be implemented using a variety of network interconnection devices, such as bridges, routers, and gateways.

Much of the software that organizations use to implement a client/server application architecture allow individual application components to be built as if there were a simple point-to-point connection between a client component and its associated server. A good set of client/server development tools hides the complexity of the communication network from the application developer.

Many complex mechanisms are required to allow client components locate appropriate server components and to coordinate communication between clients and servers. These mechanisms should ideally be handled outside of the application components themselves.

DATA TRANSPORT PROTOCOLS

Actual data transmission in a computer network is handled by network software that conforms to a particular network architecture. Each network architecture defines a set of *protocols*, sometimes called a *protocol family* or *protocol suite*, that control communication in the network. These are some network architectures or protocol families that are often used in implementing client/server computing:

- TCP/IP
- NetWare IPX/SPX
- AppleTalk
- Systems Network Architecture (SNA) Subarea Networking
- SNA Advanced Peer-to-Peer Networking
- NetBIOS
- Open Systems Interconnection (OSI)

Development tools that are used to build computing applications in the client/server environment for the most part allow applications to be built without regard to the underlying data transport mechanisms that are used. Client/server applications normally make use of communications mechanisms that run on top of the data transport facilities provided by the networking software. These communications facilities are designed to hide the complexities of the data transport facilities from application programs. Before examining these communications mechanisms, we will look first at a set of support functions that the computing environment should provide to support client/server applications.

COMMON DISTRIBUTION SUPPORT FUNCTIONS

A number of *common distribution support functions* have been identified. It is desirable that these should eventually be made universally available in the computing environment to facilitate the development of client/server applications. Some of the more important of these are listed in Box 7.1.

Eventually, such support mechanisms will be provided on all machines in an organization's network, probably by the underlying operating system and network software. Today, it is common for only some of these mechanisms to be provided in the underlying computing infrastructure. Others are often performed by the applications themselves or by specialized software that runs in support of client/server applications. Some of today's client/server database software provides many of these common support functions.

COMMUNICATIONS MECHANISMS

At a higher level than the data transport protocols and the common distribution support functions, there are a number of communications mechanisms that application components invoke for doing the actual work of exchanging information between client and

---

BOX 7.1   Common distribution support functions.

- **Network Transport Independence.** A wide variety of network architectures are in use today, each with its own set of data transport protocols. These architectures include DEC-net, SNA, OSI, TCP/IP, AppleTalk, Novell IPX/SPX, and so on. For the most part, all of these data transport protocol families provide a similar range of functions. It should eventually be possible for client/server applications to run using any available network transport mechanism. Most client/server database software already supports a variety of transport mechanisms, and the database developer seldom needs to be concerned with the specific protocols that will be used to carry data through the network.

- **Process Activation Mechanisms.** Distributed applications typically employ a large number of independent processes that run on computing systems distributed throughout a network. In order to make the best use of computing resources, it is desirable that software components should execute only when the processing they perform is actually required. Therefore operating systems and network software subsystems should provide networkwide mechanisms for loading application components into memory and executing them on demand.

- **Client/Server Rendezvous Mechanisms.** A fundamental task that must be performed when a client component makes a request for a service is to locate a computing system on which an appropriate server component is available. Networkwide directory facilities will provide this facility in most environments.

- **Thread Management Mechanisms.** A thread consists of the execution of a procedure that can operate concurrently with the execution of the same or different procedures within the same application program. Servers often allow multiple threads to execute the same procedures concurrently for the purpose of being able to serve multiple clients at the same time. Client processes can also often benefit from multithreaded operation by making requests of multiple servers concurrently. Many operating systems that are commonly used in the client/server environment are multithreading operating systems.

- **Security Mechanisms.** Security mechanisms are as important for distributed applications as they are for centralized applications. However, they are more difficult to implement in the distributed environment. An important aspect of security is *authentication*. Network-wide authentication mechanisms make it possible for one software component to verify the identity of users or other software components. Another aspect of security is *authorization*. Authorization facilities control which users are given access to which resources in the distributed environment. A third important security facility is *data encryption*. Encryption is used to prevent unauthorized parties from eavesdropping on transmissions that take place between two communicating parties.

- **Data Definition and Encoding Mechanisms.** Mechanisms should be available that allow the data structures that are exchanged between communicating partners to be defined and encoded for transmission in a way that is independent of any particular computing or communications technology. Distribution technologies employ a wide range of methods for defining data structures, such as the international standard Abstract Syntax Notation One (ASN.1) data definition notation.

---

server components. In some cases, client and server components invoke these communications services directly. In other cases, the development tools used to create the client/server applications handle the interface to the specific communications mechanism that is used.

Like the application components themselves, the communications mechanisms that application components employ to exchange information can be made independent of the specific data transport protocol employed in the network.

The technologies that are currently available for creating distributed computing applications have matured to the point where a great many choices now often face the application developer who wishes to create client/server applications. Each of these choices represents a particular type of distribution mechanism that has a set of specific characteristics, and each is typically well suited for specific types of applications.

Choosing a communications technology has some similarities to choosing a particular programming language for an application. An application developer may choose a particular language for a number of reasons. The chosen language may offer the best performance for a given environment, it may have language constructs that are well suited to the application, the developer may be more familiar with a particular language, and so on.

In the same way, a number of factors govern the particular communications technology that a developer may choose to use. There are engineering tradeoffs to be made, and what may seem like an optimal solution to one developer may seem less desirable to someone else. Like the choice of a programming language, there is often no clear cut choice in selecting a distribution mechanism, and often a number of different distribution mechanisms may have to be combined to meet the needs of a particular application.

The following sections describe four distinct technologies that are commonly used in the client/server environment for handling communications between application components:

- Message-passing mechanisms
- Remote procedure call mechanisms
- Peer-to-peer communications mechanisms
- Message-queuing mechanisms

Given any particular application situation, it is likely that more than one of the above four communications mechanisms will be suitable for that application. Also, in sophisticated distributed applications, it is likely that it will be necessary or desirable to employ more than one of the communications mechanisms in combination. Therefore, the four distribution technologies described here should by no means be considered to be mutually exclusive, nor are they the only possible communications mechanisms that can be used, and many more will be introduced as client/server computing matures.

The following sections describe each of the above four communications mechanisms that are often used in implementing communications in the client/server environment.

MESSAGE-PASSING MECHANISMS

Message-passing mechanisms consist of the direct exchange of units of data between client and server components that are running on different computing systems. With message passing, client A sends into the network a message whose destination is server B.

Server B receives the message, performs required processing, and then sends a set of messages carrying results back to client A (see Fig. 7.6). Distributed applications of great complexity that implement any client/server configuration can be built using simple message-passing mechanisms.

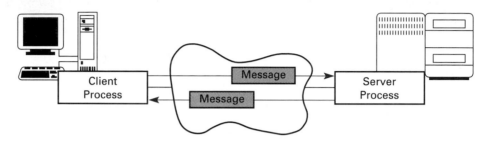

Figure 7.6   Using a message-passing mechanism.

Two forms of message-passing mechanisms can be provided for implementing distributed applications: connectionless and connection-oriented mechanisms.

Connectionless Mechanisms

With a *connectionless* data delivery mechanism, sometimes called a *datagram* mechanism, the source application simply sends a message into the network and indicates the destination or destinations to which the message is to be sent. The message-passing mechanism makes a best-efforts attempt to deliver the message to its intended destination or destinations, but the source application is not informed as to whether delivery was actually accomplished. With a connectionless message-passing service, a source application can send a message to one or more destination applications in a single operation.

Connection-Oriented Mechanisms

With a *connection-oriented* message-passing mechanism, two communicating processes exchange control messages with each other to establish a logical association, called a *connection*, between them. The connection is used for the purpose of ensuring that messages are exchanged reliably between the two processes. With a connection-oriented service, mechanisms are generally provided for detecting and recovering from situations in which messages are lost, duplicated, or corrupted during transmission. With a connection-oriented message-passing mechanism, a source application can send a message in a single operation to only one destination. A separate connection is required for each destination if multiple destinations are involved.

Both connectionless and connection-oriented message-passing mechanisms can be used to create reliable distributed applications. However, when a connectionless service is used, the application itself must implement more sophisticated reliability controls than if a connection-oriented service is available.

No matter what type of service is used to implement a distributed application, there can be no guarantee that a function that is invoked remotely will actually be executed. This is because even if a message is delivered to its destination reliably, the destination application process may fail before it is able to process the message. For this reason client/server applications that employ message-passing services generally implement their own mechanisms to ensure reliability.

REMOTE PROCEDURE CALL MECHANISMS

Remote procedure call (RPC) mechanisms extend the familiar procedure call programming paradigm from the local computing system environment to a distributed environment. With an RPC facility, the calling procedure and the called procedure can execute in different computing systems in the network (see Fig. 7.7). RPC mechanisms make it possible to hide from the application programmer the fact that distribution is taking place. A primary goal of an RPC mechanism is to make it appear to the programmer that remote procedures are invoked in exactly the same manner as local procedures.

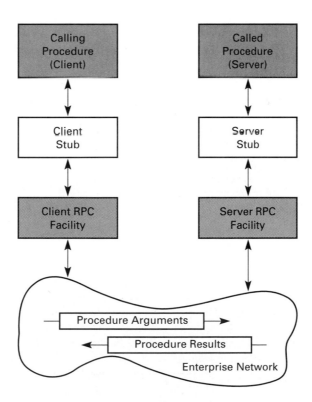

Figure 7.7   RPC facility functional model.

It is not possible to achieve complete transparency because the semantics of distributed operations are often substantially different from those of the same operation performed locally. For example, when the called procedure is executing on a different computing system from the calling procedure, a number of problems can occur that do not occur when the two procedures are running on the same computing system, including the following:

- Either of the two software components can independently fail in such a way that the other component is not aware of the failure.

- There can be a temporary loss of connectivity between the two components as they execute.

- The two applications have no access to shared memory that can be used for passing parameters and results.

- Problems can occur that relate to management and security issues that do not arise in the local environment.

Most RPC mechanisms, however, provide facilities for maintaining conventional programming methods as much as possible and for handling many of the complexities that are inherent in the distributed environment.

RPC mechanisms are typically built on top of a message-passing mechanism and implement a simple request-response protocol. The calling procedure makes a request for the execution of the called procedure and may pass a set of parameters to the called procedure. The called procedure then executes and may pass a set of results back to the calling procedure. An RPC mechanism handles the formatting and delivery of network messages that must flow between the calling procedure and the called procedure using a process called *marshaling*.

The main reason for using RPC mechanisms in the distributed environment is that they automatically handle much of the work involved in distributing functions, and they make it easier for application developers to design, implement, and maintain distributed applications.

PEER-TO-PEER COMMUNICATIONS MECHANISMS

Peer-to-peer communications mechanisms are similar to message-passing mechanisms but provide integrated support for using two-phase commit operations in a transaction processing context (see Chapter 6). These mechanisms allow client and server application components to communicate asynchronously and still retain a shared context across a dialog that may consist of multiple interactions. With this type of communications mechanism, communication takes place between two or more software components that are organized hierarchically with the initiator of the first message exchange at the root.

There are several protocol and application programming interface (API) standards for peer-to-peer communications mechanisms. The most well known is IBM's SNA logical unit 6.2 protocol and its associated Common Programming Interface for Communication (CPI-C) and Advanced Program-to-Program Communication (APPC) application programming interfaces.

MESSAGE-QUEUING MECHANISMS

With a *message-queuing* mechanism, sometimes called a reliable messaging service, an application component running on one computing system can submit messages that are addressed to other application components that may be running on other computing systems (see Fig. 7.8).

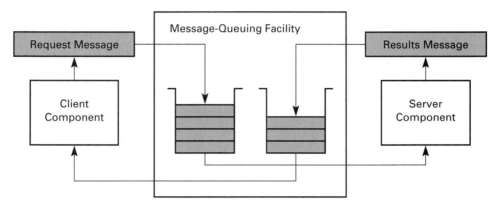

Figure 7.8   Message-queuing mechanism.

In many cases, the messages submitted by the source component do not require immediate responses. This makes it possible for a message-queuing mechanism to support asynchronous processing. The source process submits a message and does not wait for a response but immediately performs other work. The destination component may or may not be active at the time the message is submitted. If the destination component is not active, the message-queuing mechanism may wait for the destination component to become active before delivering the message, or it may take steps to activate the destination process, depending on application requirements.

SUMMARY

Client/server computing is allowing the centralized processors of an earlier era to be replaced by networks of distributed computers. With client/server computing, a client component executing in one computing system requests a service of a server component executing in another computing system. A communications network is used to allow client and server components to exchange messages. Client and server components can be configured in a variety of ways. This book examines functions performed by the various application components making up a client/server database application. It does not cover technical details concerning how the communications network is built.

In the three-tier model of client/server computing, computing applications consist of components that perform user interface processing, function processing, and data-access processing. The three types of components can be combined in various ways to create the single computing system model, the user interface distribution model, the data access distribution model, and the function distribution model.

The networking software that supports communications between components in a client/server application generally conforms to a particular network architecture and implements a particular set of data transport protocols. Transport mechanisms are often hidden from client/server applications. Client/server application components access a set of common distribution support functions that should be provided in the computing environment. These include mechanisms for network transport independence, process activation, client/server rendezvous, thread management, security, and data definition and encoding.

Client and server components in a distributed application invoke a variety of communications mechanisms for exchanging data. These mechanisms access the underlying data transport facilities on behalf of the application components. Important communications mechanisms include message passing, remote procedure calls, peer-to-peer communications, and message queuing.

There are many complexities involved in the software that is required to manage remote and distributed databases. Chapter 8 explores some of the configurations that are possible for building client/server database applications.

Client/Server Database Configurations

Different variations of the three-tier model of client/server computing described in Chapter 7 can be combined to create distributed computing configurations of any desired degree of complexity. This book concentrates on the data access distribution model of client/server computing, and this chapter discusses different variations of this model.

The data access distribution model is the most commonly used form of the client/server distribution models described in Chapter 7. It is the form of client/server distribution that is typically used in conjunction with database software in which more than one processor is used to implement a database application.

The data access distribution model can be further broken down by showing how the components associated with data access processing can be configured. We will look at how the following three components, common to all database applications, can be configured:

- Application processing components
- Database software components
- The database itself

CLIENT/SERVER DATABASE CONFIGURATIONS

The various models of database processing differ according to where instances of the above three categories of components reside. This chapter begins by examining five architectural models that are all based on the data access distribution configuration of client/server computing:

- Centralized database model
- File-server database model
- Database extract processing model

- Client/server database model
- Distributed database model

As with the models of client/server applications described in Chapter 7, the above five architectural models can be used in combination to create a wide variety of client/server database application configurations.

Centralized Database Model

In the *centralized* model, shown in Fig. 8.1, application processing components, the database software, and the database itself all reside on the same processor.

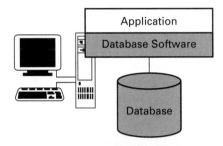

Figure 8.1   The centralized database model.

For example, a personal computer user might run application programs that use Oracle database software to access a database residing on the personal computer's internal hard disk. Since the application components, the database software, and the database itself all reside on the same personal computer, the application conforms to the centralized model.

Much of the mainstream information processing performed by many organizations still conforms to the centralized model. For example, a mainframe processor running IBM's IMS or DB2 database software may provide terminal operators at widely distributed locations with fast access to a central pool of data. However, in many such systems, all three components of the database application execute on the same mainframe. Thus this configuration also conforms to the centralized model.

File-Server Database Model

In the *file-server* model, shown in Fig. 8.2, the application components and the database software reside on one computing system, and the physical files making up the database reside on some other computing system.

Such a configuration is often used in a local area network environment in which one or more computing systems play the role of file servers that store data files to which other computing systems have access. In the file-server environment, networking software is employed that makes the application software and the database software running on an end-user system think that a file or database stored on a file server is actually attached to the end-user machine.

The file-server model is similar to the centralized model. The files implementing the database reside on a different machine from the application components and the data-

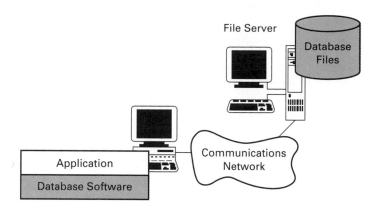

Figure 8.2   The file-server database model.

base software; however, the application components and the database software may be the same as those designed to operate in a centralized environment. In effect, the networking software tricks the application software and database software into thinking that they are accessing a local database.

Such an environment can be more complex than the centralized model because the networking software may implement concurrency mechanisms that permit more than one end user to access the same database without those users interfering with one another.

Database Extract Processing Model

Another way in which a remote database can be accessed using conventional database software is called *database extract processing*, shown in Fig. 8.3.

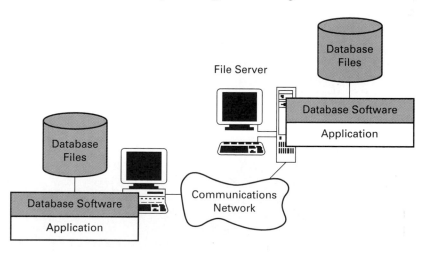

Figure 8.3   The database extract processing model.

With the database extract processing model, the user, possibly at a personal computer, makes a connection with the remote computing system where the desired data is located. The user then interacts directly with the software running on the remote machine and formulates a request to extract the required data from the remote database. The user then transfers the desired data from the remote machine to the user's own computer and hard disk. The user then processes the local copy of the data using local database software.

With this approach, the user must know where the data is located and also how to access and interact with the remote computer that maintains the database. Complementary application software must be available on both computing systems to handle database access and the transfer of data between the two systems. However, the database software running on the two machines need not be aware that remote database processing is taking place, since the user interacts with them separately.

Client/Server Database Model

In the true client/server database model, shown in Fig. 8.4, the database again resides on a machine other than those that run the application processing components. But the database software is split between the client system that runs the application program and the server system that stores the database.

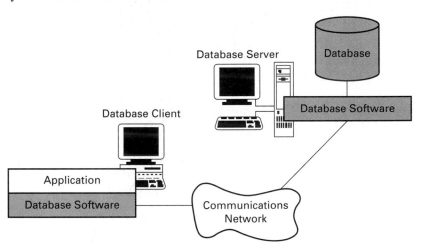

Figure 8.4   The client/server database model.

In this model, the application processing components on the client system make requests of the local database software. The local database software component in the client machine then communicates with complementary database software running on the server. The server database software makes requests for accesses to the database and passes results back to the client machine.

At first glance, the client/server database model may seem similar to the file-server model. However, the client/server model has many advantages over the file-server model. With the file-server model, information associated with each physical database access must flow across the network. A database operation that requires many database accesses may generate a lot of network traffic.

Suppose an end user makes a query request for summary data. The request requires that data element values from 1000 database records be examined. With the file server approach, the entire contents of all 1000 records must flow across the network. This is because the database software, which is running in the end-user machine, must access and examine each record to satisfy the user's request. With the client/server database approach, only the initial query and the final result need flow across the network. The database software operating in the machine that stores the database may be capable of accessing the required records, examining them, and performing the processing necessary to produce the final result.

Front-End Software

In the client/server database model, it is common to refer to front-end software and back-end software. *Front-end software* typically runs on a personal computer or desktop workstation and serves the computing needs of a single individual. The front-end software typically plays the role of the client in a client/server database application and performs functions that are oriented to the needs of the end user. Front-end software generally falls into one or more of the following categories listed in Box 8.1.

Back-End Software

Back-end software consists of the client/server database software and network software that runs on a machine playing the role of database server.

BOX 8.1   Categories of front-end software.

- **End-User Database Software.** This database software can be employed by end users on their own desktop systems to create and access small local databases as well as to connect to larger databases stored on database servers.

- **Simple Query and Reporting Software.** This software is designed to provide an easy-to-use means of retrieving data from a database and preparing simple reports from the data.

- **Data Analysis Software.** This software, in addition to providing retrieval functions, may also perform complex analyses on the data on behalf of the end user.

- **Application Development Tools.** This software typically provides language capabilities that professional information systems staff uses to produce custom database applications. Tools in this category range from simple interpreters and compilers to full-function Computer Aided Software Engineering (CASE) tools that automate all the steps in the application development process and automatically generate code for a custom database application.

- **Database Administration Tools.** These software tools allow database administrators to use a personal computer or workstation to perform database administration tasks, such as defining databases and performing backup and recovery operations.

Distributed Database Model

The file-server model and the client/server database model both assume that the database resides on one processor and that the application program that accesses the database resides on some other processor. The true distributed database model, shown in Fig. 8.5, assumes that the database itself can reside on more than one machine.

The remainder of this chapter describes some mechanisms that are useful in implementing distributed databases. Chapter 9 describes three different architectural models on which a distributed, client/server database environment can be based.

DATA DISTRIBUTION MECHANISMS

There are three major approaches, or distribution mechanisms, that can be used to manage access to a database: centralization, partitioning, and database copying. The following sections discuss each of these approaches.

Centralization

The centralization approach is used with the centralized model described earlier, in which the database is not physically distributed at all. The entire database is maintained on a single server machine in a central location, and client components running on other

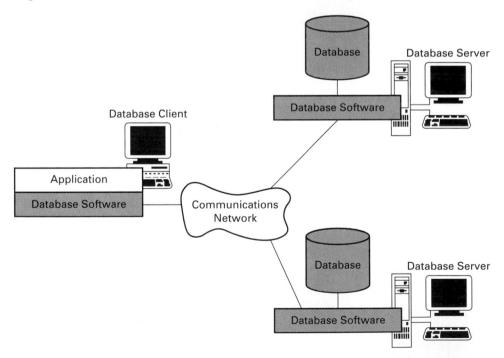

Figure 8.5   Distributed database model.

machines access the central server. The database itself is centralized, even though access to the database may be distributed.

In many environments, a centralized approach works best. It allows all database updates to be performed in a single place, and there is no need to maintain multiple copies of the data. However, with a centralized approach, the database server becomes a single point of failure for the entire database system. If the database server fails, no one has access to any of the data.

Partitioning

With *partitioning*, certain database records are stored on one machine, and certain others are stored on one or more other machines. However, with partitioning, no single piece of data is stored in more than one place, thus allowing update mechanisms to remain relatively simple.

Many partitioning schemes can be devised. For example:

- All the tables for any one database can be stored in one place, with different databases residing in different locations. All the databases may be processed by the same database software.
- Different tables from the same relational database can be stored in different locations.
- The data elements making up a given table can be split, either by rows or by columns.

With partitioning, the challenge for the database software is to be able to quickly find the location of the desired data. The database software itself may store all the information concerning the location of each data element, or a networkwide directory service might be used to help the database software locate different parts of the database.

Database Extraction and Replication

With the centralization and partitioning approaches, no additional copies are made of any data elements in the database; each data element value is stored in only one place. Two additional approaches involve making one or more copies of all or a portion of the database.

A distinction is generally made between two types of copying techniques:

- **Extraction.** A database copy is called an *extract* when the copy is intended to be used on a read-only basis. Data element values in an extract are not intended to be updated.
- **Replication.** A database copy is called a *replica* when data element values in the copy can be updated.

With extraction and replication, certain data element values from the database are stored in multiple locations, possibly to make the database more available and resistant to failures or to enhance performance. Entire databases can be copied, or, if partitioning is also used, selected partitions can be copied.

The following sections describe differences between extraction and replication techniques.

Extraction

Extraction can be used in many circumstances in which it is desirable to distribute copies of the database to multiple locations. An extract can consist of a copy of the entire database, or extraction can be combined with partitioning in which extracts are made of particular database partitions.

Various types of extracts can be made that differ with respect to mechanisms that allow application programs to determine how outdated an extract is. An extract can include no information that can be used to determine the validity of extracted data, an extract may contain a timestamp value that indicates the date and time the extract was made, or an extract can contain information, such as a checksum value, that application programs can use to determine how out of synchronization the extract is with respect to the main database.

Replication

Replication is similar to extraction except that a replica is intended to allow updating. With replication, the challenge for the database software is to ensure that data element values in replicas remain in synchronization with their associated values in the main database. Since there may potentially be many replicas of a given data element value, it is necessary to insure that updates to a given data element value are eventually applied to all database replicas that store copies of that value.

Many mechanisms have been devised for bringing replicas into convergence. In some cases, once a replica is made, only the replica can be updated. Updated data element values in the replica are then migrated back into the main database. In other cases, updates are allowed to the main database as well as to one or more replicas.

The database software might be designed to propagate changes that are made in one replica as quickly as possible to the main database and to other replicas. With some schemes, a particular replica may be designated the *master replica*, with all other replicas considered *secondary replicas*. A database update operation might be designated as complete when the master replica has been successfully updated. The database software component that is responsible for the master replica might then be responsible for propagating the update to all the secondary replicas at some future time.

Another possible scheme is to implement a separate *convergence function* that is responsible for synchronizing the replicas of the database and bringing them into agreement with the main database. The convergence function is a distributed function, components of which must be run on all the machines storing replicas of the database. The convergence function might be run frequently or infrequently depending on the convergence requirements that have been identified for a particular database.

The database software may provide for a variety of synchronization mechanisms. The database designer or database administrator might then be able to specify the synchronization mechanisms that are to be applied to each individual database or to each set of replicas. However, no matter what types of synchronization functions are employed, no distributed database that employs replication can be 100% in synchronization 100% of the time.

UPDATING REPLICATED DATABASES

When all or a portion of a database will be replicated, then the mechanisms employed to bring the various replicas into convergence may place restrictions on the types of updates that can be made to the database. In a highly replicated environment, the types of updates that are easiest for convergence functions to handle are those that meet the following three characteristics:

- **Total.** An update that is *total* can be applied to a data element value without regard to any update that may have previously been applied to that data element value.
- **Idempotent.** An update that has the *idempotent* characteristic has the same effect on the database no matter how many times it is applied.
- **Commutative.** A series of updates that are *commutative* have the characteristic that they can be applied in any sequence and produce identical results.

The total and idempotent update characteristics are facilitated by allowing only limited types of update operations to be performed. For example, updates that completely replace data element values with new values are total and idempotent; updates that add or subtract values are not. With total and idempotent updates, the database software need not implement mechanisms that ensure that a particular update is applied *only once*. It is enough to ensure that the update is applied *at least once*, a much simpler problem to solve. A series of updates can be made commutative through the use of time stamps. All updates can be time-stamped so that the updates can be applied in time sequence. The update entering the system most recently will then always be applied last.

Updates that are already total, idempotent, and commutative are those that can be most easily handled by convergence algorithms. If the database software allows users to make updates that lack one or more of these characteristics, then more complex mechanisms must be implemented in the convergence functions.

LOCATION SENSITIVITY

The ultimate goal of distributed database software is to permit users and application programs to be completely independent of the physical location of data. The user should be able to make requests for data, and the application program should be able to issue appropriate data access statements, without regard to where the data is stored. However, complete transparency is difficult to implement. Until the transparency objective can be fully achieved, the database software may place constraints on how a database can be partitioned and replicated and what types of updates are allowed.

SUMMARY

The data access distribution model is the form of client/server distribution that is typically used in conjunction with client/server database software. In the data access distribution model, three types of components are important: application processing components, database software components, and the database itself. These components can be combined in different ways to form the centralized database model, the file-server database model, the database extract processing model, the client/server database model, and the distributed database model.

With a centralized approach, the entire database is stored in one place and only access to the database is distributed. With partitioning, a database is divided up so that certain database records are stored in one place, and certain others are stored elsewhere. With extraction and replication, certain data element values from the database are stored in multiple locations, possibly to make the database more available and resistant to failures or to enhance performance. An important goal of distributed database software is to permit users and application programs to be completely independent of the physical location of data.

Chapter 9 looks at a number of different architectures that have been developed to facilitate the implementation of remote database access and distributed database access in database software.

Chapter **9**

Distributed Database Software Architectures

An implementation of a distributed database system can be simple or complex. In a homogeneous environment, the types of computing systems that process the database can be tightly controlled. Therefore, the distributed database software can be relatively simple. Some schemes for database distribution have been designed for a particular platform, consisting of specific hardware, operating system, and networking software. For example, many networks consist entirely of personal computers using Intel-architecture microprocessors. In many of these networks, the client machines run Microsoft operating systems, and the servers run Novell network operating systems. The designers of software targeted specifically for such a homogeneous environment can make many assumptions that simplify distributed database software functions.

On the other hand, a goal of many vendors of distributed database software is to support a completely heterogeneous environment. Computing systems might be mainframes, minicomputers, or personal computers running various microprocessor chips (Intel, Motorola, IBM, etc.) A variety of operating systems might be supported, including Apple, IBM, Microsoft, various Unix-type operating systems, and the proprietary operating systems often used on mainframes and minicomputers. It might also be desirable to support a variety of different communication mechanisms (message passing, remote procedure call, message queuing, etc.) and data transport protocols (SNA, TCP/IP, NetWare IPX/SPX, etc.). The functions that the distributed database software must perform in a heterogeneous environment are orders of magnitude more complex than the functions required in a homogeneous environment.

To facilitate the creation of a heterogeneous distributed database environment, three different software architectural models have proven to be useful.

- Gateway model
- Standard interface model
- Standard protocol model

GATEWAY MODEL

Each database software subsystem is designed to use a particular API. Application programs that wish to use the services of a database software subsystem must formulate database access statements using the API the database software recognizes (see Fig. 9.1). A database software vendor's end-user access facility can replace the database application program in an environment where end users access database software facilities directly (see Fig. 9.2).

The gateway model of distributed database processing allows an application program written using a given database API to request the services of database software that supports some other API. The gateway model is based on using a gateway component to perform a conversion from one application programming interface (API) to another.

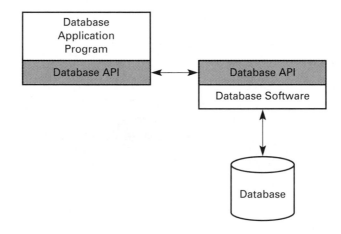

Figure 9.1   Database application programming interface (API).

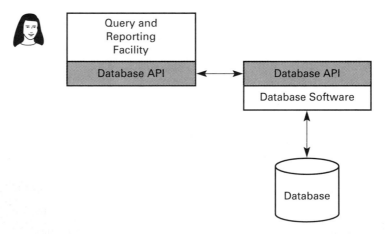

Figure 9.2   Database API with end-user query and reporting facility.

With the gateway distributed database access architecture, an application program uses one API. A separate software component called a gateway converts from one API to another to allow a program written for one API to access database software that supports some other API.

For example, Fig. 9.3 shows an application program written to access an Oracle database. It accesses a gateway that converts from the Oracle API to the DB2 API. The gateway then accesses DB2 database software on behalf of the client. In effect the gateway plays tricks on both the application program and the database software. The application program thinks it is accessing an Oracle database, and the DB2 database software thinks it is supporting a DB2 application program.

A gateway architecture can support any desired distributed database configuration. In the simplest case, the application program, the gateway component, and the database software all reside in the same machine. In a more complex case, they all reside in different machines. Other combinations are possible.

In a distributed environment, additional *communications client* and *communications server* components are required to handle the data transmission among the various machines (see Fig. 9.4). With the gateway approach to distributed database, a vendor of database software might write gateway software and communications client and server components. The gateway components must be tailored to a particular database API that some population of database users are known to be employing. The communications client and server components must support a particular communications mechanism and data transport protocol family.

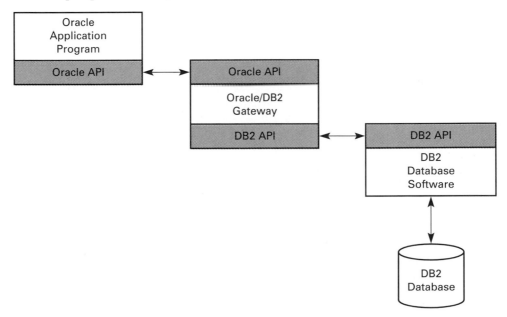

Figure 9.3   Gateway allowing an Oracle application program to access a DB2 database.

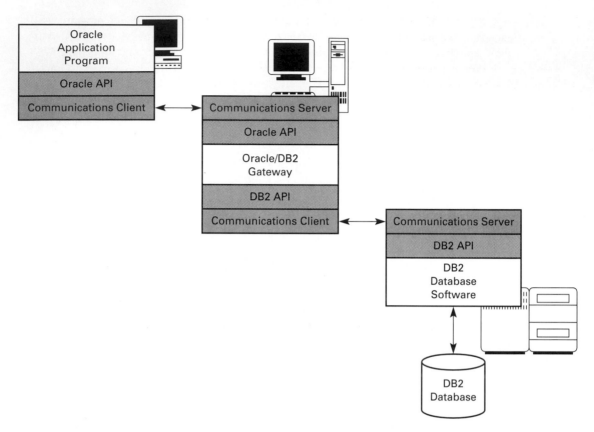

Figure 9.4   Application program, gateway, and database software implemented in separate machines.

   With the gateway model, the gateway component and the communications client
and server components must typically be designed by the same vendor. This is because
there are no standards governing interfaces, services, or functions in this environment.
The vendor can employ existing database APIs and existing end-user data access languages. This environment can also make use of existing database software that need not
itself support distributed databases.
   A vendor can design gateway software to allow programs written to the APIs of
other database software to access the vendor's own database software. Alternatively, a
vendor can design gateway software to allow users writing application programs to the
vendor's database API to access database software of other vendors. However, a vendor is
likely to support only that vendor's own database software, or only those packages the
vendor decides it is advantageous to be compatible with.
   Many distributed database vendors currently implement the gateway model, as it is
the simplest of the three models described here. However, if an installation adopts the

gateway model of distributed database access, that installation may be locked into a single vendor's approach.

STANDARD INTERFACE MODEL

Like the gateway model, the standard interface model is designed to allow an application program written using a given database API to request the services of database software that supports some other API. The software running on a server machine is called a *data source*. It consists of database software and communications server software. The software running on a client machine contains one or more driver components designed to interface with a particular type of data source (see Fig. 9.5).

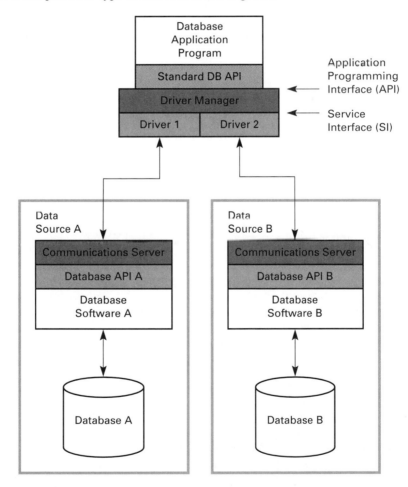

Figure 9.5   Standard interface distributed database model.

The software in a client machine includes a *driver manager* component that implements two standard interfaces:

- **Service Interface.** This is the API that drivers use to interface with the driver manager. Vendors of database software write drivers that conform to the service interface to allow their database software to interface with the driver manager.
- **Application Programming Interface.** This is the API that application programs use to request database services.

Because of its dependence on drivers and a driver manager, the standard interface model is sometimes called the *driver model*. The standard interface model has many similarities to the gateway model. The major difference is that this model depends on a standard API that all database applications employ. Database application developers that wish to participate in a distributed environment based on the standard interface model must program to the standard API or use software that converts from some other API to the standard API .

MICROSOFT'S OPEN DATABASE CONNECTIVITY (ODBC)

For the driver model to be useful in a heterogeneous environment, some sufficiently powerful organization must create and publish the required API and driver interface standards, and a sufficiently large population of users and database software vendors must agree to adhere to those standards. In the personal computer environment, Microsoft is such an organization.

Microsoft has created a database interface standard, called *Open Database Connectivity* (ODBC), that conforms to the standard interface model. A number of database software vendors who market to the personal computer community have created ODBC drivers for their packages, and ODBC has become a useful de facto distributed database access standard for the personal computer environment.

Application developers benefit from the ODBC approach to distributed database by being able to develop database applications without regard to the specific data source that will be used. The application will work properly with any vendor's driver and any compatible data source that implements the ODBC architecture. Database software vendors benefit because they need only supply appropriate driver software for each platform they choose to support.

STANDARD PROTOCOL MODEL

Figure 9.6 shows the database access protocol architectural model. This architectural model, instead of standardizing the application programming interfaces that are employed, depends on standardizing the protocol used in communicating between the various machines in the distributed environment. The standard protocol model allows any APIs to be used as long as software conforms to the protocol standard.

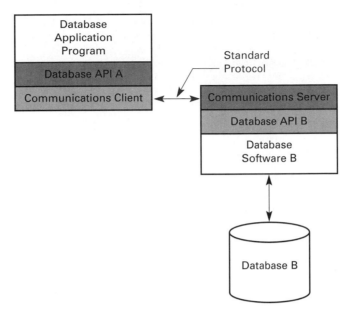

Figure 9.6   Standardized protocol distributed database model.

The term *protocol* is widely used in computer networking literature. It is used to refer to the *formats* of the messages that are exchanged over a network between two communicating machines and the *rules* that govern how those messages are exchanged.

The advantage to standardizing the protocol rather than the APIs is that different software vendors can work independently to produce different software components that may all use different APIs. As long as all components conform to the same protocol (pass standard messages over the network and follow the same rules) they should interoperate with one another in the distributed environment.

IBM'S DISTRIBUTED RELATIONAL DATABASE ARCHITECTURE (DRDA)

Again, in order for a standard protocol implementation to be useful, some sufficiently powerful organization must create and publish the protocol standard. A sufficiently large population of users and database software vendors must then agree to adhere to the standards and implement communications client and server components that implement the standard protocol. In the mainframe environment, IBM is such an organization.

IBM has created a database access protocol standard called the *Distributed Relational Database Architecture* (DRDA). IBM originally created DRDA to support its efforts with mainframe DB2 software. The original intention was to allow computers of all types to access DB2 databases maintained by mainframes. The scope of DRDA has since been broadened, and a number of vendors who market database software for the minicomputer and personal computer communities have now implemented their own database software that adheres to the DRDA protocol standards.

Levels of Distributed Database Access

IBM's DRDA defines four levels of distributed database access based on the complexity of the transactions the application can construct, the range of functions the database software must support to handle each type of transaction, and the capability of the standard protocol for communicating between components. At the time of writing, not all four levels have been implemented in IBM database products.

The four levels are as follows:

- **Remote Request.** With this level of access, the database software supports transactions that each contain a single SQL statement that accesses a single remote database. The database software needs no special transaction-processing functions to support this level of access.

- **Remote Unit of Work.** With this level of access, the database software supports transactions that can each contain a series of related SQL statements that all access the same remote database. The database software must be able to coordinate the commitment and rollback processing across all the SQL statements issued as part of the transaction. This requires that the database software support a remote commit capability.

- **Distributed Unit of Work.** With this level of access, the database software supports transactions that can each contain a series of SQL statements that may each access a different remote database. However, each individual SQL statement must reference only one database. This requires that the database software support a distributed update capability, in which a single transaction may update a database residing on different machines.

- **Distributed Request.** This level of access is similar to distributed unit of work, except now each individual SQL statement can reference information that is stored in different databases, perhaps residing on different machines. This requires that the database software provide support for distributed Join operations in which information from multiple databases, perhaps residing on different machines, is brought together. (Join operations are described in Chapter 18.)

The following sections further describe each of the above levels of distributed database access.

Remote Request

The *remote request* configuration requires the least assistance from the database software of the four client/server database approaches defined by DRDA. It allows database software that is not specifically designed for remote database access to be used in a distributed environment.

With this technique, an application program running in the local computer system generates a request for a database access and passes the request to a communications client component. The application program and the communications client component both run on the local computing system. The communications client component then sends a message across the network to a complementary software function, called the *database server*. A standard protocol defined by DRDA is used for the communication between the client and server components. The communications server component, the database software, and the database itself reside on the remote computing system. The remote request processing configuration is shown in Fig. 9.7.

The communications server component running on the remote computing system submits database access requests that it receives to the database software running there. The communications server then sends the results of the database access back to the communications client in the local system. The communications client component then passes the requested data to the local application program.

Any database API can be used in both the client and server machines as long as the communications client and server components implement the standard DRDA protocol.

With remote request processing, all the distribution functions are handled by the communications client and server components. The database software in the remote machine need not be aware that a distributed database access is taking place. The data request is submitted to the database software in the remote machine by the communications server function. The communications server appears to the database software as an ordinary application program running in the remote machine.

The database software running on the remote machine may set and release locks and may perform any required database recovery processing on behalf of the communications server function. However, if there is a failure in the network or if the application program that accesses the database client component fails, the failure must be handled by the application program, the communications client component, or the communications server component. The database software in the remote machine is unaware of failures that occur in the machine running the application program or failures that occur in the network.

Remote Unit of Work

With the *remote unit of work* configuration, complementary database software is implemented on the local machine and on the remote machine. With this approach, the database software itself performs the communications client and server functions and

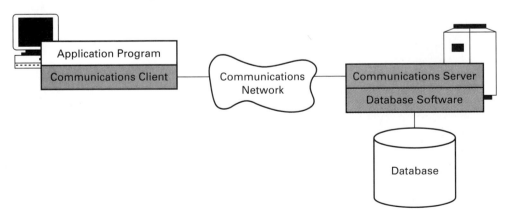

Figure 9.7   Remote request configuration.

implements the DRDA protocol for sending and receiving messages across the network. Figure 9.8 illustrates the remote unit of work remote database access configuration.

With remote unit of work processing, a given application can access a single relational database that resides on a single remote computing system. The application program can issue multiple SQL statements that may all be part of the same transaction. The two complementary database software components maintain state information relative to the progress of the entire transaction across the multiple SQL statements. They are thus able to handle commitment and rollback processing for the transaction as a whole.

The remote unit of work configuration makes many types of failures transparent to the application program. Since the communication between the two machines is handled by the database software itself, the database software can be designed to recover from failures that occur in the local machine, in the remote machine, or in the communication network. Since the entire database resides on a single machine, the transaction management functions that are required to handle recovery and roll back processing are relatively straightforward. A complex two-phase commit protocol is not required to implement this level of remote database access.

Distributed Database Configurations

The previous two levels of DRDA remote database access support allow a program to access a single database that resides on a single remote machine. The next two levels of support allow a program to access a distributed database that may reside on multiple remote machines. The two approaches to distributed database processing might implement a configuration that looks something like that shown in Fig. 9.9.

Distributed Unit of Work

With the *distributed unit of work* configuration, an application program can access the data maintained in a remote database that is spread over two or more machines. The application program can invoke any number of SQL statements within the scope of each transaction. However, with this approach, each individual SQL statement must refer to data that is stored on a single remote computing system. The data that is required to satisfy a given single SQL statement cannot be spread over multiple machines.

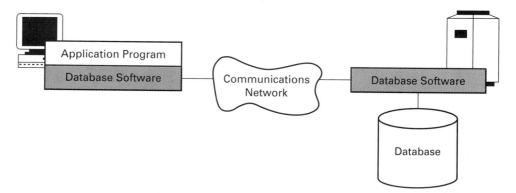

Figure 9.8   Remote unit of work configuration.

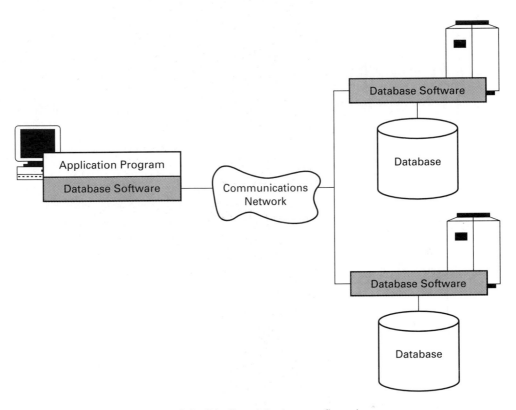

Figure 9.9   Distributed database configuration.

The database software running in the local machine and the database software running in the remote machines work together to coordinate recovery processing. Because multiple separate machines may be involved in remote unit of work processing, the database software must implement two-phase commit protocols that allow commit/rollback and recovery processing to be synchronized across the various systems.

Distributed Request

The most transparent, and least restrictive, form of DRDA distributed database processing is the *distributed request* configuration. With the distributed request configuration, the database can be spread over any number of remote machines, and a single SQL statement is allowed to reference data that may be stored on multiple separate computing systems. With this approach, the application program is completely independent of the location of the data. The distributed database can be reorganized, and the location of data changed, without requiring changes to the application programs. The database software must provide all the support necessary to provide transparent access to data maintained by the remote computing systems.

As with the distributed unit of work environment, with distributed request processing, the database software must use a two-phase commit protocol to handle commitment and rollback operations.

X/Open's Relational Database Access (RDA) Standard

Another example of a database access protocol standard is the *Relational Database Access* (RDA) standard that has been defined by X/Open, an international standards organization. X/Open's RDA conforms to the same general model as IBM's DRDA and has the same overall goals. But RDA defines a different protocol than DRDA.

ARCHITECTURAL MODEL COEXISTENCE

It is possible for an organization to employ products that conform to more than one distributed database software architectural model. As we have seen, Microsoft's ODBC standardizes the application programming interface while IBM's DRDA standardizes the database access protocol. The two architectural models are complementary rather than competing, and the use of one model does not preclude the use of the other. Some distributed database software employs the ODBC API and the DRDA protocol for communication. It is also possible for ODBC to be used in conjunction with X/Open's RDA.

DISTRIBUTED DATABASE OBJECTIVES

In the fifth edition of his popular book, *An Introduction to Database Systems, Volume 1* [1], C. J. Date discusses requirements for distributed database software. According to Date, the ultimate goal that should govern the design of any distributed database system is to make the distributed system look to the end user exactly like a nondistributed system. In other words, all of the mechanisms that are used to achieve database distribution must effectively be hidden from the user.

A distributed database should present the image of a single logical database that is physically distributed among multiple sites. The important point is that if the distribution is done right, with the right database software mechanisms, the user won't know the difference between a single local database and one that is distributed among a number of remote machines. Achieving this fundamental goal leads to other requirements that Date has described in terms of twelve general objectives, which he states as *rules*, that should govern the design of distributed database systems.

The following sections briefly describe each of Date's twelve objectives for distributed database systems. Date's twelve objectives form the basis of a good checklist that the reader may find useful in evaluating database software and possible approaches to database distribution. It is interesting to note that many of Date's objectives are equally applicable to distributed systems in general and are not necessarily limited to database systems.

Objective 1. Local Autonomy

This objective states that it is desirable for all the various locations in a distributed database system to be independent of one another. This means that operations that take place at a given location should be controlled by software running at that location alone. Operations that take place only at one site should not depend on operations that are taking place elsewhere in the distributed system. This implies that data residing at a particular location should be controlled by software operating at that location, even though it is capable of being accessed by computing systems located in other places in the distributed system.

This objective is difficult to achieve in practice, since in distributed systems it is sometimes necessary for more than one location to be involved in satisfying a data access request. Date concedes that it might be better to add the qualifier "to the maximum extent possible" to this objective.

Objective 2. No Reliance on a Central Site

The local autonomy objective implies that all locations in a distributed system should operate as peers and that there should be no reliance required on a single location that might perform some central service for the distributed system as a whole. Reliance on a central location for some service might lead to the central location becoming a resource bottleneck, and would make the entire distributed system vulnerable to failure should a failure occur at the central location.

Objective 3. Continuous Operation

It should be possible to design the distributed database system so that there is never a requirement to shut the entire system down in order to perform a required function, such as adding a new location to the distributed system or upgrading the software at a particular site.

Objective 4. Location Independence

The location independence objective might better be stated as *location transparency*. An end user or an application program should not have to be concerned with the physical location of required data when requesting a data access operation. The distributed database system should make the distributed data appear as if it were all stored in a single logical database that resides at the user's own location. This objective is really just an extension of the general database objective of data independence that we described in Chapter 1.

Objective 5. Partitioning Independence

This objective states that database software should allow the database to be partitioned so that different parts of the database can be moved to different locations in the distributed environment. This objective is important for performance reasons. Partitioning permits groups of data elements to be stored at locations at which they are most frequently accessed.

Date identifies two types of partitioning: horizontal and vertical. With horizontal partitioning, the database is partitioned such that all the occurrences of the set of data elements that represents a given business entity are stored in one location. For example, in an order entry database, information about orders might be stored in one location, information about customers in another, and information about inventory in still another.

With vertical partitioning, different sets of occurrences of the same data element type are stored in different locations. For example, order inventory information for Chicago orders might be stored in Chicago, order information for New York might be stored in New York, and so on.

The partitioning independence objective also implies partitioning transparency, which is really a subset of location independence. It should not be necessary for an end user or an application program to be aware of the partitioning scheme that is being used in a distributed database. The entire database should *appear* to be a single logical database that is not partitioned.

Objective 6. Replication Independence

It should be possible for a distributed database system to maintain multiple replicas of the same set of data element occurrences at multiple locations. As we introduced in Chapter 8, replication is often desirable in a distributed database system to increase availability and to improve performance. Again, such replication should be transparent to end users and application programs. The user should obtain the same result no matter which replica of the database is accessed. And a change that a program applies to one replica of the database should be automatically propagated to all other replicas.

Objective 7. Distributed Query Processing

This objective states that when an end user or application program at one location makes a query request, the query itself should be capable of being sent to the location containing the data required to satisfy the query. This point was discussed in Chapter 7 when we discussed the important difference between the file-server model and the client/server database model. If all the query processing is processed at location A, and the data resides at location B, then a great deal of information may have to be sent between the two locations in order to satisfy the query. If the query itself is sent from location A to location B, only the query and the final results may need to flow between the two locations.

To fully satisfy this objective, it should also be possible for the distributed database system to divide a query among a number of locations if the data necessary to satisfy the query reside in multiple locations. Such a capability makes it possible for the database software to optimize query processing.

Objective 8. Distributed Transaction Management

As we saw in Chapter 6, transaction management concerns the idea of a transaction. A transaction consists of a set of processing, possibly involving multiple database accesses, that is considered as an atomic unit with respect to recovery processing and concurrency control. The entire set of processing must be executed as a unit. If any part of the transaction fails, then the results of all previous parts of the transaction must be removed from the system.

A distributed database system should support distributed recovery processing in which data elements residing at different physical locations may have to be updated as part of a transaction's processing. If any part of the transaction fails, then any database updates that have been made to other parts of the database must be backed out in order to restore the entire distributed system to the state at which it existed prior to the transaction's beginning.

A distributed database system must also support distributed concurrency control. The distributed system must support appropriate mechanisms that allow multiple programs concurrently to access different portions of the database, and to prevent deadlocks from occurring when two components of the same distributed application issue conflicting update operations.

Distributed transaction processing is generally handled through two-phase commit operations that employ database locking facilities. Locking facilities and two-phase commit processing are discussed in Chapter 6.

Objective 9. Hardware Independence

The remaining of Date's distributed database objectives might all be subsumed under a single objective called platform independence. Hardware independence states that it should be possible for a distributed database system to be made up of computing systems of different types, such as IBM mainframes, DEC VAX processors, and Intel-based personal computers.

Objective 10. Operating System Independence

Operating system independence is partly implied by Objective 9. It should be possible for a distributed system to be created using computing systems that run different operating systems, such as IBM's MVS, DEC's OpenVMS, and Microsoft's Windows NT. Objectives 9 and 10 can be considered separately, however, because portable operating system software makes it possible to run the same operating system on different vendor machines. Also, the availability of different operating systems for the same machine permits a distributed system to be constructed using homogeneous hardware and heterogeneous system software.

Objective 11. Network Independence

Today, a computing system platform is often considered to be characterized by a particular type of hardware, running a particular operating system, and employing a particular type of network transport software, such as IBM's SNA, TCP/IP, or Novell's NetWare. It should be possible for different network transport software to be employed in different parts of the distributed system without end users of application programs having to be aware of such differences.

Objective 12. Database Software Independence

This objective states that it should be possible for a distributed database system to be constructed using different database software subsystems running at different locations in the distributed environment. This objective is not likely to be achieved in the short term unless greater standardization of interfaces becomes the rule rather than the exception. The distributed database architectures that vendors such as IBM and Microsoft are creating, discussed earlier in this chapter, are helping us to move in the direction of database software independence.

SUMMARY

To facilitate the creation of a heterogeneous distributed database environment, three different software architectural models have proven to be useful: the gateway model, the standard interface model, and the database access protocol model.

With the gateway model, a client machine that uses one database API communicates with a gateway machine. The gateway then accesses the database facilities provided by a database server whose database software uses some other API. The gateway function translates the requests that an application program makes into requests that the database software understands.

With the standard interface model, driver software running on the client machine handles the establishment of network connections and translates requests formulated in a standard database API into the database access requests that are accepted by the database software. Microsoft's Open Database Connectivity (ODBC) API standard implements the standard interface model of remote database access.

With the standard protocol model, the protocol is standardized that controls communication between the various software components in the distributed environment. IBM's Distributed Relational Database Architecture (DRDA) and X/Open's Relational Database Access (RDA) standard are two approaches to remote database access that standardize the database access protocol. DRDA defines four levels of remote database access. The remote request and remote unit of work forms of distributed database access permit access to a single remote database. The distributed unit of work and distributed request configurations permit access to a distributed database.

C. J. Date has identified twelve objectives that distributed database software should be designed to meet: local autonomy, no reliance on a central site, continuous operation, location independence, partitioning independence, replication independence, distributed query processing, distributed transaction management, hardware independence, operating system independence, network independence, and database software independence.

Chapter 10 begins Part IV of this book, which explores the relational data model that is at the heart of modern client/server database software.

REFERENCE

1. C. J. Date, *An Introduction to Database Systems, Volume 1 (fifth edition)*. Addison Wesley Publishing Company, Reading, MA, 1990.

PART **IV**

THE RELATIONAL DATA MODEL

Relational Architecture

The fundamental technology behind modern database software is generally based on the *relational data model*, first described in an article published in 1970 by Dr. E. F. Codd. The relational data model presents a generalized way of thinking about data and is described in terms of *objects*, *operators that can be applied to these objects*, and a set of *integrity rules*. Most of today's database packages implement many of the ideas defined by the relational model and embody many of its characteristics. However, at present, most database packages do not implement quite all aspects of the relational data model as described by Codd.

In this chapter, we introduce the concepts associated with the relational data model. The formal definition of the relational data model was stated by Codd using precise mathematical terminology, but we will not attempt to describe it here in a rigorous mathematical fashion. Instead, we will rely on informal explanations and examples of the important relational concepts. We will begin by examining the objects that are part of the relational data model.

TABLES

With the relational data model, data is stored in a *relational database*, which we will refer to simply as a *database*. A database is represented by, and perceived by its users as, a set of *tables* that contain *rows* and *columns*. A table represents an *entity type*—the type of person, object, or concept about which we are storing information. A column represents an *attribute* of the entity type—one type of information that we are storing about the entity. A row represents a particular *entity occurrence*, or *entity instance*. A particular row contains a set of *data elements values*, one for each column in the table.

Figure 10.1 shows an example of a possible table. Most of the illustrations in this chapter consist of windows displayed by Access, a relational database software product marketed by Microsoft. The table in Figure 10.1 represents the Vessel entity type from the

Table: Vessel

Vessel_#	Hold_Size	Vessel_Details
00165	12765	Tanker
00205	28775	Freighter
00276	12756	Tanker
00339	28775	Freighter
00463	12756	Tanker

Record: 1 of 5

Figure 10.1 Vessel table.

shipping system database. The columns in the table represent information about the ships owned by the shipping company. Each row in the table stores a set of data elements that describe a particular ship.

ALTERNATIVE TERMINOLOGY

In this book, we use the terms *table*, *column*, *row*, and *data element* to describe the data stored in a relational database. In the more formal terminology used to define the relational data model, a column is called an *attribute*, a row is called a *tuple* (rhymes with couple), and an entire table, consisting of a *set of tuples*, is called a *relation*. If a relation has *n* columns, it is said to be of *degree n*, and the tuples are called *n-tuples*. A table is also sometimes referred to in the literature as a *flat file*.

When discussing the way in which a table might be stored in a conventional computer data storage system, the column structure of the table might describe a particular *record type*, with each column being one of the record type's *fields*. Each row can be thought of as a particular *record occurrence* in the file.

TABLE PROPERTIES

The tables that make up a relational database have certain properties. The properties of the tables stored in a relational database are as follows:

- Each row-column entry in a table consists of a single, or *atomic,* data element.
- All the data elements in a given column are of the same type. The relational data model specifies that for each column, a *domain* must be defined that describes the set of values that are allowed for the data elements in that column. For example, we might define the domain for the Hold_Size column in the Vessel table as the set of all allowable short integer values. Or, we might define a certain range of values, or a particular set of values, as being valid. All relational database systems allow the user to specify a particular data type for each column. Some, but not all, database packages also support the concept of a domain.
- Each column in a table has a unique name within that table.
- The relational data model specifies that all the rows in a table must be unique. Although it is possible with most relational database systems to impose this condition on a table, uniqueness is not always required. Most relational database systems allow tables to contain duplicate rows.

• In the relational data model, the sequence of the rows and columns in a table is not meaningful; the rows and the columns can be viewed in any sequence without affecting either the information content or the semantics of any function that uses the table. It is possible with most relational database systems to impose a sequence on the rows or columns of a table. However, the basic definition of a table often does not assume any particular sequence.

NORMALIZED DATA STRUCTURES

As described above, each row-column entry in a table consists of an atomic data element; a single table entry cannot store a repeating data element or a repeating group of data elements. A data structure from which repeating data elements or repeating groups have been removed in order to place the data into tabular form is called a *normalized data structure*. The Vessel table shown in Figure 10.1 is an example of a normalized data structure.

Suppose, however, we had an Employee record that stores Skill information for employees and each employee can have any number of skills. The Skill attribute might be implemented in the form of a repeating data element, as shown in Fig. 10.2.

Figure 10.2 Repeating data element.

Given a data structure with a repeating data element or a repeating group of data elements, all the attributes representing a single entity occurrence cannot be stored in a single row of a table. Therefore, in order to store the data in relational form, the repeating group must first be removed by moving the Skill data elements to a separate table. Doing this creates a normalized data structure consisting of the two new tables, as shown in Fig. 10.3. Notice that the EmpNo data element type must be included in each of the tables so that we can still determine which employee has which skills.

The process of removing repeating groups is called placing the data into *first normal form*. Higher levels of normalization, including second normal form, third normal form,

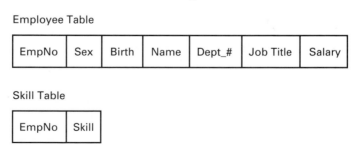

Figure 10.3 Normalized data structure.

fourth normal form, and fifth normal form, are also possible. It is generally desirable to place the data in relational databases into at least third normal form to achieve stability. However, first normal form is the only level of normalization that is addressed by the relational data model itself. Data normalization is described in detail in Chapters 13 and 14.

KEYS

As discussed earlier, one of the properties of a table, as defined by the relational data model, is that each row must be unique. This means there must be a column, or a set of columns, that uniquely identifies each row. This column, or set of columns, is called the table's *primary key*. For some tables a single column can be found that uniquely identifies each row. For example, in the Vessel table, the Vessel_# column has a unique data element value in each row and can serve as the table's primary key.

Database software uses various methods for indicating a table's primary key. For example, Microsoft Access places a "key" icon next to the column or columns that make up the primary key when presenting a table definition, as shown in Figure 10.4. If it is important to point out a table's primary key when illustrating that table's contents, we may highlight it as shown in Figure 10.5. However, Access does not do this when displaying table contents.

With many tables, two or more columns must be combined to provide unique identification. In the worst case, all the columns must be combined to uniquely identify each row, thus forming an *all-key table*. Two or more columns that are combined to serve as a primary key are called a *concatenated key*, as shown in Figure 10.6.

The primary key of a table has two important properties:

- **Unique identification.** The value of the primary key in each row must be different from the value of the primary key in any other row.

	Field Name	Data Type	Description
🔑	Vessel_#	Text	Unique vessel Identifier
	Hold_Size	Number	Capacity of vessel's cargo hold in cubic feet
	Vessel_Details	Text	Gives additional information about the vessel

Figure 10.4   Primary key shown in a table description window.

Table: Vessel

Vessel_#	Hold_Size	Vessel_Details
00165	12765	Tanker
00205	28775	Freighter
00276	12756	Tanker
00339	28775	Freighter
00463	12756	Tanker

Record: 1   of 5

Figure 10.5   Primary key highlighted in a table display window.

	Field Name	Data Type	Description
🔑	Vessel_#	Text	Unique vessel identifier
🔑	Port_#	Text	Unique port identifier
	Arrival_Date	Date/Time	Date the vessel is scheduled to arrive in port
	Departure_Date	Date/Time	Date the vessel is scheduled to leave the port

Figure 10.6   Vessel_# and Port_# together make up the concatenated key of the Port table.

- **Nonredundancy.** If a primary key consists of more than one column, then none of the columns that make up the primary key can be discarded without destroying the property of unique identification.

Many relational database packages depart from the formal relational model with respect to primary keys and allow duplicate rows to exist in a table. With many relational database packages that allow duplicate rows, it is not necessary to identify a primary key for a table if the application does not require one. However, in practice, most tables do have primary keys even if the database software does not strictly require them for all tables.

In many cases, a table may appear to have more than one possible key. For example, in a personnel application, an Employee_Name column and an Employee_Number may both have unique data element values. It might thus appear as if either column might serve as the table's primary key. The different possible keys for a table are called *candidate keys*. One of the candidate keys must be chosen as the primary key for the table.

Judgment must be applied in choosing among apparent candidate keys. For example, in an actual Personnel database, it might be possible for two employees to have the same name; thus we would not ordinarily consider Employee_Name to be a true candidate key.

REPRESENTING RELATIONSHIPS

Another characteristic of the relational data model is that all relationships between entity types are expressed in the form of data stored in the tables. There are no special *pointer* data types as there are in many implementations of the hierarchical and network database models.

Figure 10.7 shows how the one-with-many association between the Vessel table and the Port table is implemented using data element values in the Vessel_# column of the Vessel table and the Vessel_# column of the Port table.

Notice that we have used the same Vessel_# column name in both the Vessel and Port tables. Although column names must be unique within a single table, there is typically no requirement that they be unique among the various tables that make up a relational database. Using the same column name in two tables is one way of making clear a relationship that exists between the tables. However, each specific relational database system provides an explicit means to define relationships between tables, whether or not column names are duplicated from one table to another.

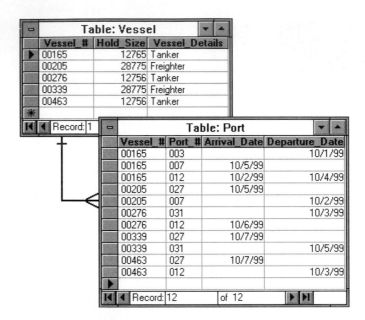

Figure 10.7   One-with-many association between the Vessel and Port tables.

Representing all relationships through stored data has two advantages. First, it makes a relational database easy to use, since the user or application program does not have to be aware of structural relationships that may not be immediately obvious. Second, it contributes to data independence. As discussed in Chapter 1, it is undesirable for application programs to be dependent on structural relationships and to refer to structural relationships explicitly in navigating the database. Such dependence causes changes that are made to the database structure to require that changes be made to the application programs that access the database. With a relational database, changes in relationships are made simply by changing data, and such changes are less likely to require changes in application programs.

SUMMARY

The relational data model defines data objects, operators, and integrity rules. In a relational database, data is represented in the form of tables consisting of rows and columns. A table represents an entity type, a column represents an attribute of the entity type, and a row represents a particular occurrence of the entity type. Each row contains a set of data values, one for each attribute of the entity type. More formal descriptions of the relational data model sometimes uses the term attribute for column, tuple for row, and relation for table.

In the relational data model, a table has a number of characteristics. Each row-column entry consists of a single, atomic data item; repeating groups are not allowed. All the data items in a given column are of the same data type, and their values are taken from the same domain. Each column in a table has a unique name within that table, and each row in the table must be unique. The sequence of a table's rows and columns is not meaningful, and the rows and columns of a table can be viewed in any sequence.

A data structure from which repeating groups have been removed to permit storage in a relational database table is called a normalized data structure, and the data is said to be in first normal form. Additional levels of normalization are also desirable.

Since each row in a table must be unique, there must exist a column, or set of columns, called the primary key, that uniquely identifies each row. A primary key has two important properties: unique identification and nonredundancy. A primary key that must consist of two or more columns to ensure uniqueness is called a concatenated key.

All relationships between tables are expressed by data stored in the tables. Two advantages of representing relationships using data stored in the database are ease of use and data independence.

Chapter 11 examines the types of operations that the relational data model defines for manipulating the data stored in the tables of a relational database.

Chapter 11

Relational Operations

As we pointed out in Chapter 10, the relational data model defines a set of operators that can be used to perform operations on the tables that make up a relational data structure. This chapter describes the relational operators that can be used to perform operations on the tables making up a relational data structure.

RELATIONAL ALGEBRA

The relational operators defined by the relational data model make up a *relational algebra* that is used to specify operations that can be performed on data represented in relational form. The operators that form the relational algebra share two common characteristics.

The first common characteristic of all relational operators is that they operate on an *entire table*; they do not operate on individual *rows* of a table. Most relational database software packages define functions that can be performed in application programs on table data a row at a time using an object called a *cursor*. But these types of operations are not defined by the relational data model itself. The use of cursors in application programs that use SQL is discussed in Chapters 21 and 22.

The second common characteristic is that when a relational operator is applied to one or more tables, the operation always results in another complete table. This is important for two reasons:

- All data in a relational database, including that derived as a result of relational operations, takes the form of tables.

- Operations can be nested; a second relational operator can always be applied to the result of a previous operation.

The relational data model defines eight relational operations that can be performed on tables:

- Restrict
- Project
- Join
- Divide

- Union
- Intersection
- Difference
- Cartesian Product

Keep in mind as you read this chapter that the actual languages that are provided by relational database software, including the Structured Query Language (SQL), often do not use the same verbs or operators as those of the relational data model. However, all or most of the relational operations defined by the formal relational algebra can typically be expressed using the data access languages supported by relational database software.

THE RESTRICT OPERATOR

The *Restrict* operator allows a result table to be formed that contains all the columns from *selected rows* in the original table. The Restrict operator is often called the *Select* operator in relational database literature. However, this is an unfortunate choice of terminology as it can lead to confusion with the SELECT statement of SQL. The SQL SELECT statement can be used to perform Restrict relational operations, as well as other types of relational operations.

In Fig. 11.1, an example of a relational Restrict operation, the resulting table contains only those rows from an Employee table that have a data element value of "02" in the Dept_# column. This Restrict operation might be used to obtain a list of those employees that are in department 02.

Use of the Restrict operator can make a database easier to use by providing access to only that part of the database that is of interest to the user. A Restrict operation could also be used to limit access to only those rows that a given user is allowed to access.

THE PROJECT OPERATOR

The *Project* operator is used to produce a new table that contains all the rows from the original table, but only a subset of the columns. The Project operation shown in Fig. 11.2 produces a new table that contains all the columns from the Employee table except for the Salary column. As with the Restrict operation, a Project operation can be used to make a database easier to use by presenting only pertinent information, or it can be used to limit access to only those columns that the user is authorized to access.

Depending on the columns chosen in the Project operation, the initial table that results from the Project operation might be one that contains duplicate rows, as shown in Fig. 11.3. Notice that the first step in eliminating the unwanted columns results in rows containing duplicate Dept_#/Skill combinations. Since this preliminary result violates the uniqueness rule of the relational data model, the Project operation continues by eliminating duplicate rows in producing the result table.

Employee Table

Emp_#	EmpName	Dept_#	Salary
301	Hansen	01	2000
482	Michaels	02	1800
127	Robinson	04	1100
185	Donatelli	02	5000
079	Smith	01	1700
246	Chapman	03	2000

Restrict (Dept_# = '02')

Result Table

Emp_#	EmpName	Dept_#	Salary
482	Michaels	02	1800
185	Donatelli	02	5000

Figure 11.1   Relational Restrict operation.

Employee Table

Emp_#	EmpName	Dept_#	Salary
301	Hansen	01	2000
482	Michaels	02	1800
127	Robinson	04	1100
185	Donatelli	02	5000
079	Smith	01	1700
246	Chapman	03	2000

Project (Emp_#, EmpName, Dept_#)

Result Table

Emp_#	EmpName	Dept_#
301	Hansen	01
482	Michaels	02
127	Robinson	04
185	Donatelli	02
079	Smith	01
246	Chapman	03

Figure 11.2   Project operation.

Employee Table

Emp_#	EmpName	Sex	Birth	Dept_#	Skill	JobTitle	Salary
373	Jones	M	100335	04	73	Accountant	2000
871	Blanagan	M	101019	17	43	Plumber	1800
355	Lawrence	F	090932	04	02	Clerk	1100
963	Rockefeller	M	011132	09	11	Consultant	5000
597	Roplay	M	021242	17	43	Plumber	1700
188	Smith	M	091130	04	73	Accountant	2000
645	Rainer	M	110941	04	02	Clerk	1200
161	Horace	F	071235	17	07	Engineer	2500
190	Hall	M	011030	17	21	Architect	3700
292	Fair	F	020442	09	93	Programmer	2100

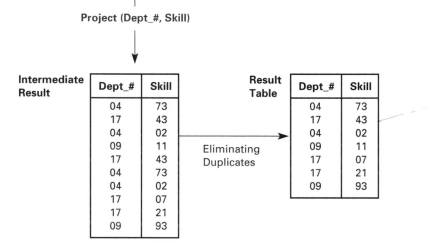

Project (Dept_#, Skill)

Intermediate Result

Dept_#	Skill
04	73
17	43
04	02
09	11
17	43
04	73
04	02
17	07
17	21
09	93

Eliminating Duplicates →

Result Table

Dept_#	Skill
04	73
17	43
04	02
09	11
17	07
17	21
09	93

Figure 11.3   Project operation with duplicate rows.

THE JOIN OPERATOR

The *Join* operator combines the columns from two tables, resulting in a third, wider table. A Join operation must be based on one or more columns from each of the two tables whose data values share a common domain. The result table is formed in such a way that in each row, the data values from the two columns (or sets of columns) on which the Join is based have the same data element values.

In the example of a Join operation shown in Fig. 11.4, we are joining the Employee table and the Department table on the Dept_#_A and Dept_#_B columns. In performing this Join, each Dept_#_A value is compared against *all* the Dept_#_B values. Where the values are equal, the row from the Employee table is combined with the row from the Department table to form a row in the resulting table. This particular Join operation could be used to obtain a complete list of the locations at which each employee works.

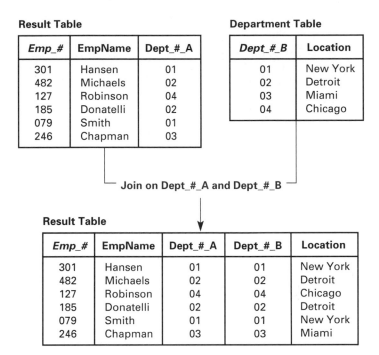

Result Table

Emp_#	EmpName	Dept_#_A
301	Hansen	01
482	Michaels	02
127	Robinson	04
185	Donatelli	02
079	Smith	01
246	Chapman	03

Department Table

Dept_#_B	Location
01	New York
02	Detroit
03	Miami
04	Chicago

Join on Dept_#_A and Dept_#_B

Result Table

Emp_#	EmpName	Dept_#_A	Dept_#_B	Location
301	Hansen	01	01	New York
482	Michaels	02	02	Detroit
127	Robinson	04	04	Chicago
185	Donatelli	02	02	Detroit
079	Smith	01	01	New York
246	Chapman	03	03	Miami

Figure 11.4   Join operation.

Equijoin

Because we made an *equal* comparison in performing the Join, the operation is known, formally, as an *Equijoin*. We can also perform Joins using other types of comparisons. For example, we might perform a Greater-than Join, a Less-than-or-equal-to Join, and so on. In such cases, the columns on which the Join is performed will not have equal values; instead the values in each row will be related according to the type of comparison made. The most common type of Join operation in practice, however, is the Equijoin.

Natural Join

Because of the way the Equijoin operation is defined, the resulting table from an Equijoin contains two columns that have identical data element values. In the previous example, these were columns Dept_#_A and Dept_#_B. We can, if we like, eliminate one of the two columns, as shown in Fig. 11.5.

An Equijoin with one of the identical columns eliminated is called a *natural join*. When we use the term Join without qualification, we generally mean an Equijoin that is also a natural join.

In Fig. 11.4, we explicitly named the columns from each table on which the Join operation is based. In some cases, a Join operation might be constructed without naming

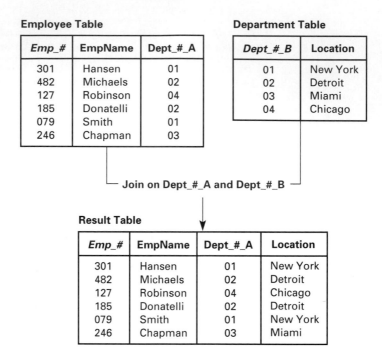

Employee Table

Emp_#	EmpName	Dept_#_A
301	Hansen	01
482	Michaels	02
127	Robinson	04
185	Donatelli	02
079	Smith	01
246	Chapman	03

Department Table

Dept_#_B	Location
01	New York
02	Detroit
03	Miami
04	Chicago

Join on Dept_#_A and Dept_#_B

Result Table

Emp_#	EmpName	Dept_#_A	Location
301	Hansen	01	New York
482	Michaels	02	Detroit
127	Robinson	04	Chicago
185	Donatelli	02	Detroit
079	Smith	01	New York
246	Chapman	03	Miami

Figure 11.5   Equijoin operation.

the joining columns. When this is done, the two tables being joined generally have columns that share a common name.

In Fig. 11.6 the column on which the Join is performed is implied, and the two tables are joined based on the data element values in the Department column.

Inner Join Operations

The relational data model itself originally defined only the type of Join operation described in the previous section. A number of different types of Join operations are useful in practice, and the original form of Join operation is an example of what is now typically called an *inner join* operation. With an inner join operation, there is a possibility that some of the rows from either or both of the tables being joined will not be represented in the result table.

For example, examine Fig. 11.7, showing an example of an inner join operation using different table contents than the previous examples. Notice that there are no corresponding rows in the Department table for the Leben and Martin entries in the Employee table. Also, there are no corresponding rows in the Employee table for the Los Angeles and Houston entries in the Department table. By the rules of the Inner Join operation, information for Leben, Martin, Los Angeles, and Houston is not included in the resulting table.

In many applications, the above result would be the one required by the application. However, there are some applications in which we would like to perform a form of Join

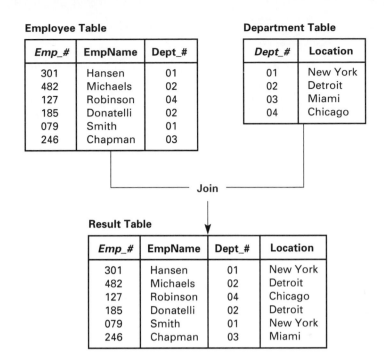

Employee Table

Emp_#	EmpName	Dept_#
301	Hansen	01
482	Michaels	02
127	Robinson	04
185	Donatelli	02
079	Smith	01
246	Chapman	03

Department Table

Dept_#	Location
01	New York
02	Detroit
03	Miami
04	Chicago

Join

Result Table

Emp_#	EmpName	Dept_#	Location
301	Hansen	01	New York
482	Michaels	02	Detroit
127	Robinson	04	Chicago
185	Donatelli	02	Detroit
079	Smith	01	New York
246	Chapman	03	Miami

Figure 11.6 Natural join operation.

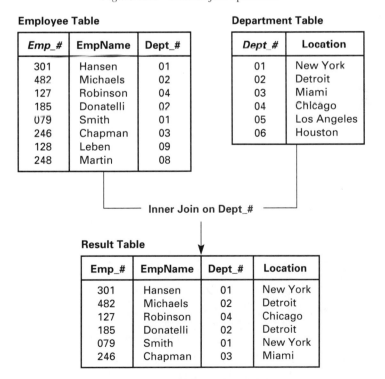

Employee Table

Emp_#	EmpName	Dept_#
301	Hansen	01
482	Michaels	02
127	Robinson	04
185	Donatelli	02
079	Smith	01
246	Chapman	03
128	Leben	09
248	Martin	08

Department Table

Dept_#	Location
01	New York
02	Detroit
03	Miami
04	Chicago
05	Los Angeles
06	Houston

Inner Join on Dept_#

Result Table

Emp_#	EmpName	Dept_#	Location
301	Hansen	01	New York
482	Michaels	02	Detroit
127	Robinson	04	Chicago
185	Donatelli	02	Detroit
079	Smith	01	New York
246	Chapman	03	Miami

Figure 11.7 Inner join operation.

operation in which data in one or both of the source tables is not lost in the result table when data values do not match.

Outer Join Operations

Join operations that retain in the result table information from all the rows in one or more of the tables being joined are called *outer join operations*.

To understand outer join operations, it is useful to view a Join operation as if it produced three different result tables, as in Fig. 11.8. Outer join operations combine the inner join result with one or more of the tables containing the rows that were not included from the two source tables.

The following are descriptions of the three types of outer join operations that are possible when two tables are being joined, illustrated in Fig. 11.9.

- **Left Outer Join.** A *left outer join* operation consists of the results of an inner join operation plus the information from the rows in the source table on the left that were excluded from the result of the inner join.

Employee Table

Emp_#	EmpName	Dept_#
301	Hansen	01
482	Michaels	02
127	Robinson	04
185	Donatelli	02
079	Smith	01
246	Chapman	03
128	Leben	09
248	Martin	08

Department Table

Dept_#	Location
01	New York
02	Detroit
03	Miami
04	Chicago
05	Los Angeles
06	Houston

Join on Dept_#

Inner Join Result Table

Emp_#	EmpName	Dept_#	Location
301	Hansen	01	New York
482	Michaels	02	Detroit
127	Robinson	04	Chicago
185	Donatelli	02	Detroit
079	Smith	01	New York
246	Chapman	03	Miami

Rows from Employee Not in Result

Emp_#	EmpName	Dept_#	Location
128	Leben	09	--
248	Martin	08	--

Rows from Department Not in Result

Emp_#	EmpName	Dept_#	Location
--	--	05	Los Angeles
--	--	06	Houston

Figure 11.8 Outer join operation components.

Employee Table

Emp_#	EmpName	Dept_#
301	Hansen	01
482	Michaels	02
127	Robinson	04
185	Donatelli	02
079	Smith	01
246	Chapman	03
128	Leben	09
248	Martin	08

Department Table

Dept_#	Location
01	New York
02	Detroit
03	Miami
04	Chicago
05	Los Angeles
06	Houston

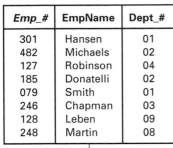

Outer Joins on Dept_#

Left Outer Join Result Table

Emp_#	EmpName	Dept_#	Location
301	Hansen	01	New York
482	Michaels	02	Detroit
127	Robinson	04	Chicago
185	Donatelli	02	Detroit
079	Smith	01	New York
246	Chapman	03	Miami
128	Leben	09	--
248	Martin	08	--

Right Outer Join Result Table

Emp_#	EmpName	Dept_#	Location
301	Hansen	01	New York
482	Michaels	02	Detroit
127	Robinson	04	Chicago
185	Donatelli	02	Detroit
079	Smith	01	New York
246	Chapman	03	Miami
--	--	05	Los Angeles
--	--	06	Houston

Full Outer Join Result Table

Emp_#	EmpName	Dept_#	Location
301	Hansen	01	New York
482	Michaels	02	Detroit
127	Robinson	04	Chicago
185	Donatelli	02	Detroit
079	Smith	01	New York
246	Chapman	03	Miami
128	Leben	09	--
248	Martin	08	--
--	--	05	Los Angeles
--	--	06	Houston

Figure 11.9 Outer join operation result tables.

- **Right Outer Join.** A *right outer join* operation consists of the results of an inner join operation plus the information from the rows in the source table on the right that were excluded from the result of the inner join.

- **Full Outer Join.** A *full outer join* operation consists of the results of an inner join operation plus the information from the rows in both source tables that were excluded from the result of the inner join.

Notice that the result tables that are created by outer join operations contain null values in those rows for which department values do not match in both tables.

We can interpret the null values as representing information that is *missing* or that is *not known*. In most of the examples in this book, we are showing fields containing null values using hyphens. Some relational database software packages display null values as blanks. Keep in mind, however, that a field containing a null value is different from an alphanumeric field containing blanks or a numeric field containing the value zero.

The previous discussion represents somewhat of an oversimplification of the outer join concept. Outer joins are relatively straightforward when only two tables are being joined, but they become more complex when we attempt to perform outer join operations on three or more tables. The table that results from such an operation may be different depending on the sequence in which the tables are joined. Discussions of complex outer join operations are beyond the scope of this book.

THE DIVIDE OPERATOR

The processing performed by the *Divide* operator is also based on a comparison of data element values contained in columns from two tables. One table is the dividend table and the other the divisor. The dividend and divisor tables must have one or more matching columns, and the dividend table must have one or more additional columns not in the divisor table. The results of the Divide operation consists of a result table containing only *columns* from the dividend table that are not in the divisor table. The result table contains only *rows* from the dividend table that satisfy the comparison for *all* rows in the divisor table.

Suppose we have an Employee_Skill table containing an Emp_# column and a Skill column and a Skill table containing only a Skill column. We might perform a Divide operation by dividing the Employee_Skill table (the dividend) by the Skill table (the divisor) based on the Emp_# and Skill columns in the Employee_Skill table and the Skill column in the Skill table. To perform such a Divide operation, the Skill data element value for each Emp_# value in the Employee_Skill table is compared with all the Skill data elements in the Skill table.

The result of the Divide operation is a new table that contains only Emp_# values where there are Emp_#/Skill pairs in the Employee_Skill table that match all the Skill values in the Skill table. Such a Divide operation is shown in Fig. 11.10.

The result of the Divide operation is a table with Emp_# values 301 and 482, since these are the only two Emp_#/Skill pairs in the Employee_Skill table that have Skill values of both 02 and 11. We might use such a Divide operation to produce a list of those employees that have both skills 02 and 11.

SET-ORIENTED RELATIONAL OPERATIONS

Relational theory draws heavily upon the branch of mathematics called *set theory*. In addition to the four basic relational operators we have described thus far, the relational data model defines four additional operators that correspond to operations that are used

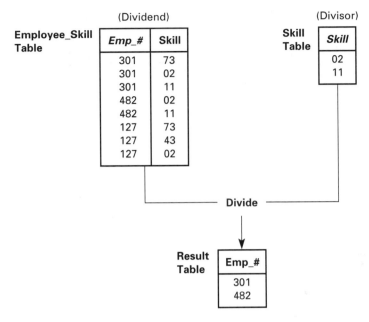

Figure 11.10   Divide operation.

to perform manipulations on sets: Union, Intersection, Difference, and Cartesian Product.

THE UNION OPERATOR

The *Union* operator combines the rows from two similar tables to form a new table, usually having more rows than either of the two source tables. The new table consists of those rows that are in *either* or *both* of the original tables.

The Venn diagrams used in set theory can help make clear the set operations that can be performed on tables. The Venn diagram in Fig. 11.11 illustrates the Union operation. If the two tables each contain a different set of unique rows, then the result of a Union operation on the two tables consists of a new table with all the rows from both original tables. If some of the rows are duplicated in the two tables, then the duplicates are removed from the resulting table as part of the Union operation.

In Fig. 11.12, showing a Union operation, the resulting table contains all the rows that are in the Welders table, the Programmers table, or in both tables. Suppose the Welders table represents employees that can weld and the Programmers table describes employees that can program. This Union operation might then be used to obtain a list of all employees that can weld, can program, or can both weld and program.

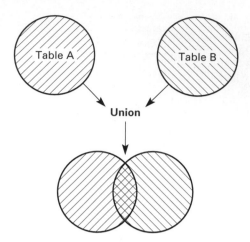

Figure 11.11   Venn diagram showing the function of a Union relational operation.

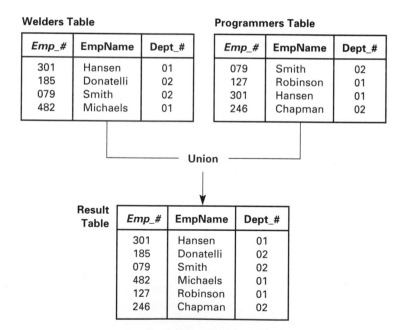

Welders Table

Emp_#	EmpName	Dept_#
301	Hansen	01
185	Donatelli	02
079	Smith	02
482	Michaels	01

Programmers Table

Emp_#	EmpName	Dept_#
079	Smith	02
127	Robinson	01
301	Hansen	01
246	Chapman	02

Union

Result Table

Emp_#	EmpName	Dept_#
301	Hansen	01
185	Donatelli	02
079	Smith	02
482	Michaels	01
127	Robinson	01
246	Chapman	02

Figure 11.12   Union operation.

THE INTERSECTION OPERATOR

The *Intersection* operator combines the rows from two similar tables to form a third table that is typically smaller than either of the tables being combined. The new table consists of only those rows that are in *both* of the original tables. Figure 11.13 shows a Venn diagram that illustrates the Intersection relational operation.

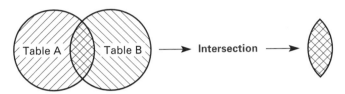

Figure 11.13 Venn diagram showing the function of an Intersection relational operation.

The Intersection operation shown in Fig. 11.14 produces a table that contains only those rows that are in both the Welders table and the Programmers table. We might use the result of an Intersection operation on the Welders table and the Programmers table to obtain a list of those employees that can both weld and program.

THE DIFFERENCE OPERATOR

The *Difference* operator combines two tables to produce a third table that contains those rows that are in the first table and are not also in the second table. Figure 11.15 shows a Venn diagram that illustrates the Difference operation.

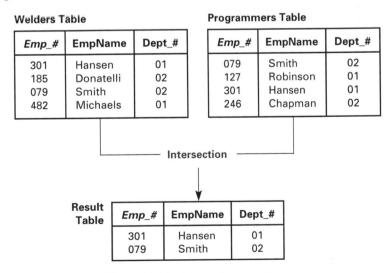

Figure 11.14   Intersection operation.

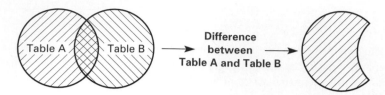

Figure 11.15   Venn diagram showing the function of a Difference relational operation.

In the Difference operation shown in Fig. 11.16, the two rows of the resulting table are those that are in the Welders table but are not in the Programmers table. Notice that the Union and Intersection operators are associative, but that the Difference operator is not. The result of one Difference operation performed on the Welders table and the Programmers table could be used to obtain a list of those employees that can only weld and cannot program. The result of another Difference operation can be used to give the opposite result—a list of those employees that can only program and cannot weld (see Fig. 11.17).

THE CARTESIAN PRODUCT OPERATOR

The previous three set-oriented relational operators work with tables that are essentially similar in that they have the same column structure. Tables with the same column structure are called *Union-compatible* tables.

The final set operator—the *Cartesian Product* operator—works with two tables whose column structures are different. To form the result of a Cartesian Product operation applied to two tables, we concatenate each row of the first table with each row of the

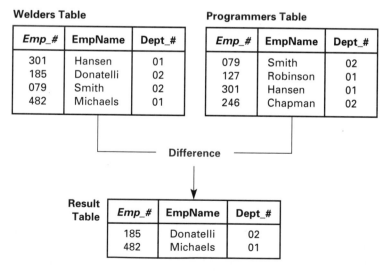

Figure 11.16   Difference operation.

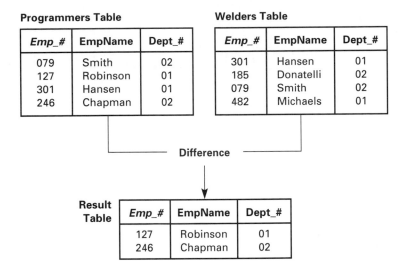

Figure 11.17   Alternative Difference operation.

second table. Thus the number of rows in the resulting table is the product of the number of rows in the first table and the number of rows in the second table.

Figure 11.18 shows the result of a Cartesian Product operation performed on the Employee table and a Room table that maintains information about room numbers and ID numbers assigned to the locks on those rooms.

Notice that each row from the Employee table is repeated three times, once for each of the rows in the Room table. Suppose that the Employee table represents employees in department 01 and that the Room table represents room numbers and lock identifiers for the rooms in department 01. The Cartesian Product of the Employee table and the Room table might then be used to obtain a list of the room numbers and lock identifiers that can be accessed by each of the employees in department 01.

The Cartesian Product operation is not very useful in practice, and most relational database systems do not directly provide a verb to form a Cartesian Product. This operator is included in the definition of the relational model for conceptual reasons and because the database software may need to form a Cartesian Product as an intermediate step in performing a Join operation that is based on a comparison that is other than an equal comparison.

SUMMARY

The relational model defines a set of relational operators that make up a relational algebra. Relational operations apply to an entire table and not to individual rows, and when a relational operator is applied to a table or group of tables, the result of the operation is always another table.

When the Restrict relational operator is applied to a table, a result table is formed that contains all the columns from selected rows in the original table.

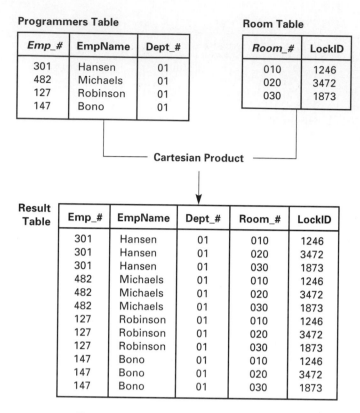

Figure 11.18   Cartesian Product operation.

The Project operator is used to produce a result table that contains all the rows from the original table but only a subset of the columns.

The Join operator combines the columns from two tables to produce a third, wider table. A Join operation is based on a comparison that is made between one or more columns from the tables being joined that contain similar data items. The Join operation resulting from an equal comparison is called an Equijoin operation. Joins can be classified as either inner joins or outer joins. With an inner join, only the rows that satisfy the Join comparison are placed on the result table. With an outer join, all the rows of one or more of the source tables can be placed in the result table. Outer joins can be classified as left outer joins, right outer joins, or full outer joins.

A Divide relational operation is based on a comparison of data element values contained in columns from two tables. The dividend and divisor tables must have one or more matching columns, and the dividend table must have one or more additional columns not in the divisor table. The results of the Divide operation consist of a result table containing only columns from the dividend table that are not in the divisor table, and only rows from the dividend table that satisfy the comparison for all rows in the divisor table.

The Union operation combines the rows from two similar tables to form a new table, usually having more rows than either of the two source tables. The new table consists of rows that are in either or both of the original tables.

The Intersection operator combines the rows from two similar tables to form a third table that is typically smaller than either of the tables being combined. The new table consists of only those rows that are in both of the original tables.

The Difference operator combines two tables to produce a third table that contains those rows that are in the first table and are not also in the second table.

The Cartesian Product operator works on tables that have different column structures. It produces a result table that consists of a concatenation of each row of the first table with each row of the second table. The number of rows in the result table is the product of the number of rows in the first table and the number of rows in the second table.

Chapter 12 examines integrity constraints that can be placed on relational tables to help control the consistency of the information they store.

Integrity Constraints

In the previous two chapters, we saw how the relational data model defines a number of objects and a set of operators that can be applied to those objects. In this chapter, we see how the relational data model also defines two types of *integrity constraints* that concern the data element values that can be placed in tables. These two integrity constraints are called *entity integrity* and *referential integrity*.

ENTITY INTEGRITY

The *entity integrity* rule states that no column that is part of a primary key can have a null value. This rule is necessary if the primary key is to fulfill its role of uniquely identifying the rows in a table. If we allowed a primary key value to be completely null, we would be saying that there is some particular entity occurrence that could not be distinguished from other entity occurrences. This is a contradiction, since two entity occurrences that cannot be distinguished from one another must be the same occurrence. Similar arguments can be made for disallowing partial null key values.

Most relational database systems implement the entity integrity rule. Many systems implement primary keys by means of objects called *indexes*. Such a database package may ensure entity integrity for a given table only if a unique index is defined for that table. If a table is defined with no unique index associated with it, the entity integrity rule may not be enforced for that table.

REFERENTIAL INTEGRITY

It is possible for one table to contain a column, or set of columns, that contain data element values drawn from the same domain as the column or columns that form the primary key in some other table. This column or set of columns is called a *foreign key*.

In the example shown in Fig. 12.1, the DeptManager column in the Department table is a foreign key because each DeptManager value is drawn from the same domain

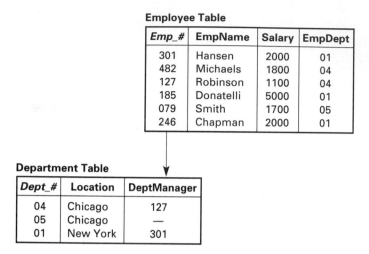

Employee Table

Emp_#	EmpName	Salary	EmpDept
301	Hansen	2000	01
482	Michaels	1800	04
127	Robinson	1100	04
185	Donatelli	5000	01
079	Smith	1700	05
246	Chapman	2000	01

Department Table

Dept_#	Location	DeptManager
04	Chicago	127
05	Chicago	—
01	New York	301

Figure 12.1   The DeptManager column is a foreign key.

as the Emp_# values in the Employee table. In this case, the domain is the set of valid employee numbers.

The referential integrity rule states that every foreign key value must either match a primary key value in its associated table, or it must be wholly null. In other words, any value of DeptManager in the Department table must either be null or it must match an Emp_# value in the Employee table. The referential integrity rule guarantees that the Department table will not reference a manager who is not also an employee. Allowing a null value in the foreign key, however, does allow the Department table to contain a row for a department that currently has no manager.

HIERARCHICAL STRUCTURES

A foreign key creates a hierarchical relationship between the two associated tables, with the table containing the foreign key being the *child*, or *dependent*, and the table containing the column from which foreign key values are obtained being the *parent*. We might illustrate such a parent-child relationship in a database diagram using an arrow, with the arrow pointing from the parent table to the dependent table, as shown in Fig. 12.2.

MULTIPLE-LEVEL HIERARCHIES

As we have seen, a referential integrity relationship links two tables—a parent table and a dependent table. However, it is possible for more than two tables to be linked by referential constraints, thus forming more complex structures. There may be special considerations related to a complex referential structure, particularly in the way the deletion of rows is handled.

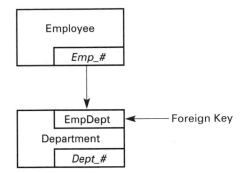

Figure 12.2   Foreign key hierarchical relationship.

Suppose our Department and Employee tables are related in a new way together with a Project table, as shown in Fig. 12.3. In this, the following foreign key relationships are in effect:

- The Employee table has an EmpDept foreign key that identifies the department to which each employee belongs. The EmpDept foreign key takes its values from Dept_#, the primary key of the Department table.
- The Project table has a ProjLeader foreign key that identifies the project leader of each project. The ProjLeader foreign key takes its values from Emp_#, the primary key of the Employee table.

The structure in Fig. 12.3 is a multiple-level hierarchy. The Project table is a dependent of the Employee table, since it contains a foreign key, with the Employee table as the parent table for this relationship. The Employee table is a dependent of the Department table and is also the parent of the Project table.

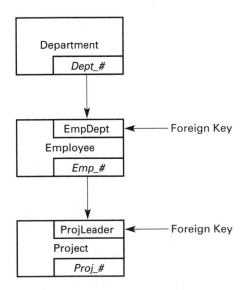

Figure 12.3   Three-level foreign key hierarchy.

In a multiple-level hierarchy, any table below a parent table, at any level in a hierarchy, is called a *descendant*. Employee and Project are both descendants of Department. A parent table may have multiple dependents, and a dependent table that has multiple foreign keys defined has multiple parents. Such relationships can lead to hierarchies with quite complex structures, such as the structure shown in Fig. 12.4.

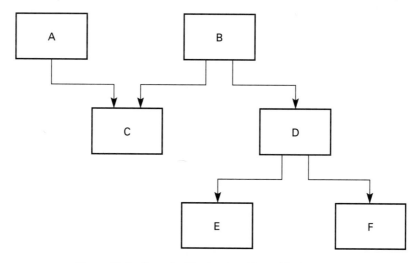

Figure 12.4   Complex foreign key hierarchical structure.

CYCLES

A *cycle* is a structure in which a table is a descendent of itself. Suppose we defined the following referential constraints on the Department and Employee tables:

- The Department table has a DeptManager foreign key that identifies each employee's manager. The DeptManager foreign key takes its values from Emp_#, the primary key of the Employee table.
- The Employee table has an EmpDept foreign key that identifies the department to which each employee belongs. The EmpDept foreign key takes its values from Dept_#, the primary key of the Department table.

We can represent these relationships as shown in Fig. 12.5. Here, the Department table is a dependent of the Employee table, and the Employee table is a dependent of the Department table. Therefore, the Department table is a descendent of itself, thus constituting a cycle.

Multiple-Level Cycles

A cycle can involve multiple levels of tables, as shown in Fig. 12.6.

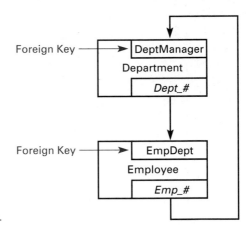

Figure 12.5   Foreign key cycle.

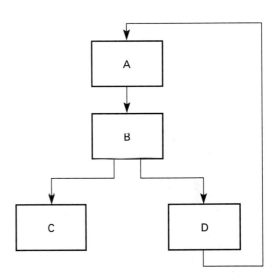

Figure 12.6   Foreign key multiple-level cycle.

Self-Referencing Cycles

A table may also have a foreign key that references itself. For example, suppose our Employee table contains an EmpManager column that identifies each employee's manager, who is also an employee. An example of such a relationship is shown in Fig. 12.7.

The foregoing structure is called a *self-referencing cycle*. The referential constraint defined in the previous example ensures that the EmpManager column contains only values that are also valid Emp_# values (or are null).

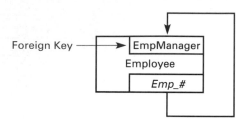

Figure 12.7 Self-referencing cycle.

REFERENTIAL INTEGRITY DELETE CONSIDERATIONS

Suppose a program issues a Delete request to the database software to delete a row in a parent table, such as invoking a DELETE SQL statement. To enforce the referential integrity rule, the Delete request may also affect tables that are referentially related to it.

Most relational database software allows a *delete rule* to be specified when a foreign key is defined. The delete rule specifies the way in which the database software handles requests for row deletions when referential integrity constraints are in effect. Each database software package defines its own set of delete rules that it supports. Commonly implemented delete rules include restrict, cascade, and set null:

- **Restrict Delete Rule.** The *restrict* delete rule specifies that a row in a parent table cannot be deleted if there are one or more rows in dependent tables that contain matching foreign key values. With this delete rule, if appropriate rows in the dependent tables are not explicitly deleted before issuing the delete operation for the row in the parent table, the delete operation will fail.

- **Cascade Delete Rule.** The *cascade* delete rule specifies that when a row is deleted from a parent table, the database software should also automatically delete any rows in dependent tables that contain matching foreign key values.

- **Set Null Delete Rule.** The *set null* delete rule says that if a row is deleted from a parent table, the database software should change to null values all matching foreign key values in dependent tables.

As an example of how delete rules work in conjunction with referential integrity constraints, suppose we have defined the foreign keys shown in Fig. 12.8 and have specified the cascade delete rule for each of them.

With the above structure, if we delete a department from the Department table, the database software will also delete dependent rows for that department from the Employee table. The rows deleted from the Employee table may in turn cause dependent rows to be deleted from the Project table.

The term *delete-connected* is sometimes used to designate all dependent tables, plus any other descendent tables that are under a dependent table that specify the cascade delete rule. Delete-connected tables are tables that can have rows automatically deleted when a deletion occurs in a parent table.

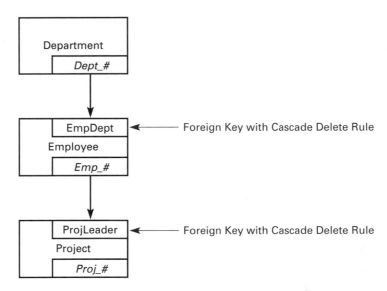

Figure 12.8   Foreign key hierarchy with the cascade delete rule specified.

CUSTOM RULE-BASED PROCESSING

The integrity rules that are defined by the relational data model provide powerful tools for maintaining the integrity of the data in a relational database. However, they do not always provide the tools necessary for implementing integrity constraints, or other types of processing, based on specific business rules rather than on fundamental data relationships.

Intelligent-database features, such as stored procedures and database triggers (see Chapter 5), can be used to extend the functions of the database software to implement integrity constraints based on specific business rules. Such facilities can be used to extend the functions of the database to include any desired processing.

For example, an organization may want to implement a new business rule saying that whenever the inventory quantity on certain parts or subsystems falls below some minimum quantity, a special report should be generated and sent to an inventory manager.

A complex inventory management application may consist of a great many application programs that may all play a role in maintaining inventory quantities for the parts in question. A special program could be written that examines the appropriate table column, makes the required decisions, and formats the required report. This new program could then be run periodically to generate the required report.

By using stored procedures and database triggers, the database software used to manage the inventory database could be directed to implement this new business rule and could itself run the required procedure to generate the inventory report at the appropriate times.

To do this, a database trigger might be designed that activates each time an UPDATE statement is issued for the inventory quantity table column. The trigger might execute a stored procedure that examines the required Inventory table columns after each pertinent update is performed. Whenever one of the specified inventory quantity values falls below the specified minimum, the stored procedure could then invoke additional procedural code to format the required report and send it to the appropriate inventory manager. With this technique, no existing application programs need be modified to add this application function to the inventory system.

By using intelligent-database facilities, the functions of the database software can be extended to provide rule-based processing of whatever kind is needed to serve the needs of the database application.

SUMMARY

The entity integrity constraint states that no column that is part of a primary key can have a null value. This rule guarantees that a primary key value always uniquely identifies its row.

The referential integrity rule is based on foreign keys. A foreign key consists of a column or group of columns whose data values are drawn from the same domain as that defined for the primary key of an associated table. The referential integrity rule states that every foreign key value in the first table must either match a primary key value in the second table or it must be wholly null.

A foreign key creates a hierarchical relationship between two tables. The table containing the foreign key is the child, or dependent table, and the table containing the column from which foreign key values are obtained is the parent. Foreign key hierarchical relationships can form multiple-level hierarchies, cycles, and self-referencing cycles.

Referential integrity constraints can define various types of delete rules that specify how deletions are handled when rows in parent tables are deleted. The cascade delete rule specifies that when a row in a parent table is deleted, associated rows in dependent tables should also be deleted. The set null delete rule specifies that when a row in a parent table is deleted, associated rows in dependent tables should have their foreign key values set to null values.

By using intelligent-database features, such as stored procedures and rule-based processing activated by database triggers, the functions of the database software can be extended to perform processing that is based on specific business rules.

Chapter 13 begins an examination of the normalization process. Normalization helps the database designer arrange data elements in tables so that the entire relational structure is as stable as possible and represents the inherent properties of the data.

Chapter **13**

Third Normal Form

Normalization theory, first described by E.F. Codd in conjunction with the relational data model, has been used to aid in database design. Normalization is a design technique that is widely used in designing all types of databases; its use is not limited to relational database structures.

Normalization theory, like the relational data model itself, can be described in rigorous mathematical terms. However, its underlying ideas are simple in nature and have much to do with ordinary common sense. Using the same approach with normalization that we took with the relational data model, we rely on simple explanations and examples to show how further normalization of relational data structures can help build stability into relational databases.

The overall goals of the normalization process are to:

- Arrange data so that it can be represented in tables, where each row-column position contains a single data element (no repeating data elements or groups).
- Ensure that data elements are associated with the correct keys, thereby minimizing data redundancy and increasing stability.

Normalization involves a series of steps that change the column structure of the various tables that make up a relational database by placing the data into a series of different forms called *first normal form*, *second normal form*, and so on.

FIRST NORMAL FORM

The first step in the normalization process is to place the data into *first normal form*. As we discussed in Chapter 10, this involves the removal of repeating groups. A table that contains no repeating groups and can be represented as a tabular data structure is a normalized data structure and is in at least first normal form. Therefore, if we already have a set of data in the form of tables, then it is already in first normal form. Any relational database table is automatically in first normal form, since each item in a table must be a single data element.

Removing Repeating Groups

We can remove repeating groups from a data structure by simply creating a separate row for each of the elements in the repeating group. Suppose we begin with the employee data shown in Fig. 13.1.

Here, a given record stores information about a number of different projects that a particular employee has worked on. In order to represent this data in tabular form, we generate a row for each project on which an employee has worked by repeating the employee information in each row (see Fig. 13.2).

In Chapter 10 we learned that the relational data model requires that we define a primary key for each table, and we will assume here that we are following this principle in defining relational database tables. Both the Emp_# and Project_# columns are needed to uniquely identify each row, so Emp_# and Project_# comprise a concatenated key for the table. This is shown in Fig. 13.3.

Data Redundancy

We have said that one of the goals of the normalization process is to reduce data redundancy. In fact, we have actually increased data redundancy by placing the data into first normal form. Job_# and JobTitle data element values are repeated many times, and the same Completion values are stored multiple times as well. This increase in data redun-

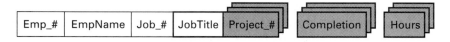

Figure 13.1   Unnormalized data structure with a repeating group.

Employee Table

Emp_#	EmpName	Job_#	JobTitle	Project_#	Completion	Hours
120	Jones	1	Programmer	01	7/17	37
120	Jones	1	Programmer	08	1/12	12
121	Harpo	1	Programmer	01	7/17	45
121	Harpo	1	Programmer	08	1/12	21
121	Harpo	1	Programmer	12	3/21	107
270	Garfunkel	2	Analyst	08	1/12	10
270	Garfunkel	2	Analyst	12	3/21	78
273	Selsi	3	Designer	01	7/17	22
274	Abrahms	2	Analyst	12	3/21	41
279	Higgins	1	Programmer	01	7/17	27
279	Higgins	1	Programmer	08	1/12	20
279	Higgins	1	Programmer	12	3/21	51
301	Flannel	1	Programmer	01	7/17	16
301	Flannel	1	Programmer	12	3/21	85
306	McGraw	3	Designer	12	3/21	67

Figure 13.2   Data structure in first normal form.

Employee Table

Emp_#	Project_#	EmpName	Job_#	JobTitle	Completion	Hours
120	01	Jones	1	Programmer	7/17	37
120	08	Jones	1	Programmer	1/12	12
121	01	Harpo	1	Programmer	7/17	45
121	08	Harpo	1	Programmer	1/12	21
121	12	Harpo	1	Programmer	3/21	107
270	08	Garfunkel	2	Analyst	1/12	10
270	12	Garfunkel	2	Analyst	3/21	78
273	01	Selsi	3	Designer	7/17	22
274	12	Abrahms	2	Analyst	3/21	41
279	01	Higgins	1	Programmer	7/17	27
279	08	Higgins	1	Programmer	1/12	20
279	12	Higgins	1	Programmer	3/21	51
301	01	Flannel	1	Programmer	7/17	16
301	12	Flannel	1	Programmer	3/21	85
306	12	McGraw	3	Designer	3/21	67

Figure 13.3 Emp_# and Project_# make up the concatenated key of the Employee table.

dancy is an important argument for why further normalization steps are required in order to produce a stable design.

A table that is in first normal form only may have many undesirable characteristics, of which data redundancy is only one. We will see how subsequent steps in the normalization process will reduce the redundancy that we have introduced and how additional normalization steps improve our data structure in other important ways as well.

SECOND NORMAL FORM

The second step in the normalization process places our data into *second normal form*. Second normal form involves the idea of *functional dependence*.

Functional Dependence

In general, a given column, say column B, is functionally dependent on some other column, say column A, if for any given value of column A there is a single value of column B associated with it. Saying that column B is functionally dependent on column A is equivalent to saying that column A *identifies* column B. Notice in our table, shown in Fig. 13.4, that there are three rows that have an Emp_# value of 121, but in each of those rows, the EmpName data element value is the same—Harpo.

A similar relationship exists between the Emp_# and EmpName columns in the other rows that have the same Emp_# value. Therefore, as long as we assume that no two employees can have the same employee number, EmpName is functionally dependent on Emp_#. We can use the same argument to show that Job_# and JobTitle are also functionally dependent on Emp_#.

Employee Table

Emp_#	Project_#	EmpName	Job_#	JobTitle	Completion	Hours
120	01	Jones	1	Programmer	7/17	37
120	08	Jones	1	Programmer	1/12	12
121	01	Harpo	1	Programmer	7/17	45
121	08	Harpo	1	Programmer	1/12	21
121	12	Harpo	1	Programmer	3/21	107
270	08	Garfunkel	2	Analyst	1/12	10
270	12	Garfunkel	2	Analyst	3/21	78
273	01	Selsi	3	Designer	7/17	22
274	12	Abrahms	2	Analyst	3/21	41
279	01	Higgins	1	Programmer	7/17	27
279	08	Higgins	1	Programmer	1/12	20
279	12	Higgins	1	Programmer	3/21	51
301	01	Flannel	1	Programmer	7/17	16
301	12	Flannel	1	Programmer	3/21	85
306	12	McGraw	3	Designer	3/21	67

Figure 13.4   EmpName is functionally dependent on Emp_#.

Full Functional Dependence

In some cases, a column will not be functionally dependent on a single column but will be functionally dependent on a *group* of columns. For example, Hours is functionally dependent on the combination of Emp_# and Project_#. This leads to the idea of *full functional dependence*. A column can be said to be fully functionally dependent on some collection of other columns when it is functionally dependent on the entire set but not on any subset of that collection. Hours is fully functionally dependent on Emp_# and Project_#. However, Completion is not fully functionally dependent on Emp_# and Project_#, since Completion is functionally dependent on Project_# alone.

In order to place a group of columns that are in first normal form into second normal form, we identify all the full functional dependencies that exist and create a separate table for each set of these. We begin by identifying a likely key—in this case Emp_#—and determining which other columns are fully functionally dependent on that key. EmpName, Job_#, and JobTitle are functionally dependent on Emp_#, so we leave them in the Employee table, which has Emp_# as its primary key (see Fig. 13.5).

Employee Table

Emp_#	EmpName	Job_#	JobTitle
120	Jones	1	Programmer
121	Harpo	1	Programmer
270	Garfunkel	2	Analyst
273	Selsi	3	Designer
274	Abrahms	2	Analyst
279	Higgins	1	Programmer
301	Flannel	1	Programmer
306	McGraw	3	Designer

Figure 13.5   The columns that are functionally dependent on the Emp_# column form an Employee table.

Of the remaining columns, Completion is dependent on Project_#, so we move the Project_# and Completion columns to a separate Project table that has Project_# as the primary key, as shown in Fig. 13.6.

Project Table

Project_#	Completion
01	7/17
08	1/12
12	3/21

Figure 13.6   The column that is functionally dependent on the Project_# key forms a Project table.

This leaves the Hours column. Hours is fully functionally dependent on the concatenated key that consists of Emp_# and Project_#. So we create a third table, called Hours, that consists of Emp_#, Project_#, and Hours. The key of the Hours table consists of Emp_# and Project_# (see Fig. 13.7).

Hours Table

Emp_#	Project_#	Hours
120	01	37
120	08	12
121	01	45
121	08	21
121	12	107
270	08	10
270	12	78
273	01	22
274	12	41
279	01	27
279	08	20
279	12	51
301	01	16
301	12	85
306	12	67

Figure 13.7   The column that is fully functionally dependent on the Emp_# and Project_# concatenated key forms an Hours table.

We can now say that the new set of three tables represents a data structure that is in second normal form. All three tables are in first normal form, and every non-key column is fully functionally dependent on the primary key of its table.

Duplicated Columns

Notice in Fig. 13.8 that we have included the Emp_# column in two of the tables and that we have included the Project_# column in two of the tables. Duplicating columns is perfectly valid and often occurs when converting a group of columns to second normal form. By duplicating columns in multiple tables, we are able to use relational operations to combine the tables in various ways to extract the data we need from them.

Employee Table

Emp_#	EmpName	Job_#	JobTitle
120	Jones	1	Programmer
121	Harpo	1	Programmer
270	Garfunkel	2	Analyst
273	Selsi	3	Designer
274	Abrahms	2	Analyst
279	Higgins	1	Programmer
301	Flannel	1	Programmer
306	McGraw	3	Designer

Hours Table

Emp_#	Project_#	Hours
120	01	37
120	08	12
121	01	45
121	08	21
121	12	107
270	08	10
270	12	78
273	01	22
274	12	41
279	01	27
279	08	20
279	12	51
301	01	16
301	12	85
306	12	67

Project Table

Project_#	Completion
01	7/17
08	1/12
12	3/21

Figure 13.8   Employee data in second normal form.

Second Normal Form Advantages

Notice that placing the data into second normal form has reduced much of the value redundancy that existed in the original table. Job_# and JobTitle data element values now appear only once per employee, and Completion data element values appear only once per project. Now that we have our data in second normal form, we can point out another undesirable characteristic of a table that is in first normal form only.

When our data was in first normal form only, we had a single table whose primary key consisted of Emp_# and Project_#. Because of the entity integrity constraint, we need to have valid values for both Emp_# and Project_# in order to create a new row. This means that we would be unable to store a row for an employee that is currently not assigned to a project (null Project_# value). Similarly, we would be prevented from storing a row for a project that currently has no employees assigned to it (null Emp_# value).

With our columns in second normal form, we can add a new employee by adding a row to the Employee table without having to change either of the other two tables. After the new employee has been assigned to a project and has logged some time on that project, we can add a row to the Hours table to describe the project assignment and the number of hours worked. In a similar manner, we can add a row to the Project table to describe a new project without changing either the Employee or Hours tables. Both of these functions would be impossible if our tables were not in second normal form.

THIRD NORMAL FORM

The third step in the normalization process involves the idea of *transitive dependence*.

Transitive Dependencies

Suppose we have a table with columns A, B, and C:

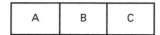

If column C is functionally dependent on column B, and column B is functionally dependent on column A, then column C is functionally dependent on column A. We can show this by drawing links between columns:

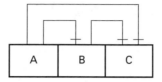

In the above diagram, we are using crow's-foot notation in which the bar at the end of each link indicates a *one cardinality*. In other words, for each value of A there is one and only one value of B, for each value of A there is one and only one value of C, and for each value of B there is one and only one value of C.

In most cases, similar dependencies exist in the opposite direction as well. A is functionally dependent on B, and B is functionally dependent on C:

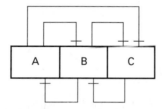

If similar dependencies are *not* true in the opposite direction (i.e., column A is *not* functionally dependent on column B or column B is *not* functionally dependent on column C), then column C is said to be transitively dependent on column A, as in this example:

Transitive Dependency

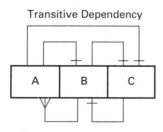

In the above diagram, the link with the *crow's-foot* symbol from B to A indicates that for each value of B there can be many values of A associated with it.

We said earlier that Job_# and JobTitle were functionally dependent on Emp_# (we are omitting the EmpName data element for clarity):

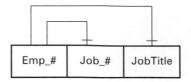

Assuming there is only one job title associated with a given job code, JobTitle is functionally dependent on Job_#:

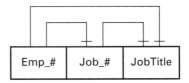

In the reverse direction Job_# is functionally dependent on JobTitle as long as a given job title is associated with only one job code. However, many employees may have the same job code. So Emp_# is not functionally dependent on Job_#. This means that JobTitle is transitively dependent on Emp_#:

Transitive Dependency

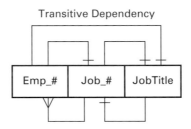

Removing Transitive Dependencies

In order to place our employee data into third normal form, we must remove transitive dependencies. This is done by placing the JobTitle column in a separate table called Jobs with Job_# as the primary key. The third normal form of the employee data is shown in Fig. 13.9.

A table is said to be in third normal form if it is in second normal form *and* every non-key column is nontransitively dependent on its primary key.

We can give a simpler definition of third normal form by saying that in a table that is in third normal form, all the columns of a table are functionally dependent on the key, the whole key, and nothing but the key.

Third Normal Form Advantages

Placing data into third normal form eliminates more potentially undesirable characteristics of data that is in only first or second normal form. The above set of tables shows that a job title associated with a given job code now appears in only one place rather than appearing for each employee that has that job code. This makes it easier to change a job title, since the change has to be made in only one place. Also, we can now add a new job code with its

Employee Table

Emp_#	EmpName	Job_#
120	Jones	1
121	Harpo	1
270	Garfunkel	2
273	Selsi	3
274	Abrahms	2
279	Higgins	1
301	Flannel	1
306	McGraw	3

Hours Table

Emp_#	Project_#	Hours
120	01	37
120	08	12
121	01	45
121	08	21
121	12	107
270	08	10
270	12	78
273	01	22
274	12	41
279	01	27
279	08	20
279	12	51
301	01	16
301	12	85
306	12	67

Project Table

Project_#	Completion
01	7/17
08	1/12
12	3/21

Jobs Table

Job_#	JobTitle
1	Programmer
2	Designer
3	Analyst

Figure 13.9 Employee data in third normal form.

associated job title even though no employee has yet been assigned that job code. And we will not lose the job title if we temporarily have no employees assigned a given job code.

SUMMARY

Placing data into first normal form involves the removal of repeating groups so that each data element can be represented by a single row/column entry in a relational database table. One or more columns of the resulting table are designated the primary key so that each primary key value uniquely identifies one of the table's rows.

Placing data into second normal form involves the idea of full functional dependence. Data that is already in first normal form can be placed into second normal form by ensuring that all the data elements in each table are completely identified by the primary key of that table. Placing data into second normal form often reduces data redundancy that exists in tables that are in first normal form only.

Placing data into third normal form involves the removal of transitive dependencies, in which dependencies are not true in both directions. All the columns in a table that is in third normal form are dependent on the key, the whole key, and nothing but the key. Data that is in third normal form is more stable than data that is in second normal form only and has better update behavior.

In most cases, ensuring that a relational data structure is in third normal form is enough. However, there are some logical data structures that can benefit from further normalization. Fourth normal form and fifth normal form are discussed in Chapter 14.

Higher Levels of Normalization

In the great majority of cases, placing data into third normal form provides a sufficient level of normalization. Higher levels of normalization are possible, however, and it is occasionally beneficial to place data into *fourth normal form* and even sometimes into *fifth normal form*. This chapter introduces these two higher levels of normalization.

FOURTH NORMAL FORM

Suppose that an employee can be assigned to several projects concurrently. Also suppose that an employee can possess multiple skills. If we record this information in a single table, we need to use all three columns as the key, since no other column grouping produces unique row identification. This is shown in Fig. 14.1.

Using a single table like this is not desirable because values have to be repeated, which could cause consistency problems when updating. However, since there are no columns in this table that are not part of the key, the table is in third normal form.

We can represent the relationships in this table in a simpler manner if we place them into fourth normal form. To do that, we split the table into the two separate all-key tables shown in Fig. 14.2.

Employee_Project_Skill Table

Emp_#	Project_#	Skill
120	01	Design
120	01	Program
120	01	Document
120	08	Design
120	08	Program
120	08	Document

Figure 14.1 Emp_#, Project_#, and Skill data in third normal form.

Employee_Project Table

Emp_#	Project_#
120	01
120	08

Employee_Skill Table

Emp_#	Skill
120	Design
120	Program
120	Document

Figure 14.2   Emp_#, Project_#, and Skill data in fourth normal form.

Multivalued Dependencies

Fourth normal form involves the idea of *multivalued dependencies*, in which a given value for a single column identifies multiple values of another column. A multivalued dependency is defined in terms of the set of values from one column that is associated with a given pair of values from two other columns. Figure 14.3 shows the original three-column table.

Employee_Project_Skill Table

Emp_#	Project_#	Skill
120	01	Design
120	01	Program
120	01	Document
120	08	Design
120	08	Program
120	08	Document

Figure 14.3   Emp_#, Project_#, and Skill data in third normal form.

The relationship between Emp_# and Project_# is a multivalued dependency because for each pair of Emp_#/Skill values in the table, the associated set of Project_# values is determined only by Emp_# and is independent of Skill. Similarly, the relationship between Emp_# and Skill is a multivalued dependency, since the set of Skill values for an Emp_#/Project_# pair is independent of Project_#.

It can be shown that multivalued dependencies in all-key tables always occur in pairs, as in this example. Conversion to fourth normal form involves decomposing the original table into multiple tables so that the multivalued dependencies are eliminated.

Fourth Normal Form Advantages

The two tables in fourth normal form better represent the true relationships between the columns because there is no real relationship between projects and skills. Also, there is less redundant data in the two separate tables, and the update behavior of the two separate tables is better as well. For example, if an employee acquires a new skill, we simply add a new row to the Employee_Skill table. With the single table, we would have to add multiple rows, one for each project the employee is assigned to.

Repeating Groups

Another way of looking at data that is in third normal form but not in fourth normal form is that the data contains multiple repeating groups. We could view the original set of data in the following manner, where Project_# and Skill each takes the form of a repeating group, as shown in Fig. 14.4.

Figure 14.4 Repeating group made up of Project_# and Skill_#.

Placing the data into fourth normal form simply eliminates the repeating groups by placing each of them into a separate table. In actual practice, the earlier steps of normalization often identify such repeating groups and removes them, thus producing third-normal-form tables that are already also in fourth normal form.

FIFTH NORMAL FORM

After all of the normalization steps we have discussed thus far, we would be able to use the relational Project operation to split a table into two of its projections and still retain all the data contained in the original table. In other words, we can perform a Join operation on the two constituent tables to re-create the original table. There exist, however, some tables, in fourth normal form, that cannot be split into two projections without changing the original data in some way.

Consider the table shown in Fig. 14.5. In this table, an employee is assigned to one or more projects and uses one or more skills on each project. In this case, though, the particular combination of data element values that occur in the table imply that there is a relationship not only between employees and skills (an employee *has* a particular skill) but also between projects and skills (certain skills are *used* on each project). We can interpret these relationships to mean that an employee uses a skill that he or she possesses on a project only if the skill is used by that project. This means that employees may *have* skills that are not *used* on projects to which they are assigned.

Employee_Project_Skill Table

Emp_#	Project_#	Skill
120	01	Design
120	08	Program
120	01	Program
205	01	Program

Figure 14.5 Emp_#, Project_#, and Skill information in fourth normal form.

At first glance, Fig. 14.5 seems to have the same characteristics as the table in the previous example. Suppose we decompose the table in Fig. 14.5 into two of its projections as we did earlier. This is shown in Fig. 14.6.

If we now perform a Join operation on these two tables, we get the result shown in Fig. 14.7. Notice that the result table has an extra row that the original table did not have (the second row). Project 08 now appears to use design skills when the original data shows no employee using the design skill for that project. The reason that this occurs is that the two projections we created from the original table do not accurately represent the associations inherent in the original table. In this case, there *does* exist a relationship

Employee_Project Table

Emp_#	Project_#
120	01
120	08
205	01

Employee_Skill Table

Emp_#	Skill
120	Design
120	Program
205	Program

Figure 14.6   Decomposing the information into two projections.

Employee_Project_Skill Table

Emp_#	Project_#	Skill
120	01	Design
120	08	Design
120	01	Program
120	08	Program
205	01	Program

Figure 14.7   Rejoining the two projections.

between projects and skills; each project only uses certain types of skills. This relationship is lost when we decompose the table into the two projections shown in Fig. 14.6.

Note that the original table does not contain multivalued dependencies, and thus is already in fourth normal form. The set of Project_# values associated with each Emp_#/Skill pair is dependent on both Emp_# and Skill and not just on Emp_#. Similarly, Skill value sets are dependent on both Emp_# and Project_#. Thus we cannot separate the table into two projections as we did before. The table can, however, be further normalized by placing it into *fifth normal form*. This involves decomposing the table into *three* of its projections, thus retaining the true relationships between the various columns, as shown in Fig. 14.8.

Employee_Project Table

Emp_#	Project_#
120	01
120	08
205	01

Employee_Skill Table

Emp_#	Skill
120	Design
120	Program
205	Program

Project_Skill Table

Project_#	Skill
01	Design
08	Program
01	Program

Figure 14.8   Decomposing the data into three projections.

We can now join the first two tables to form the combined table having the spurious row as we did previously. This intermediate table corresponds to all the skills that *might* be used on projects. The third table specifies that skills that each project *actually* uses. When we then join the intermediate table with the third table above, using both the Project_# and Skill columns for the Join operation, we eliminate the spurious row and get a result that is identical to the original table (see Fig. 14.9).

Join Dependencies

The three tables shown in Fig. 14.8, which *can* be rejoined to produce the original relation, are in fifth normal form. A constraint on which projections can be validly rejoined is called a *Join dependency*.

Employee_Project_Skill Table

Emp_#	Project_#	Skill
120	01	Design
120	08	Program
120	01	Program
205	01	Program

Figure 14.9   Rejoining the three projections.

The Join dependency in the original table causes the table to have a somewhat bizarre update behavior. Consider the table shown in Fig. 14.10, in which an employee uses Design skills on one project and Programming skills on a different project.

Employee_Project_Skill Table

Emp_#	Project_#	Skill
247	11	Design
247	28	Program

Figure 14.10   Employee_Project_Skill table.

Suppose we added a new employee to the table, who uses Programming skills on project 11 (see Fig. 14.11). The addition of that one row to the table on first glance seems to be valid. But let us now again use a relational Project operation to decompose the above table into three of its projections, as shown in Fig. 14.12.

Employee_Project_Skill Table

Emp_#	Project_#	Skill
247	11	Design
247	28	Program
308	11	Program

Figure 14.11   Adding a new employee to the Employee_Project_Skill table.

Employee_Project Table

Emp_#	Project_#
247	11
247	28
308	11

Employee_Skill Table

Emp_#	Skill
247	Design
247	Program
308	Program

Project_Skill Table

Project_#	Skill
11	Design
28	Program
11	Program

Figure 14.12   Decomposing the table into three projections.

We now rejoin the three above tables, producing the result shown in Fig. 14.13. Notice that this table has one extra row that the table we began with did not have. This result at first seems intuitively wrong. Does this mean that the three projections are not in fifth normal form? No, it means that it is not valid to add only that one row to the non-

Employee_Project_Skill Table

Emp_#	Project_#	Skill
247	11	Design
247	28	Program
247	11	Program
308	11	Program

Figure 14.13   Rejoining the three projections.

fifth-normal-form table. By adding the one new row to the non-fifth-normal-form table, we are actually stating three facts:

1. Employee 308 has been assigned to project 11

2. Employee 308 has Programming skills

3. Project 11 now uses Programming skills

By analyzing the contents of the original table together with the above facts, we can see that when we add the new row for employee 308, project 11, and the Programming skill, then we must also add a new row for employee 247, project 11, and the Programming skill. This is because employee 247 already had the Programming skill and was already assigned to project 11; thus, employee 247's Programming skill is now available to project 11.

By using the three projections rather than the composite table, we can be sure that all three facts are reflected properly and completely in the table data.

Update Anomalies

The Join dependencies that exist in the single table that is not in fifth normal form create constraints on the updating of the table. If the table is left in fourth normal form, then we must sometimes add two rows to the table at a time instead of only one. There can be similar problems with deletions. It is often quite difficult to determine when these updating anomalies occur. By placing the data into fifth normal form, we can add the employee 247 data in a straightforward manner by simply adding a new row to each of the three individual tables. The two new rows will then automatically appear in the result if we rejoin the three fifth-normal-form individual tables.

Placing the data into fifth normal form also allows us to add data that couldn't be added to the composite table. For example, we can show an employee with a particular skill, even though no project currently uses that skill, by adding a row only to the Employee_Skill table. This information cannot be added to the composite table, since it would require a null Project_# value. Null values are not allowed in columns that make up the key of a table.

HIGHER LEVELS OF NORMALIZATION

Research is continuing on normalization, and even higher forms of normalization have been identified. However, it can be shown that fifth normal form is the highest form of normalization possible with respect to the relational operations of Project and Join. Thus, fifth normal form is the highest form of normalization that is generally required in practice.

SUMMARY

Fourth normal form involves the idea of multivalued dependencies in which a given value of a single column identifies multiple values of another column. Multivalued dependencies sometimes occur in all-key tables. Placing data into fourth normal form involves identifying and removing multivalued dependencies by splitting an all-key table into multiple tables in which no multivalued dependencies exist. Placing tables into fourth normal form often reduces data redundancy and improves update behavior.

Fifth normal form involves the idea of Join dependencies in which the semantics of the data prevent a table's projections from being rejoined to recreate the original table. Placing data into fifth normal form involves splitting a table into a set of projections that better represent the true relationships among the columns.

Any number of possible languages can be devised for working with data stored in databases, and, in the early years of database, most software vendors developed their own unique database languages. Today, most database software supports the *Structured Query Language* (SQL) that application programs use to manipulate the data in relational databases. Part V of this book concentrates on SQL.

PART **V**

STRUCTURED QUERY LANGUAGE

Chapter **15**

SQL Language Characteristics

The main language used by most client/server database software products is *Structured Query Language* (SQL). The chapters in the final part of this book examine the SQL language in detail and show examples of its use.

This chapter examines the characteristics of the SQL language, describes the environment in which SQL implementations are intended to operate, and introduces the types of database queries we will be looking at in the remaining chapters of this book.

SQL DIALECTS

The Structured Query Language has been standardized, and its structure is documented in an accepted international standard. The standards document that is most current at the time of writing is published by the American National Standards Institute, 11 West 42nd Street, New York, NY 10036 as ANSI X3.135-1992. Previous versions of the SQL standard that did not define all the facilities in the 1992 version of the standard were also published in 1986 and in 1989.

Many features were added to the language during the years that standardization was underway, and a wide variety of vendors have implemented different variations of the language. Because the development of SQL implementations proceeded in parallel with the development of the standard itself, each vendor's implementation of an SQL product is slightly different from those of other vendors. This situation is likely to improve over time as more vendors bring their SQL implementations into conformance with the SQL standard.

In showing examples of SQL language statements, we will attempt to remain faithful to the ANSI X3.135-1992 standard. Where it is necessary to depart from the standard, we will use examples of SQL as it is implemented by the following database software products:

- **Oracle.** Oracle Corporation's Oracle family of relational database software products.
- **Access.** Microsoft's Access database system for personal computers.
- **DB2.** IBM's DB2 and DB2/2 relational database software products for mainframes and personal computers.

It is not the intention of this book to provide a complete description of the 1992 version of the SQL standard.

THE SQL ENVIRONMENT

As we introduced in Chapter 5, the SQL standard defines a number of different types of objects that make up the total *SQL environment*. As shown in Fig. 15.1, the SQL environment can be viewed as being made up of two broad classes of objects: *data-related objects* that are associated with the data stored in relational databases and *program-related objects* that are associated with entities that operate on the data stored in those databases. We will examine each of these classes of objects and then discuss the client/server orientation of the current SQL standard.

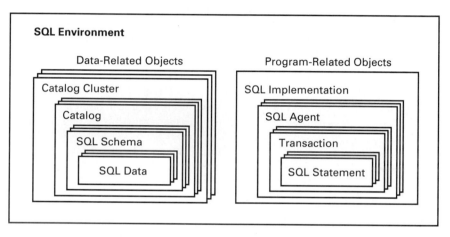

Figure 15.1   The SQL environment.

DATA-RELATED OBJECTS

The data making up relational databases in the SQL environment consists of *SQL data* that is defined by an *SQL schema*. SQL schemas are defined in *catalogs* that may be grouped in *catalog clusters*. The following sections describe each of these categories of objects.

SQL Data

SQL data consists primarily of *tables* that are made up of rows and columns. SQL tables are similar to the relational tables we discussed in Part III. The SQL standard also defines additional objects that fall under the SQL data classification, such as *views*, *domains*, and *cursors*. Many relational database systems also define objects that are not specifically referenced in the SQL standard, such as *indices*.

Box 15.1 summarizes the various types of SQL data objects that most client/server database packages implement.

BOX 15.1   SQL data objects.

- **Table.** A *table* is a set of data elements arranged in a two-dimensional array of columns and rows. A table is often called a *base table* to distinguish a table from a view.

- **View.** A *view* is an alternative arrangement of the rows or columns from one more base tables that may define a subset of the data contained in the base tables.

- **Domain.** A *domain* is a set of permissible values from which the values in one or more columns can be taken.

- **Cursor.** A *cursor* is an object that refers to a particular row in a table or view. A cursor is useful in application programs for processing the results of a relational operation one row at a time.

- **Index.** An *index* typically consists of a set of pointers to the rows in a table. An index that is defined for a table can be used for a variety of purposes, including placing the rows of a table into a particular sequence to provide more efficient access to data and to enforce integrity constraints. Although the SQL standard does not reference indices, indices are implemented by most relational database software. A *unique index* is a particular type of index that can be used to ensure that no two rows in a table have the same key values. The primary key of a table is typically implemented in the form of a unique index.

SQL Schemas

The data making up a particular collection of objects that defines one or more relational databases is defined by an object called an *SQL schema*. An SQL schema has a name that is unique within a particular catalog, defines the owner of the SQL schema, and contains descriptions of all the SQL data defined by the SQL schema. An SQL schema is essentially the definition of a relational database.

Catalogs and Catalog Clusters

One or more SQL schema definitions can be defined by an optional object called a *catalog*. When it is used, a catalog contains information about one or more SQL schemas. A catalog always contains a schema named INFORMATION-SCHEMA that contains information about the other SQL schemas in that catalog. A catalog is effectively a system database that contains information about other databases.

Catalogs can be grouped into implementation-defined collections of catalogs called *catalog clusters*. Catalog clusters are used to group schemas that are associated in some way. SQL data objects—such as tables and views—that are referenced in the same relational operation, must be defined in catalogs that are part of the same catalog cluster. For example, when an SQL statement specifies that two tables be joined using a Join relational operation, the two tables must be part of the same catalog cluster. The way in which catalogs are grouped into catalog clusters is strictly an implementation issue, and the SQL standard does not preclude the possibility of a particular catalog being a member of more than one catalog cluster.

PROGRAM-RELATED OBJECTS

Program-related objects are objects in the SQL environment that operate on the data-related objects that make up the organization's relational databases. The major program-related objects shown in Fig. 15.1 are *SQL statements* that are grouped to make up *SQL transactions*. The sequences of SQL statements making up SQL transactions are executed by entities called *SQL agents*. These program-related objects in the SQL environment are described next.

SQL Statements

SQL statements are statements that conform to the rules of the SQL language. SQL statements operate directly on the data-related objects. The functions of commonly used SQL statements that make up the SQL language are introduced later in this chapter, and examples of many of them are shown in the remaining chapters in this book.

SQL Transactions

An SQL transaction is a sequence of SQL statements that are atomic with respect to recovery. The SQL statements making up a transaction must all be executed completely or they must not be executed at all. If the execution of any SQL statement making up a transaction fails, then the results of all the SQL statements that have already been executed as part of that transaction must be rolled back. If any part of a transaction fails, any SQL data objects must be reset to the condition in which they existed before the transaction began its execution.

SQL Agents

An SQL agent is defined by the SQL standard as an implementation-defined entity that causes the execution of the SQL statements in one or more transactions. In effect, SQL agents are the application programs that execute SQL statements.

CLIENT/SERVER ORIENTATION

The SQL standard makes the assumption that an SQL implementation may contain separate components that play the roles of clients and servers. The client/server orientation of the SQL standard simplifies the implementation of the database distribution configurations and architectures described in Chapters 8 and 9. Figure 15.2 illustrates the client/server environment that the SQL environment describes.

SQL Clients and Servers

A particular SQL agent that executes a set of SQL statements making up one or more transactions is bound to an entity called an *SQL client*. The SQL agent and the SQL client typically execute in the same computing system and may share the same address space.

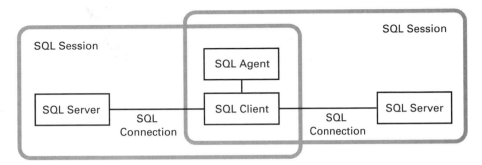

Figure 15.2　SQL client/server environment.

SQL Connections

An SQL client component establishes *SQL connections* with one or more *SQL server* components. An SQL connection is an abstract entity, and the SQL standard does not specify how SQL connections are implemented.

In practice, SQL connections are typically implemented by networking software that provides the services required to allow the SQL client to communicate with the SQL server over a communication network. The networking software typically handles the task of locating a particular server and establishing a communication channel between the client and the server. The details concerning network communication are generally hidden from the database software implementing the SQL agent, SQL client, and SQL server components.

SQL Sessions

Each combination of an SQL agent, an SQL connection, and an SQL server is called an *SQL session*. The SQL client component and the SQL server component in a session may execute in the same or in different computing systems.

During the operation of an SQL session, the contents of SQL statements, the results of the execution of SQL statements, and diagnostic information may flow over the SQL connection between the SQL client component and the SQL server component.

A user or an application programmer typically interacts only with an SQL agent. Therefore, the details concerning the client/server distribution of database operations can easily be hidden from the user or the application program. A user can perceive a database as residing on the user's local computing system even though it may actually be stored in a networked computer system located some distance away.

SQL LANGUAGE FACILITIES

Although SQL has the term *query* in its name, SQL is more than simply a query language. As we introduced in Chapter 5, different subsets of the statements making up the SQL language allow SQL to be used in three different ways:

- **Data Manipulation Language.** The statements making up a *data manipulation language (DML)* allow SQL to be used to retrieve data from a relational database, to update and delete existing data, to insert new data.
- **Data Description Language.** The statements making up a *data description language (DDL)* allow SQL to be used to create, alter, and delete the various objects—including tables, views, domains, and indices—that are used to implement a relational database.
- **Data Control Language.** The statements making up a *data control language (DCL)* allow SQL to be used to perform administrative procedures relating to SQL objects, such as granting authorization to users for their access and establishing synchronization points to control database recovery processing.

It is important to note that not all implementations of SQL provide the same level of support in all three of the areas that the full SQL defines. For example, the Microsoft Access implementation of SQL for the personal computer environment concentrates on the use of SQL as a data manipulation language. Data description language and data control language functions are provided in Access through graphical user interface functions rather than through SQL. Other database products, such as IBM's DB2 and DB2/2 products make explicit use of the DML, DDL, and DCL features of SQL.

Box 15.2 lists the most commonly used SQL statements that make up the SQL data manipulation language, data description language, and data control language. Although

---

BOX 15.2   SQL statement summary.

SQL Data Manipulation Language Statements

- SELECT. Used to specify database retrievals and to create alternative views of the data contained in one or more base tables.
- UPDATE. Used to change the values in existing rows in base tables or views.
- INSERT. Used to add new rows to tables or views.
- DELETE. Used to delete rows from tables or views.

SQL Data Description Language Statements

- CREATE. Used to define a new SQL object, such as a table, view, or domain.
- ALTER. Used to modify the characteristics of an existing SQL object.
- DROP. Used to delete an existing SQL object from the SQL environment.

SQL Data Control Language Statements

- GRANT. Used to give users authorization to access an SQL object.
- REVOKE. Used to remove a user's authorization to access an SQL object.
- COMMIT. Used to establish a synchronization point to indicate that all changes that have been made to SQL objects up to that point are to be made permanent.
- ROLLBACK. Used to indicate that changes that have been made to SQL objects up to the most recent synchronization point are to be reversed, thus restoring those objects to the condition in which they existed prior to the establishment of that synchronization point.

various implementations of SQL have different rules regarding the use of capital and lower case letters in SQL statements, we will use all upper case in referring to the names of the statements making up the SQL language.

AN SQL IMPLEMENTATION

The following sections describe the statements that make up a particular implementation of SQL. The example we use is IBM's DB2 database software product. The DB2 SQL implementation supports DDL statements for describing tables and other DB2 objects and DML statements for retrieving and manipulating the data stored in tables. DB2's SQL includes statements that can be used to define user views, logical data models, and physical storage structures. It also includes statements that can be used to retrieve and manipulate data and to handle the special processing requirements associated with DB2 applications, including security, integrity, recovery, and dynamic SQL execution.

In this chapter, we also use the Microsoft Access database software for personal computers to present query examples and to display examples of SQL statements that database software generates to support query processing.

Data Description

SQL DDL statements associated with logical data description are used to define and describe tables and views. These statements are concerned with the way data is logically represented to and accessed by end users and application programs. SQL DDL statements associated with physical data description are used to create and drop databases, indices, storage groups, and table spaces, and to alter these objects. Box 15.3 lists the SQL statements used for data description.

Data Retrieval and Manipulation

SQL DML statements associated with retrieving and manipulating data are used to perform relational operations on tables, to delete rows, to insert rows, and to modify existing

---

BOX 15.3　SQL data description language statements.

Logical Data Description

These statements are used to define and describe tables and views:

- ALTER TABLE
- COMMENT ON
- CREATE TABLE
- CREATE SYNONYM
- CREATE VIEW
- DECLARE TABLE

- DESCRIBE
- DROP TABLE
- DROP SYNONYM
- DROP VIEW
- INCLUDE
- LABEL ON

(Continued)

BOX 15.3   *(Continued)*

Physical Data Description

The following statements are used to define and describe databases, indices, storage groups and table spaces:

- ALTER INDEX
- ALTER STOGROUP
- ALTER TABLESPACE
- CREATE DATABASE
- CREATE INDEX
- CREATE STOGROUP

- CREATE TABLESPACE
- DROP DATABASE
- DROP INDEX
- DROP STOGROUP
- DROP TABLESPACE

---

rows. The statement used to retrieve data and to perform many types of relational operations on tables is the SELECT statement. The result of a SELECT statement is another table that often contains multiple rows.

The conventional programming languages used to develop SQL applications are typically not designed to operate on entire tables. To accommodate these languages, SQL uses an object called a *cursor* to process rows one at a time. Box 15.4 lists the SQL statements used for data retrieval, data manipulation, and cursor processing.

PROCESSING SUPPORT

SQL includes statements that can be used to control authorization to access various SQL objects and to perform certain types of operations on them, to control data integrity by

---

BOX 15.4   SQL data manipulation statements.

Data Retrieval and Manipulation

The following statements are used for basic data manipulation:

- SELECT
- DELETE

- INSERT
- UPDATE

Cursor Manipulation

The following statements are used to define and manipulate cursors to do row-at-a-time processing:

- DECLARE
- OPEN

- FETCH
- CLOSE

placing locks on table data, and to control whether and when changes are committed, or made permanent. There are also statements that allow SQL statements to be dynamically constructed and executed during program execution, rather than requiring the SQL statements to be compiled into the program. Box 15.5 lists the SQL statements used to provide processing support.

BOX 15.5 SQL processing support statements.

Security, Integrity and Recovery

The following statements are used to provide for security, data integrity, and recovery:

- GRANT
- REVOKE
- LOCK TABLE
- COMMIT
- ROLLBACK

Dynamic Processing

The following statements are used to dynamically construct and execute SQL statements:

- DECLARE STATEMENT
- EXECUTE
- EXECUTE IMMEDIATE
- PREPARE

ORDER ENTRY DATABASE

The database access examples in this chapter and in the remaining chapters in this part of the book are based on an Order Entry database consisting of the tables shown in Fig. 15.3. We will assume that the tables have already been created and loaded and that they are available for our use.

In the Order Entry database, the primary key of the Inventory table is Inv_Part_#, the primary key of the Quotations table is a concatenated key made up of a combination of the Quo_Supp_# and Quo_Part_# columns, and the primary key of the Suppliers table is Sup_Supp_#. The Inventory table and the Quotations table are related based on Inv_Part_# and Quo_Part_# column values, and the Quotations table and the Suppliers table are related based on Quo_Supp_# and Sup_Supp_# column values.

DATABASE QUERIES

Many client/server database software products allow SQL statements to be entered interactively through a user-interface device to specify database accesses. Others provide alternative methods for allowing users to formulate requests for access to relational databases. Some database products also provide facilities that allow SQL statements to be executed as part of a stored procedure or to be embedded in an application program written in a conventional programming language.

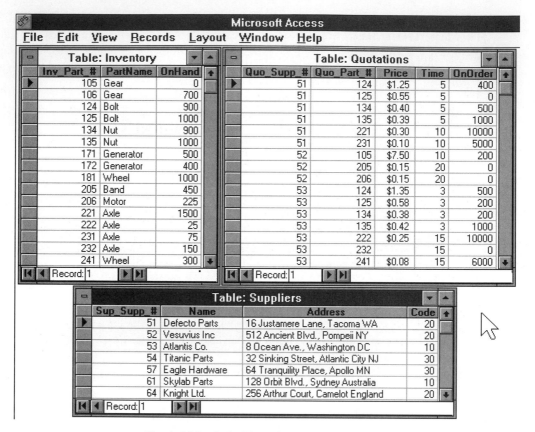

Figure 15.3 Order Entry database table contents.

Graphical Query Facility

Fig. 15.4 shows how we might request a list of all the rows in the Quotations table using the graphical query facility supported by Microsoft Access. Microsoft Access implements a form of the Query by Example (QBE) language. QBE is described further in Appendix C.

The upper part of the display shows the column structure of the Quotations table from the Order Entry database. The column name in bold indicates the primary key of the table.

The lower part of the display describes our query. In this example, the * character following the table name Quotations indicates that we want a list of the data in all the columns in the Quotations table.

Generated SQL Statements

Many relational database software products that support an easy-to-use query facility for formulating access requests convert those queries to SQL in order to actually process the query against the database and to support client/server database distribution. Some data-

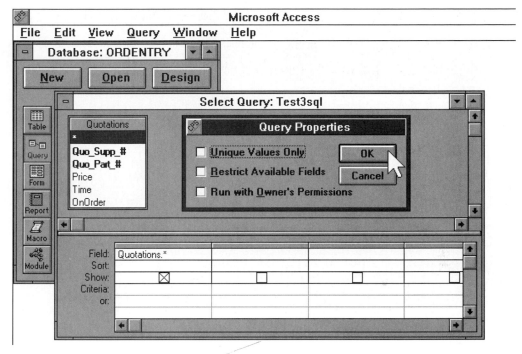

Figure 15.4   Database query using Microsoft Access.

base software allows the user to request a display of the SQL statements that are generated as a result of a query request. Figure 15.5 shows an example of the SQL display that Microsoft Access presents when requested.

Query Results

Figure 15.6 shows the results of the previous query as it might be displayed by Microsoft Access.

SQL QUERY FORMAT

In this part of the book we examine SQL as a language. The chapters in this part are intended to be independent of any particular implementation of the SQL language. For clarity, we will show the results of SQL statements as if they had been entered using a database package that allows SQL statements to be entered interactively at a character-oriented user interface device.

A slightly simpler form of the previous query can be formulated directly in SQL as follows:

```
SELECT    *
FROM      Quotations
```

202Structured Query LanguagePart V

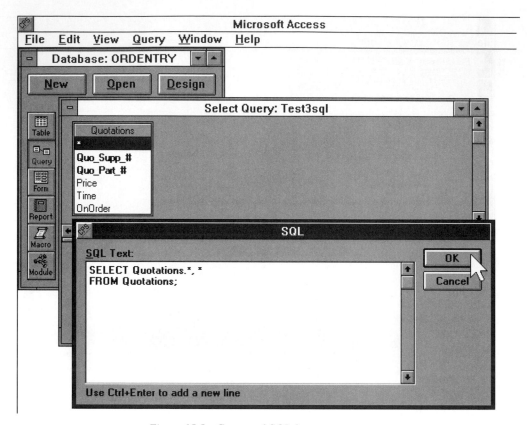

Figure 15.5   Generated SQL language statement.

The following shows the above query and its results in the style we will use for the sample queries in the remaining chapters in this part:

```
SELECT     *
FROM       Quotations
```

Quo_Supp_#	Quo_Part_#	Price	Time	OnOrder
51	124	1.25	5	400
51	125	0.55	5	0
51	134	0.40	5	500
51	135	0.39	5	1000
51	221	0.30	10	10000
51	231	0.10	10	5000
52	105	7.50	10	200
52	205	0.15	20	0
52	206	0.15	20	0
53	124	1.35	3	500
53	125	0.58	3	200
53	134	0.38	3	200

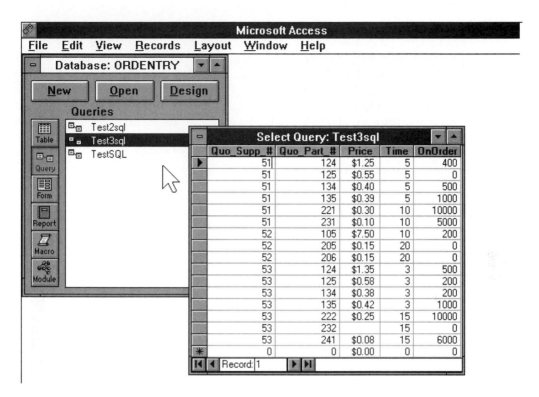

Figure 15.6   Microsoft Access query results display.

53	135	0.42	3	1000
53	222	0.25	15	10000
53	232	–	15	0
53	241	0.08	15	6000

SUMMARY

The Structured Query Language is defined by the ANSI X3.135-1992 standard. However, a number of dialects of the language are in common use. The SQL examples in this book are based on the ANSI standard.

The SQL environment described in the ANSI SQL standard defines data-related objects and program-related objects. The data-related objects consist of catalog clusters, catalogs, SQL schemas, and SQL data objects. The program-related objects consist of SQL implementations, SQL agents, transactions, and SQL statements.

The SQL language has a client/server orientation, in which an SQL agent that executes SQL statements is bound to an SQL client. SQL clients exchange information with SQL servers via SQL connections. Each combination of an SQL agent, an SQL client, and an SQL server constitutes an SQL session.

The SQL language defines facilities that allow SQL to be used as a data manipulation language (DML), a data description language (DDL), and a data control language (DCL). SQL DML statements include SELECT, UPDATE, INSERT, and DELETE. SQL DDL statements include CREATE, ALTER, and DROP. SQL DCL statements include GRANT, REVOKE, COMMIT, and ROLL-BACK.

Although most client/server database systems support the use of SQL for making database queries, many database products also provide easier to use methods for accessing relational databases, such as variations of the Query by Example query language.

Chapter 16 continues the discussion of SQL by examining the functions that can be performed with different variations of the SQL SELECT statement.

The SELECT Statement

This chapter begins our investigation of SQL facilities by discussing the many uses to which the SELECT statement can be put in formulating queries against a relational database. We start this chapter by showing simple examples of the SQL SELECT statement followed by the results they produce. We then show examples of somewhat more complex queries.

Please note that the SQL SELECT statement should not be confused with the Select operator that is sometimes used as an alternative name for the Restrict operator introduced in Chapter 11. The SQL SELECT statement can be used to perform all the various relational operations on tables and is not limited to Restrict relational operations.

SQL STATEMENT FORMAT

All SQL statements consist of a verb followed by one or more optional clauses. The basic form of the SELECT statement is as follows:

SELECT	some data (the names of one or more columns)
FROM	some place (the name of a table or view)
WHERE	conditions (comparisons based on data element values)
ORDER BY	desired sequence (the names of one or more columns)

All SELECT statements must include a FROM clause, but the WHERE and ORDER BY clauses are optional.

SELECTING ALL COLUMNS, ALL ROWS

The simplest form of SQL query is to request a list of all the data contained in a table. This can be done by using the * option of the SELECT statement. For example, the following SELECT statement displays all the rows from all the columns in the Quotations table, shown in Fig. 11.3:

```
SELECT    *
FROM      Quotations
```

Quo_Supp_#	Quo_Part_#	Price	Time	OnOrder
51	124	1.25	5	400
51	125	0.55	5	0
51	134	0.40	5	500
51	135	0.39	5	1000
51	221	0.30	10	10000
51	231	0.10	10	5000
52	105	7.50	10	200
52	205	0.15	20	0
52	206	0.15	20	0
53	124	1.35	3	500
53	125	0.58	3	200
53	134	0.38	3	200
53	135	0.42	3	1000
53	222	0.25	15	10000
53	232	–	15	0
53	241	0.08	15	6000

The asterisk following the key word SELECT indicates that we would like all columns listed. The columns are typically displayed in the order in which they were defined when the table was created.

CODING CONVENTIONS

In practice, each SQL statement must often end with an implementation-defined terminator character, which is a semicolon in most cases, as in the following example:

```
SELECT    *
FROM      Quotations;
```

We will not show the terminator character in most of the SQL examples shown in this part of the book. Keep in mind, however, that your database software may require you to include a terminator character at the end of each SQL statement you enter.

We often use multiple lines and indentation in the SQL examples in this book to make our intentions clear. However, SQL statements are completely freeform, and the number of lines that are used and indentations have no significance to the software that processes the SQL statements.

SPECIFYING COLUMN ORDER

The SELECT statement can be used to generate a report that lists columns in a specified order by explicitly listing the column names in the SELECT statement; the database software then displays the columns in the order in which we list them:

```
SELECT    Time, Quo_Part_#, Quo_Supp_#, OnOrder, Price
FROM      Quotations
```

Time	Quo_Part_#	Quo_Supp_#	OnOrder	Price
5	124	51	400	1.25
5	125	51	0	0.55
5	134	51	500	0.40
5	135	51	1000	0.39
10	221	51	10000	0.30
10	231	51	5000	0.10
10	105	52	200	7.50
20	205	52	0	0.15
20	206	52	0	0.15
3	124	53	500	1.35
3	125	53	200	0.58
3	134	53	200	0.38
3	135	53	1000	0.42
15	222	53	10000	0.25
15	232	53	0	—
15	241	53	6000	0.08

DISPLAYING SELECTED COLUMNS

We can limit the number of columns that are displayed simply by omitting from the SELECT statement the names of the columns that we do not want displayed. Providing a list of only selected column names in a SELECT statement is equivalent to performing a Project relational operation on the table.

In the following example, we are displaying data from only three columns:

```
SELECT    Quo_Supp_#, Quo_Part_#, Price
FROM      Quotations
```

Quo_Supp_#	Quo_Part_#	Price
51	124	1.25
51	125	0.55
51	134	0.40
51	135	0.39
51	221	0.30
51	231	0.10
52	105	7.50
52	205	0.15
52	206	0.15
53	124	1.35
53	125	0.58
53	134	0.38
53	135	0.42
53	222	0.25
53	232	—
53	241	0.08

DISPLAYING SELECTED ROWS

We can include a WHERE clause in a SELECT statement to cause the database software to display data from only selected rows in the table. This use of a WHERE clause in a SELECT statement is equivalent to performing a Restrict relational operation on the table. We use the WHERE clause to specify one or more conditions that certain data element values in a row must meet in order for data from that row to be displayed.

For example, the following SELECT statement asks the database software to display only the rows in the Quotations table for which the Quo_Part_# data element value is 124:

```
SELECT    *
FROM      Quotations
WHERE     Quo_Part_# = 124
```

Quo_Supp_#	Quo_Part_#	Price	Time	OnOrder
51	124	1.25	5	400
53	124	1.35	3	500

In the above example, we used an equal comparison (Quo_Part_# = 124) as the selection condition. Other types of comparisons can also be specified, including:

>   greater than

>=   greater than or equal to

<   less than

<=   less than or equal to

¬=   not equal to

¬>   not greater than

¬<   not less than

For example, the following statement asks for a list of all supplier, part, and price values for those parts whose price is greater than $1.00:

```
SELECT    Quo_Supp_#, Quo_Part_#, Price
FROM      Quotations
WHERE     Price > 1.00
```

Quo_Supp_#	Quo_Part_#	Price
51	124	1.25
52	105	7.50
53	124	1.35

We can also specify a WHERE condition that performs a comparison on data element values from a column that contains character data. To do this, we must enclose the comparison value in single quotation marks:

```
SELECT     *
FROM       Inventory
WHERE      PartName = 'Bolt'
```

Inv_Part_#	PartName	OnHand
124	Bolt	900
125	Bolt	1000

SELECTION USING ARITHMETIC EXPRESSIONS

We can include arithmetic expressions in WHERE selection conditions to perform calculations in condition clauses. Arithmetic operators that we can use in SELECT statements are:

+   add
−   subtract
*   multiply
/   divide

The following SELECT statement displays all supplier and part values where the quotation amount (Price + OnOrder) is greater than $500.00:

```
SELECT     Quo_Supp_#, Quo_Part_#
FROM       Quotations
WHERE      Price * OnOrder > 500.00
```

Quo_Supp_#	Quo_Part_#
51	221
52	105
53	124
53	222

SELECTION USING A LIST OR RANGE

We can use the IN and BETWEEN keywords to specify a list of values or a range of values in a WHERE condition. We use the IN keyword to specify a list of values in parentheses. Whenever a row contains a data element value that matches one of the values in parentheses following the IN keyword, the row is selected.

The following SELECT statement displays supplier, part, and price values for part numbers 105, 135, and 205:

```
SELECT     Quo_Supp_#, Quo_Part_#, Price
FROM       Quotations
WHERE      Quo_Part_# IN (105, 135, 205)
```

Quo_Supp_#	Quo_Part_#	Price
51	135	0.39
52	105	7.50

```
52              205   0.15
53              135   0.42
```

We use the BETWEEN keyword to specify a range of values as the selection criterion. The range specified includes the two specified values as well as all values that fall between them. The following statement selects quotations for all parts in the range 105 through 135:

```
SELECT    Quo_Supp_#, Quo_Part_#, Price
FROM      Quotations
WHERE     Quo_Part_# BETWEEN 105 AND 135
```

Quo_Supp_#	Quo_Part_#	Price
51	124	1.25
51	125	0.55
51	134	0.40
51	135	0.39
52	105	7.50
53	124	1.35
53	125	0.58
53	134	0.38
53	135	0.42

The IN and BETWEEN keywords can also be used to specify character values, in which case the values must be enclosed in single quotation marks.

PATTERN MATCHING

We can base a selection on the occurrence of a particular pattern of characters in a data element. This is done by using the LIKE keyword. Selection using LIKE can only be done for columns that contain character data. We can specify that any number of characters may occur either before or after the desired value by using the percent sign (%) as a wild-card character. (Some database packages use the asterisk (*) character instead of the % wild card.) We might use the following SELECT statement to select suppliers located in the state of Minnesota:

```
SELECT    Sup_Supp_#, Name, Address
FROM      Suppliers
WHERE     Address LIKE '% MN%'
```

Sup_Supp_#	Name	Address
57	Eagle Hardware	64 Tranquility Place, Apollo MN

The first "%" character in the quoted string following the LIKE keyword specifies that any number of other characters can precede " MN," and the second "%" character specifies that any number of characters can follow it.

Queries such as the above must be carefully planned. All rows with the three-character string " MN" in the address column will be selected. We included a blank preceding the "MN" in the string to ensure that the "MN" is preceded by at least one blank, thus ensuring that rows will not be selected that have the characters "MN" embedded in a street or city name.

We can also specify the number of characters that should precede or follow the desired value by using an underscore (_) wild-card character in each character position that must precede or follow the pattern character. (Some database software products use the question mark (?) instead of _ wild card.) The following SELECT statement could be used to display all parts for which the second character in the part name is "o":

```
SELECT     *
FROM       Inventory
WHERE      PartName LIKE '_o%'
```

Inv_Part_#	PartName	OnHand
124	Bolt	900
125	Bolt	1000
206	Motor	225

The above query could alternatively be performed using the SUBSTR function:

```
SELECT     *
FROM       Inventory
WHERE      SUBSTR (PartName,2,1) = 'o'
```

Inv_Part_#	PartName	OnHand
124	Bolt	900
125	Bolt	1000
206	Motor	225

The SUBSTR function is used to specify the starting position and length of a substring within a character or graphic data string. The substring can then be compared against the desired value.

ELIMINATING DUPLICATE ROWS

Depending on the selection criteria we specify and the columns that the database software selects for display, it is possible for the result to contain duplicate rows. For example, the following SELECT statement displays suppliers that have quotations with an on-order quantity greater than 200:

```
SELECT     Quo_Supp_#
FROM       Quotations
WHERE      OnOrder > 200
```

Quo_Supp_#
51
51

```
                          51
                          51
                          51
                          53
                          53
                          53
                          53
```

In this example, suppliers 51 and 53 are each listed multiple times in the resulting display, since each has multiple parts for which the OnOrder value is greater than 200. In order to produce a result that is equivalent to the result of a true Restrict relational operation, we must include the DISTINCT keyword before specifying column names. The DISTINCT keyword causes the database software to eliminate duplicate rows from the result:

```
SELECT    DISTINCT Quo_Supp_#
FROM      Quotations
WHERE     OnOrder > 200
```

```
Quo_Supp_#
          51
          53
```

MULTIPLE CONDITIONS

Selection can be based on multiple conditions by using the AND and OR Boolean operators. The following statement selects quotations for part number 124 where the price is also greater than $1.30:

```
SELECT    Quo_Supp_#, Quo_Part_#, Price
FROM      Quotations
WHERE     Quo_Part_# = 124
          AND
            Price > 1.30
```

```
Quo_Supp_#    Quo_Part_#    Price
        53          124      1.35
```

Two conditions connected by AND select a row only if the row satisfies both conditions. Two conditions connected by OR select a row if the row meets either condition. We can specify any number of conditions using combinations of AND and OR, as in the following example:

```
SELECT    *
FROM      Quotations
WHERE     Quo_Part_# < 200
          AND
            (Price > 1.00 OR Time < 10)
```

Quo_Supp_#	Quo_Part_#	Price	Time	OnOrder
51	124	1.25	5	400
51	125	0.55	5	0
51	134	0.40	5	500
51	135	0.39	5	1000
52	105	7.50	10	200
53	124	1.35	3	500
53	125	0.58	3	200
53	134	0.38	3	200
53	135	0.42	3	1000

In a WHERE clause that uses ANDs and ORs, all the ANDs are evaluated first, followed by all the ORs. We can use parentheses to control the order in which the conditions are to be evaluated, as in the previous example. Parentheses can also be used to add clarity:

```
SELECT    *
FROM      Quotations
WHERE     (Quo_Part_# < 200 AND Price > 1.00)
          OR
          Time < 10
```

Quo_Supp_#	Quo_Part_#	Price	Time	OnOrder
51	124	1.25	5	400
51	125	0.55	5	0
51	134	0.40	5	500
51	135	0.39	5	1000
52	105	7.50	10	200
53	124	1.35	3	500
53	125	0.58	3	200
53	134	0.38	3	200
53	135	0.42	3	1000

Multiple levels of parentheses can be used if required.

NULL VALUES

Depending on how a table is defined, a column may be allowed to contain data elements that have a null value. A null value means that no value has been entered for the data element in that row. As we introduced in Chapter 11, a null value is not the same as a value of blanks in a character field or zero in a numeric field. Many database products display a null value as a hyphen (-); others use blanks. We are using hyphens in the examples in this part of the book.

The Quotations table shows an example of a null value. The entry for supplier 53 and part 232 has a null Price value. We can select specifically for null values by using the NULL keyword:

```
SELECT    *
FROM      Quotations
WHERE     Price IS NULL
```

Quo_Supp_#	Quo_Part_#	Price	Time	OnOrder
53	232	—	15	0

Note that we used the keyword IS instead of the equal sign. The various comparison operators (+, >, <, etc.) cannot be used to select a null value. Null is not considered greater than, less then, or equal to any value in evaluating conditional expressions. When any operation is performed using a null value, the result is null. So, for the row shown above, the arithmetic operation Price * OnOrder results in a null value, not zero. NULL cannot be specified as one of the values in the list of values used with the IN keyword.

NEGATIVE CONDITIONS

We can specify the opposite of any condition by adding the keyword NOT to the beginning of the conditional expression. When NOT is used, rather than selecting rows that meet the condition, the database software selects rows that fail to meet the condition. For example, NOT can be used with a comparison operator:

```
SELECT    *
FROM      Quotations
WHERE     NOT Quo_Part_# = 124
```

Quo_Supp_#	Quo_Part_#	Price	Time	OnOrder
51	125	0.55	5	0
51	134	0.40	5	500
51	135	0.39	5	1000
51	221	0.30	10	10000
51	231	0.10	10	5000
52	105	7.50	10	200
52	205	0.15	20	0
52	206	0.15	20	0
53	125	0.58	3	200
53	134	0.38	3	200
53	135	0.42	3	1000
53	222	0.25	15	10000
53	232	—	15	0
53	241	0.08	15	6000

The above SELECT statement is equivalent to the following:

```
SELECT    *
FROM      Quotations
WHERE     Quo_Part_# ¬= 124
```

Quo_Supp_#	Quo_Part_#	Price	Time	OnOrder
51	125	0.55	5	0
51	134	0.40	5	500
51	135	0.39	5	1000
51	221	0.30	10	10000

```
51          231     0.10    10      5000
52          105     7.50    10       200
52          205     0.15    20         0
52          206     0.15    20         0
53          125     0.58     3       200
53          134     0.38     3       200
53          135     0.42     3      1000
53          222     0.25    15     10000
53          232      —      15         0
53          241     0.08    15      6000
```

Note that NOT precedes the entire condition. It would not be correct to code the following:

```
SELECT    *
FROM      Quotations
WHERE     Quo_Part_# NOT = 124
```

USING THE NOT OPERATOR

The NOT Boolean operator can be used with multiple conditions that are connected by AND or OR. Again, it may be necessary to use parentheses to specify to which part or parts of the conditions the NOT applies. If parentheses are not used, the NOT applies only to the condition that immediately follows it. So, the following two SELECT statements are equivalent:

```
SELECT    *
FROM      Quotations
WHERE     NOT Quo_Part_# < 200
          AND
          (Price > 1.00 OR Time < 10)

SELECT    *
FROM      Quotations
WHERE     (NOT Quo_Part_# < 200)
          AND
          (Price > 1.00 OR Time < 10)
```

No rows would be selected by either of the above SELECT statements.

To negate an entire expression, it is necessary to enclose the entire conditional expression in parentheses:

```
SELECT    *
FROM      Quotations
WHERE     NOT
          (
              Quo_Part_# < 200
            AND
              (Price > 1.00 OR Time < 10)
          )
```

Quo_Supp_#	Quo_Part_#	Price	Time	OnOrder
51	221	0.30	10	10000
51	231	0.10	10	5000
52	205	0.15	20	0
52	206	0.15	20	0
53	222	0.25	15	10000
53	232	–	15	0
53	241	0.08	15	6000

The above SELECT statement selects all rows where the part number is greater than or equal to 200, or the price is less than or equal to 1.00 and time is greater than or equal to 10.

NOT can also be used with the IN, BETWEEN, and LIKE keywords. For example the following SELECT statement lists rows with part numbers other than 105, 135, or 205:

```
SELECT    Quo_Supp_#, Quo_Part_#, Price
FROM      Quotations
WHERE     Quo_Part_# NOT IN (105, 135, 205)
```

Quo_Supp_#	Quo_Part_#	Price
51	124	1.25
51	125	0.55
51	134	0.40
51	221	0.30
51	231	0.10
52	206	0.15
53	124	1.35
53	125	0.58
53	134	0.38
53	222	0.25
53	232	–
53	241	0.08

Similarly, the following SELECT statement selects rows where the part number is less than 105 or greater than 135:

```
SELECT    Quo_Supp_#, Quo_Part_#, Price
FROM      Quotations
WHERE     Quo_Part_# NOT BETWEEN 105 AND 135
```

Quo_Supp_#	Quo_Part_#	Price
51	221	0.30
51	231	0.10
52	205	0.15
52	206	0.15
53	222	0.25
53	232	–
53	241	0.08

And this one selects suppliers whose address does not contain the value " MN":

```
SELECT    *
FROM      Suppliers
WHERE     Address NOT LIKE '% MN%'
```

Sup_Supp_#	Name	Address	Code
51	Defecto Parts	16 Justamere Lane, Tacoma WA	20
52	Vesuvius Inc.	512 Ancient Blvd., Pompeii NY	20
53	Atlantis Co.	8 Ocean Ave., Washington DC	10
54	Titanic Parts	32 Sinking Street, Atlantic City NJ	30
61	Skylab Parts	128 Orbit Blvd., Sydney Australia	10
64	Knight Ltd.	256 Arthur Court, Camelot England	20

NOT can also be used with the NULL keyword, to select entries that do not have a null value. The following SELECT statement selects all rows in which the price is not a null value.

```
SELECT    *
FROM      Quotations
WHERE     Price IS NOT NULL
```

Quo_Supp_#	Quo_Part_#	Price	Time	OnOrder
51	124	1.25	5	400
51	125	0.55	5	0
51	134	0.40	5	500
51	135	0.39	5	1000
51	221	0.30	10	10000
51	231	0.10	10	5000
52	105	7.50	10	200
52	205	0.15	20	0
52	206	0.15	20	0
53	124	1.35	3	500
53	125	0.58	3	200
53	134	0.38	3	200
53	135	0.42	3	1000
53	222	0.25	15	10000
53	241	0.08	15	6000

GENERATED COLUMNS

In addition to displaying columns selected from a table, it is possible to display values that are generated based on calculations performed on values from other columns. Earlier, we calculated the quotation amount by multiplying Price times OnOrder and used the result as part of a condition. We can also display the calculated amount as part of the resulting table:

```
SELECT    Quo_Supp_#, Quo_Part_#, Price * OnOrder
FROM      Quotations
WHERE     Price > 1.00
```

Quo_Supp_#	Quo_Part_#	Price*OnOrder
51	124	500.00
52	105	1500.00
53	124	675.00

Different SQL implementations use various conventions for naming generated columns. For example, many systems leave the names of generated columns blank. One DB2 version of SQL assigns the name "COL1" to the first generated column, "COL2" to the second, and so on. Some SQL implementations use the expression itself as the column name, as in our example above. We will adopt this convention in our examples to make the results easier to read.

NAMING OUTPUT COLUMNS

We can give a specific name to be used for a column in the output display by including an AS clause in the SELECT statement. The following statement gives the name "Price_Quote" to the generated column:

```
SELECT    Quo_Supp_#, Quo_Part_#,
          Price * OnOrder AS Price_Quote
FROM      Quotations
WHERE     Price > 1.00
```

Quo_Supp_#	Quo_Part_#	Price_Quote
51	124	500.00
52	105	1500.00
53	124	675.00

Although the above example gives a name to the generated column, any name in the output display can be explicitly named by including an AS clause for it:

```
SELECT    Quo_Supp_#       AS Supplier,
          Quo_Part_#       AS Part,
          Price * OnOrder  AS Price_Quote
FROM      Quotations
WHERE     Price > 1.00
```

Supplier	Part	Price_Quote
51	124	500.00
52	105	1500.00
53	124	675.00

SEQUENCING ROWS

The rows that are displayed as the result of a query are often displayed in the same sequence that they occur within the table from which they are selected. However, some relational database packages automatically impose a sequence on the data in some tables, especially when a primary key is defined for a table.

As we learned in Chapter 10, one of the characteristics of the relational data model is that no sequence is associated with a table's rows. If data is entered into a table in sequence, the table may appear to be sequenced when it is displayed, but this initial sequence may not be maintained by the database software. Some database software, however, provides commands that can be used to explicitly specify a sequence for table data.

When data is retrieved, we may want it displayed in an explicit sequence. We can use the ORDER BY clause in the SELECT statement to sequence the rows in the displayed table. For example, the following SELECT statement lists the selected rows in ascending part number sequence and in descending price sequence for each part number:

```
SELECT    Quo_Part_#, Quo_Supp_#, Price
FROM      Quotations
WHERE     Quo_Part_# IN (124, 125, 134, 135)
ORDER BY  Quo_Part_#, Price DESC
```

Quo_Part_#	Quo_Supp_#	Price
124	53	1.35
124	51	1.25
125	53	0.58
125	51	0.55
134	51	0.40
134	53	0.38
135	53	0.42
135	51	0.39

The ORDER BY clause specifies the sequence used for the results. The first column name listed is the primary sequence. Additional column names, if used, specify minor sort sequences. In the above example, the results are displayed in sequence by part number, and by price within part number. The keyword DESC specifies descending sequence on the Price column. The default is ascending sequence, so part numbers are listed in ascending sequence. A column that we specify in an ORDER BY clause must be included in the list of columns specified in the SELECT statement (or implicitly selected by using the * option).

SORTING ON A GENERATED COLUMN

It is possible to use a generated column as one of the ORDER BY columns. However, since a calculated column does not have a name by which it can be referenced, we must refer to it by its column number.

Here, since the generated column is the third one specified in the SELECT statement, we can refer to it by the number 3 in the ORDER BY clause:

```
SELECT    Quo_Supp_#, Quo_Part_#, Price * OnOrder
FROM      Quotations
WHERE     Price > 1.00
ORDER BY  Quo_Part_#, 3 DESC
```

Quo_Supp_#	Quo_Part_#	Price*OnOrder
52	105	1500
53	124	675
51	124	500

Column numbers can be used in place of column names for the other columns as well. The following SELECT statement is equivalent to the previous one:

```
SELECT    Quo_Supp_#, Quo_Part_#, Price * OnOrder
FROM      Quotations
WHERE     Price > 1.00
ORDER BY  2, 3 DESC
```

Quo_Supp_#	Quo_Part_#	Price*OnOrder
52	105	1500
53	124	675
51	124	500

BUILT-IN FUNCTIONS

SQL includes a set of built-in functions that can be used with the SELECT statement to perform operations on a table or on sets of rows from a table. Some commonly used functions are as follows:

Function	Operation
SUM	Calculates a total
MIN	Calculates the minimum value
MAX	Calculates the maximum value
AVG	Calculates an average value
COUNT(*)	Counts the number of selected rows
COUNT(DISTINCT column name)	Counts unique values within a set of selected rows

Built-in functions can be applied to all the values in one or more columns in a table, as in the following example:

```
SELECT    SUM(OnOrder),  SUM(Price * OnOrder),
          MAX(Price),    AVG(Price)
FROM      Quotations
```

SUM(OnOrder)	SUM(Price*OnOrder)	MAX(Price)	AVG(Price)
35000	10357	7.50	0.92333333

We can include the DISTINCT keyword with any of the functions in order to eliminate duplicate data values from the computation. For example, the following SELECT statement would calculate the average of all the unique price values in the Price column:

```
SELECT    AVG(DISTINCT Price)
FROM      Quotations
```

```
AVG(DISTINCT Price)
```
          0.978571

GROUPING ROWS

Built-in functions can be applied to selected groups of rows in a table. To do this, we use the GROUP BY clause to indicate how rows should be grouped together. Generally, GROUP BY produces one row in the resulting table for each different value it finds in the column specified in the GROUP BY clause.

The following SELECT statement uses a SUM function and a GROUP BY clause to produce a total of the OnOrder data element values for each different part number:

```
SELECT    Quo_Part_#, SUM(OnOrder)
FROM      Quotations
GROUP BY  Quo_Part_#
ORDER BY  Quo_Part_#
```

Quo_Part_#	SUM(OnOrder)
105	200
124	900
125	200
134	700
135	2000
205	0
206	0
221	10000
222	10000
231	5000
232	0
241	6000

In the above example, we group rows together based on their part-number values and apply the SUM function to the OnOrder values for each group of rows that have the same part number. Grouping rows does not guarantee that the results will be in sequence by the column specified. It is still necessary to include an ORDER BY clause, as shown above, if we wish the results to be displayed in a particular sequence.

SUMMARY DATA IN CONDITIONS

Summary data calculated by grouping rows can be referenced in a conditional expression as well as being displayed in a column. To do this we use a HAVING clause instead of a WHERE clause to specify the conditional expression when the conditional expression references group data.

For example, in this example, we use a conditional expression that references the results of a SUM function:

```
SELECT    Quo_Part_#, SUM(OnOrder)
FROM      Quotations
GROUP BY  Quo_Part_#
HAVING    SUM(OnOrder) > 0
ORDER BY  Quo_Part_#
```

Quo_Part_#	SUM(OnOrder)
105	200
124	900
125	200
134	700
135	2000
221	10000
222	10000
231	5000
241	6000

In the above example, the query results list only parts that have a total on order quantity that is greater than zero.

MULTIPLE COLUMNS IN A GROUP BY CLAUSE

If we specify more than one column name in the SELECT statement, other than those that specify built-in functions, we must list all of those columns in the associated GROUP BY clause. The database software then generates a result row when the value changes in any of the specified columns.

Suppose we have the table shown in Fig. 16.1.

Table: Invoices			
Ivo_Supp_#	Ivo_Part_#	Ivo_#	Ivo_Amount
51	124	A103	200.00
51	124	A107	200.00
51	124	A111	100.00
51	134	A106	200.00
51	135	A120	200.00
51	135	A131	190.00
52	105	A115	1000.00
52	105	A127	500.00
53	125	A109	75.00
53	125	A122	25.00
53	125	A130	16.00

Record: 1

Figure 16.1   Invoices table contents.

The following SELECT statement calculates the total invoice amount for each supplier/part pair:

```
SELECT    Ivo_Supp_#,  Ivo_Part_#, SUM(Ivo_Amount)
FROM      Invoices
GROUP BY  Ivo_Supp_#,  Ivo_Part_#
ORDER BY  Ivo_Supp_#,  Ivo_Part_#
```

Ivo_Supp_#	Ivo_Part_#	SUM(Ivo_Amount)
51	124	500.00
51	134	200.00
51	135	390.00
52	105	1500.00
53	125	116.00

SUMMARY

The SQL SELECT statement is used to retrieve data from a table. A typical SELECT statement contains SELECT, FROM, WHERE, and ORDER BY clauses.

Rows are selected by specifying, in a WHERE clause, selection conditions that are to be met. Multiple conditions can be connected with AND and OR operators, and negative conditions expressed using NOT are valid. Selection conditions can also specify null values. An ORDER BY clause can be included to specify the sequence in which the results should be displayed. Arithmetic expressions can be used to calculate values in selection conditions. These calculated values can be displayed, and they can also be included in selection conditions. The IN and BETWEEN keywords specify a list of values or a range of values in a WHERE condition. The LIKE keyword can be used to base a selection on a pattern of characters in a character string data element. Wild-card characters can be included in the comparison pattern. The DISTINCT keyword can be included in SELECT statements to eliminate duplicate rows from the results of a query.

In addition to displaying columns that are selected from a table, it is possible to include new columns that are generated based on calculations performed on columns in the input tables. The SQL implementation can be allowed to supply a name for a generated column, or an AS clause can be included to supply a name.

SQL includes a set of built-in functions that can be used in a SELECT statement to perform operations on a table or on sets of rows from a table. Commonly implemented built-in functions include SUM, MIN, MAX, AVG, and COUNT. Built-in functions can also be used to group rows in a table using a GROUP BY clause.

Chapter 17 continues the discussion of the SELECT statement by showing how SELECT statements can be nested to form subqueries.

Subqueries

One SELECT statement can be nested within another outer SELECT statement. The nested SELECT statement is typically called a *subquery*. We can reference the result of a subquery in the outer SELECT statement. Suppose we wished to list part numbers and prices for parts supplied by supplier Vesuvius Inc. To do this, we might use a subquery to determine the supplier number that corresponds to the name Vesuvius Inc. The following example shows how an outer SELECT statement references the result of the subquery:

```
SELECT    Quo_Part_#, Price
FROM      Quotations
WHERE     Quo_Supp_# = (SELECT   Sup_Supp_#
                        FROM     Suppliers
                        WHERE    Name = 'Vesuvius Inc.')
```

Quo_Part_#	Price
105	7.50
205	0.15
206	0.15

The database software evaluates the inner SELECT first and returns the value 52 for Sup_Supp_#. Based on this value, the database software evaluates the outer SELECT and returns the results shown.

Note that the subquery must be entirely enclosed in parentheses. Generally, a subquery should be used when a value that is referenced in a WHERE or HAVING clause cannot be specified directly, but must be determined based on data retrieved from a table.

BUILT-IN FUNCTIONS IN SUBQUERIES

Built-in functions can be used in subqueries, as in the following example:

```
SELECT    Quo_Supp_#, Quo_Part_#
FROM      Quotations
```

```
WHERE     Price > (SELECT   AVG(Price)
                   FROM     Quotations)
```

Quo_Supp_#	Quo_Part_#
51	124
52	105
53	124

Here the subquery determines the average price in the Quotations table (0.92), and then the main query selects supplier/part pairs that have a price higher than the average.

The following example shows a subquery used in a HAVING clause. Here, we are selecting parts with a total on order quantity greater than the average on order quantity:

```
SELECT    Quo_Part_#, SUM(OnOrder)
FROM      Quotations
GROUP BY  Quo_Part_#
HAVING    SUM(OnOrder) > (SELECT   AVG(OnOrder)
                          FROM     Quotations)
```

Quo_Part_#	SUM(OnOrder)
221	10000
222	10000
231	5000
241	6000

SUBQUERIES THAT RETURN MULTIPLE VALUES

In the subquery examples used thus far, the subquery immediately follows a comparison operator. For this to be valid, the subquery must return a single value, since we cannot perform a comparison operation on a set of values. We can, however, make use of subqueries that return multiple values by using the keywords IN, ANY, and ALL.

The following SELECT statement lists part numbers and prices for parts supplied by suppliers whose Code value is 20:

```
SELECT    Quo_Part_#, Price
FROM      Quotations
WHERE     Quo_Supp_# = ANY (SELECT Sup_Supp_#
                            FROM Suppliers
                            WHERE Code = 20)
```

Quo_Part_#	Price
124	1.25
125	0.55
134	0.40
135	0.39
221	0.30
231	0.10
105	7.50
205	0.15
206	0.15

In the above example, the subquery determines which suppliers have a code of 20 and returns a list of those supplier numbers. The main query then uses the ANY keyword to list part number and price for *every* row in Quotations that has a supplier number in the list returned by the subquery.

The keyword IN means the same thing as an equal comparison in combination with ANY. The following example lists all parts whose total on order quantity is greater than 500:

```
SELECT    Inv_Part_#, PartName, OnHand
FROM      Inventory
WHERE     Inv_Part_# IN (SELECT    Quo_Part_#
                         FROM      Quotations
                         GROUP BY  Quo_Part_#
                         HAVING    SUM(OnOrder) > 500)
```

Inv_Part_#	PartName	OnHand
124	Bolt	900
134	Nut	900
135	Nut	1000
221	Axle	1500
222	Axle	25
231	Axle	75
241	Wheel	300

If the comparison operation is other than an equal comparison, then we must use ANY. In the following example, we are using it to find all distinct supplier/part pairs with a price that is greater than any one of the prices for parts that have an on-order quantity of 0.

```
SELECT    DISTINCT Quo_Supp_#, Quo_Part_#, Price
FROM      Quotations
WHERE     Price > ANY (SELECT    Price
                       FROM      Quotations
                       WHERE     OnOrder > 0)
```

Quo_Supp_#	Quo_Part_#	Price
52	105	7.50
53	124	1.35
51	124	1.25
51	125	0.55
53	125	0.58
53	135	0.42
51	134	0.40
51	135	0.39
53	134	0.38
51	221	0.30
52	205	0.15
52	206	0.15
53	222	0.25
51	231	0.10

In the above example, the ANY specifies that we are selecting those rows that have a price greater than the lowest price of any row that has an on-order quantity greater than 0. The lowest price value of these is 0.08 (null values are not included in the selection), so all rows except for the row with price 0.08 and the row with the null price value are included in the selection.

When we use ANY, the comparison must be true for only one of the values returned by the subquery in order for the row to be selected. If we specify the ALL keyword, the comparison must be true for all values returned by the subquery.

Here we are using ALL to find the part or parts that have the highest average on-order quantity:

```
SELECT     Quo_Part_#, AVG(OnOrder)
FROM       Quotations
GROUP BY   Quo_Part_#
HAVING     AVG(OnOrder) >= ALL (SELECT     AVG(OnOrder)
                                FROM       Quotations
                                GROUP BY   Quo_Part_#)
```

Quo_Part_#	AVG(OnOrder)
221	10000
222	10000

USING NOT WITH ANY AND ALL

We must use care in testing for negative conditions involving ANY and ALL. Suppose we wished to list part number, name, and on-hand quantity for all parts that have a total on-order quantity of zero or are not included in the Quotations table. One way of doing this is by using a subquery to select part numbers with total on-order quantity greater than zero and then selecting part numbers that are not in this list:

```
SELECT     Inv_Part_#, PartName, OnHand
FROM       Inventory
WHERE      Inv_Part_# NOT IN (SELECT     Quo_Part_#
                              FROM       Quotations
                              GROUP BY   Quo_Part_#
                              HAVING     SUM(OnOrder) > 0)
```

Inv_Part_#	PartName	OnHand
106	Gear	700
171	Generator	500
172	Generator	400
181	Wheel	1000
205	Band	450
206	Motor	225
232	Axle	150

Another way of performing the subquery is as follows:

```
WHERE      Inv_Part_# ¬= ALL (SELECT    Quo_Part_#
                              FROM       Quotations
                              GROUP BY   Quo_Part_#
                              HAVING     SUM(OnOrder) > 0)
```

The above WHERE clause, in effect, selects only rows whose part numbers are different from all the part numbers returned by the subquery. If we had inadvertently used ANY instead of ALL in the above WHERE clause, it would select rows that have part numbers that are different from any one value in the list, thus selecting all the rows.

MULTIPLE LEVELS OF NESTING

If we like, we can perform subqueries within subqueries. Suppose we wish to select part information for parts supplied by suppliers whose Code value is 10. We could do this with the following query:

```
SELECT     Inv_Part_#, PartName, OnHand
FROM       Inventory
WHERE      Inv_Part_# IN (SELECT   Quo_Part_#
                          FROM     Quotations
                          WHERE    Quo_Supp_# IN (SELECT   Sup_Supp_#
                                                  FROM     Suppliers
                                                  WHERE    Code = 10))
```

Inv_Part_#	PartName	OnHand
124	Bolt	900
125	Bolt	1000
134	Nut	900
135	Nut	1000
222	Axle	25
232	Axle	150
241	Wheel	300

Nested queries are always evaluated from the innermost subquery outwards. In the above example, the subquery at level 3 is evaluated first and returns a set of supplier numbers for suppliers that have a Code value of 10. The subquery at level 2 is then evaluated, which selects part numbers for the parts supplied by those suppliers. The main query is then evaluated based on the part numbers returned by the subquery at level 2.

Most relational database products do not place an arbitrary limit on the number of levels of nesting that can be specified in a SELECT statement. However, performance considerations often make about five levels of nesting a practical limit.

CORRELATED SUBQUERIES

In the subqueries we have examined thus far, the subquery needed to be evaluated only once. In some cases, we need to use a subquery that is reevaluated for each row selected by the main query. This type of subquery is called a *correlated subquery*.

Suppose we wished to list the supplier number, part number, and price for the supplier that has the lowest price for each part. The following example shows how a correlated subquery can be used to produce the desired result:

```
SELECT     Quo_Supp_#, Quo_Part_#, Price
FROM       Quotations Row_X
WHERE      Price = (SELECT  MIN(Price)
                    FROM    Quotations
                    WHERE   Quo_Part_# = Row_X.Quo_Part_#)
```

Quo_Supp_#	Quo_Part_#	Price
51	124	1.25
51	125	0.55
51	135	0.39
51	221	0.30
51	231	0.10
52	105	7.50
52	205	0.15
52	206	0.15
53	134	0.38
53	222	0.25
53	241	0.08

The name Row_X following the table name in the FROM clause is called a *correlation variable* or a *correlation name*. It serves to identify the current row that is being processed by the main query. We can choose any name as the correlation name. In the subquery, the correlation name is used as a prefix to identify those values that are to come from the row in the main query. In the above example, the subquery is evaluated as each row from the Quotations table is processed. The subquery uses the part number from the current row to determine the minimum price offered for that part. If the price in the current row is equal to the minimum price, that row is selected. As each row is processed, the part number and the subquery result both change.

THE EXISTS KEYWORD

In addition to using a subquery to determine a value or set of values, a subquery can also be used to determine if a row exists that meets a specified condition. In its simple form, EXISTS can be used to perform the same type of processing as the IN keyword. In an earlier example, we used the following SELECT statement to list parts supplied by suppliers that have a Code value of 20:

```
SELECT     Quo_Part_#, Price
FROM       Quotations
WHERE      Quo_Supp_# IN (SELECT   Sup_Supp_#
                          FROM     Suppliers
                          WHERE    Code = 20)
```

We could produce the identical results by using a correlated subquery in conjunction with the EXISTS keyword:

```
SELECT    Quo_Part_#, Price
FROM      Quotations ThisRow
WHERE     EXISTS (SELECT    *
                  FROM      Suppliers
                  WHERE     Sup_Supp_# = ThisRow.Quo_Supp_#
                            AND
                  Code = 20)
```

Quo_Part_#	Price
124	1.25
125	0.55
134	0.40
135	0.39
221	0.30
231	0.10
105	7.50
205	0.15
206	0.15

When we use EXISTS, the subquery does not return data element values. Instead, it returns an indication of whether or not any rows in the subquery met the specified conditions. If one or more rows do meet the conditions, the EXISTS clause is considered to be true. Since no data is returned, it is not necessary to specify individual columns in the SELECT clause of the subquery, and the form SELECT * is commonly used.

In the above example, as each row in Quotations is processed by the main query, the subquery determines whether or not any rows exist in the Suppliers table with the current row's supplier number and a Code value of 20. If such a row exists, the current row in the main query is selected.

USING NOT WITH EXISTS

We can also use the NOT keyword with EXISTS to select rows that do not meet specified conditions. For example, the following query lists all parts from the Inventory table that do not have entries in the Quotations table:

```
SELECT    Inv_Part_#, PartName
FROM      Inventory Row_X
WHERE     NOT EXISTS (SELECT    *
                      FROM      Quotations
                      WHERE     Row_X.Inv_Part_# = Quo_Part_#)
```

Inv_Part_#	PartName
106	Gear
171	Generator
172	Generator
181	Wheel

In the above example, a row from the main query is selected only if no row exists in Quotations that has the same part number. Again, this query could be handled by using NOT IN instead of a correlated subquery.

USING EXISTS FOR ALL VALUES

The EXISTS keyword can be particularly useful in specifying a condition that must be met for all values in a particular column. To see an example of using EXISTS, we will assume that the Quotations and Suppliers tables contain the contents shown in Fig. 17.1.

Table: Quotations

Quo_Supp_#	Quo_Part_#	Price	Time	OnOrder
51	124	$1.25	5	400
51	125	$0.55	5	0
51	134	$0.40	5	500
51	135	$0.39	5	1000
52	105	$7.50	10	200
52	124	$1.30	10	250
52	135	$0.40	10	100
52	206	$0.15	20	0
53	124	$1.35	3	500
53	125	$0.58	3	200
53	134	$0.38	3	200
53	135	$0.42	3	1000
53	222	$0.25	15	10000

Record: 1

Table: Suppliers

Sup_Supp_#	Name	Address	Code
51	Defecto Parts	16 Justamere Lane, Tacoma WA	20
52	Vesuvius Inc	512 Ancient Blvd., Pompeii NY	20
53	Atlantis Co.	8 Ocean Ave., Washington DC	10

Record: 1

Figure 17.1 Quotations and Suppliers table contents.

Suppose we wish to list those parts that are supplied by all suppliers. This means that a part number is selected if, for every supplier number in Supplier, there is a row in Quotations with that supplier and part number. We test for this type of condition in a negative manner. We select part numbers where there *does not exist* a supplier number where the corresponding supplier and part number pair *does not exist* in Quotations.

We could use the following query to obtain the desired results:

```
SELECT    Quo_Part_#
FROM      Quotations Row_X
WHERE     NOT EXISTS
              (SELECT *
               FROM    Suppliers Row_Y
               WHERE   NOT EXISTS
                           (SELECT   *
                            FROM     Quotations
                            WHERE    Row_Y.Sup_Supp_# = Quo_Supp_#
                                  AND
                                     Row_X.Quo_Part_# = Quo_Part_#))
```

```
Quo_Part_#
    124
    135
```

For each of these part numbers, there is no supplier number in Suppliers where there is not a corresponding supplier/part entry in Quotations. In other words, for all suppliers, there is a supplier/part entry in Quotations.

SUMMARY

SELECT statements can be nested within other SELECT statements to create subqueries. A subquery is typically used to generate a value or set of values that is used as part of a selection condition. Built-in functions can be included in subqueries. When a subquery is used in a WHERE clause as part of a comparison operation, it must return a single value. The IN, ANY, and ALL keywords can be used in conjunction with subqueries that return multiple values.

Multiple levels of nesting can be used in performing subqueries within subqueries. Most relational database software implementations do not place a limit on the number of levels of nesting that are supported, but performance considerations often limit the number of levels to about five.

A correlated subquery is one that uses a value from the rows being processed by the main query. A correlated subquery is reevaluated for each row in the main query. In addition to returning values, a subquery can be used to determine whether or not a row exists that meets particular conditions.

In addition to using subqueries to determine a value or set of values, the EXISTS keyword can be included in a subquery to determine whether or not one or more rows exists that meets a specified condition. The NOT keyword can be used in conjunction with EXISTS to test for the nonexistence of rows. The EXISTS keyword is particularly useful in specifying a condition that must be met for all values in a particular column.

Chapter 18 shows how SELECT statements can be written to perform the various types of inner join and outer join operations introduced in Chapter 11.

Inner and Outer Joins

The queries shown in the previous chapters were all based on selecting data from a single table. SQL has the capability to allow data from multiple tables to be combined in various ways. In this chapter we will look at examples of SQL SELECT statements that request operations that combine tables. This chapter examines alternative methods that can be used to request inner joins, outer joins, and Union relational operations. The examples in this chapter reference the Order Entry database tables from Chapter 15 (see Fig. 15.3).

INNER JOIN OPERATIONS

As we discussed in Chapter 11, a relational Join operation involves combining rows from one table with rows from another table. The Join operation is based on a comparison that is performed between the data element values in a column from the first table and the values from a column in the second table.

Inner Join Example

With an inner join operation, only the rows that satisfy the comparison used to create the Join are included in the result. Suppose that we wished to list the part number, name, on hand quantity, supplier, and on order quantity for those parts that currently have suppliers and thus have entries in the Quotations table. To do this, we need to combine information from the Inventory and Quotations tables.

The following SELECT statement joins the two tables based on the Inv_Part_# column from the Inventory table and the Quo_Part_# column from the Quotations table:

```
SELECT    Inv_Part_#, PartName, OnHand, Quo_Supp_#, OnOrder,
FROM      Inventory, Quotations,
          Inventory INNER JOIN Quotations
          ON Inv_Part_# = Quo_Part_#
ORDER BY  Inv_Part_#, Quo_Supp_#
```

Inv_Part_#	PartName	OnHand	Quo_Supp_#	OnOrder
105	Gear	0	52	200
124	Bolt	900	51	400
124	Bolt	900	53	500
125	Bolt	1000	51	0
125	Bolt	1000	53	200
134	Nut	900	51	500
134	Nut	900	53	200
135	Nut	1000	51	1000
135	Nut	1000	53	1000
205	Band	450	52	0
206	Motor	225	52	0
221	Axle	1500	51	10000
222	Axle	25	53	10000
231	Axle	75	51	5000
232	Axle	150	53	0
241	Wheel	300	53	6000

Notice in the above SELECT statement that we listed column names from both tables and also identified both tables in the FROM clause. The FROM clause includes an additional specification that identifies the type of Join operation we are requesting on the two tables, the columns on which the Join operation is based, and the type of comparison used to implement the join. In the above example, we are requesting an Equijoin based on the Inv_Part_# and Quo_Part_# columns.

The comparison used to join the tables does not have to be for equal values, but the Equijoin is the most commonly used type of Join in practice. The above Join operation specifies, for example, that each row in the Quotations table that has a part number of 124 will be joined with the information for part 124 from the Inventory table. Only the rows for the part numbers that appear in both the Quotations and Inventory tables are included in the result. Some implementations of SQL may allow the keyword INNER to be omitted from a JOIN specification, in which case, an inner join operation is typically implied.

Alternative Join Syntax

The INNER JOIN keyword used in the previous Join operation is part of the ANSI X3.135-1992 standard, but is a relatively recent addition to the standard. Many implementations of SQL provided provisions for various types of Join operations before the specific JOIN syntax was made part of SQL. Therefore, different database systems provide various ways of expressing different Join operations. For example, a WHERE clause can be used to express the same Join operation as in the previous example:

```
SELECT    Inv_Part_#, PartName, OnHand, Quo_Supp_#, OnOrder,
FROM      Inventory, Quotations,
WHERE     Inv.Part_# = Quo_Part_#
ORDER BY  Inv_Part_#, Quo_Supp_#
```

Inv_Part_#	PartName	OnHand	Quo_Supp_#	OnOrder
105	Gear	0	52	200
124	Bolt	900	51	400

124	Bolt	900	53	500
125	Bolt	1000	51	0
125	Bolt	1000	53	200
134	Nut	900	51	500
134	Nut	900	53	200
135	Nut	1000	51	1000
135	Nut	1000	53	1000
205	Band	450	52	0
206	Motor	225	52	0
221	Axle	1500	51	10000
222	Axle	25	53	10000
231	Axle	75	51	5000
232	Axle	150	53	0
241	Wheel	300	53	6000

Notice in the above SELECT statement we simply listed column names from both tables and also identified both tables in the FROM clause. The WHERE clause specifies that we want an Equijoin based on the Inv_Part_# and Quo_Part_# columns. As in the previous inner join examples, the comparison used to join the tables does not have to be for equal values.

Join Semantics

In performing Join operations, we must take care in selecting the joining columns. It is the user's responsibility to ensure not only that the SELECT statement syntax is correct but that the semantics of the requested Join operation are also reasonable.

In most cases, Join operations should be performed on columns that contain the same type of data, such as the part numbers in the previous example. Values in the columns being joined should typically be drawn from the same domain, and it should make sense to make comparisons on them. For example, it would make no sense to perform a Join operation based on a part number from the Inventory table and an order amount from the Quotations table, even though some of the values might by chance possibly match. The database software typically checks that the joining columns contain the appropriate type of data to be compared but often performs no validation beyond this.

Multiple Inner Join Operations

More than two tables can be joined in the same SELECT statement. Suppose that in our previous example we also wished to list the supplier name from the Supplier table. We simply include an additional INNER JOIN specification in the FROM clause:

```
SELECT    Inv_Part_#, PartName, OnHand, Quo_Supp_#, Name, OnOrder
FROM      Inventory, Quotations, Suppliers,
          Inventory INNER JOIN Quotations
          ON Inv_Part_# = Quo_Part_#,
          Suppliers INNER JOIN Quotations
          ON Sup_Supp_# = Quo_Supp_#,
ORDER BY  Inv_Part_#, Quo_Supp_#
```

Inv_Part_#	PartName	OnHand	Quo_Supp_#	Name	OnOrder
105	Gear	0	52	Vesuvius, Inc.	200
124	Bolt	900	51	Defecto Parts	400
124	Bolt	900	53	Atlantis Co.	500
125	Bolt	1000	51	Defecto Parts	0
125	Bolt	1000	53	Atlantis Co.	200
134	Nut	900	51	Defecto Parts	500
134	Nut	900	53	Atlantis Co.	200
135	Nut	1000	51	Defecto Parts	1000
135	Nut	1000	53	Atlantis Co.	1000
205	Band	450	52	Vesuvius, Inc.	0
206	Motor	225	52	Vesuvius, Inc.	0
221	Axle	1500	51	Defecto Parts	10000
222	Axle	25	53	Atlantis Co.	10000
231	Axle	75	51	Defecto Parts	5000
232	Axle	150	53	Atlantis Co.	0
241	Wheel	300	53	Atlantis Co.	6000

Again, the same Join operations can also be expressed using WHERE clauses to express the Join comparisons:

```
SELECT     Inv_Part_#, PartName, OnHand, Quo_Supp_#, Name, OnOrder
FROM       Inventory, Quotations, Suppliers,
WHERE      Inv_Part_# = Quo_Part_# AND Sup_Supp_# = Quo_Supp_#,
ORDER BY   Inv_Part_#, Quo_Supp_#
```

Notice in the above examples that the comparisons we are asking the database software to perform are semantically reasonable. We are comparing part numbers in the Inventory and Quotations tables and supplier numbers in the Quotations and Suppliers tables.

Cartesian Product Operations

It is also possible to use the above form of syntax to join tables without specifying a joining condition. If we exclude the WHERE clause and simply name two tables, each row of the first table is joined with every row of the second table—in effect performing a Cartesian Product relational operation.

As we pointed out in Chapter 11, the result of a Cartesian Product operation is a table that has a number of rows that is equal to the number of rows in the first table multiplied by the number of rows in the second table. A Cartesian Product operation is allowed by some database software, but if the two tables are large executing such an operation could consume excessively large amounts of computing resources. Cartesian Product operations do not turn out to be very useful in practice.

OUTER JOIN OPERATIONS

As we discussed in Chapter 11, inner join operations sometimes do not produce the result required by the application. For example, when joining the Inventory and Quotations tables on the part number columns, there may be part numbers listed in the Inventory table that do not yet have suppliers and so do not yet have entries in the Quotations table. What is less likely is that there may be a part that has a supplier but is not currently listed in the Inventory table. (Proper use of referential integrity constraints, however, can preclude this possibility.)

Outer join operations can be used to ensure that information for all required part numbers is listed for those applications that do not want desired rows to be dropped from the result.

Left Outer Join Operation

Suppose we wish to list all part numbers and the suppliers that supply them. If a part number currently has no supplier, it should be listed with a null value displayed in the Suppliers column. This is a left outer join of the Inventory and Quotations tables based on part number values. This left outer join operation can be performed with the following statements:

```
SELECT    Inv_Part_#, Quo_Supp_#
FROM      Inventory, Quotations,
          Inventory LEFT OUTER JOIN Quotations
          ON Inv_Part_# = Quo_Part_#
ORDER BY  Inv_Part_#, Quo_Part_#
```

Inv_Part_#	Quo_Supp_#
106	
171	
172	
181	
124	51
125	51
134	51
135	51
221	51
231	51
105	52
205	52
206	52
124	53
125	53
134	53
135	53
222	53
232	53
241	53

In the above SELECT statement, a qualifier is added to the FROM clause to express the outer join operation that is desired. With most relational database packages, the keyword OUTER is optional, and LEFT JOIN produces the same result as LEFT OUTER JOIN.

Alternative Outer Join Syntax

Again, the LEFT JOIN syntax is a relatively recent addition to the SQL standard, and many relational database systems use additions to the WHERE clause syntax to express outer joins. For example, with the SQL implementation used in many Oracle database products, the user inserts a "(+)" qualifier in the WHERE clause to indicate which column should contain entries with null values when there is no matching value in the other column:

```
SELECT    Inv_Part_#, Quo_Supp_#
FROM      Inventory, Quotations,
WHERE     Inv_Part_# = Quo_Part_#(+)
ORDER BY  Inv_Part_#, Quo_Part_#
```

Inv_Part_#	Quo_Supp_#
106	
171	
172	
181	
124	51
125	51
134	51
135	51
221	51
231	51
105	52
205	52
206	52
124	53
125	53
134	53
135	53
222	53
232	53
241	53

Right Outer Join Operation

If we have not specified a referential integrity constraint as part of the database description, and it is possible for a part number to appear in the Quotations table without also being in the Inventory table, we might want to request a right outer join operation:

```
SELECT    Inv_Part_#, Quo_Supp_#
FROM      Inventory, Quotations,
          Inventory RIGHT OUTER JOIN Quotations
          ON Inv_Part_# = Quo_Part_#
ORDER BY  Inv_Part_#, Quo_Part_#
```

Inv_Part_#	Quo_Supp_#
124	51
125	51

134	51
135	51
221	51
231	51
105	52
205	52
206	52
124	53
125	53
134	53
135	53
222	53
232	53
241	53

The above query produces the same result as an inner join in this database because there are no parts referenced in the Quotations table that are not also in the inventory table.

Again, using the Oracle WHERE clause syntax, the same right outer join syntax could be expressed as follows:

```
SELECT     Inv_Part_#, Quo_Supp_#
FROM       Inventory, Quotations,
WHERE      Inv_Part_#(+) = Quo_Part_#
ORDER BY   Inv_Part_#, Quo_Part_#
```

Full Outer Join Operations

We can also request a full outer join operation to include in the resulting table a row for each part number, whether the part number is referenced only in the Inventory table, only in the Quotations table or in both tables:

```
SELECT     Inv_Part_#, Quo_Supp_#
FROM       Inventory, Quotations,
           Inventory FULL OUTER JOIN Quotations
           ON Inv_Part_# = Quo_Part_#
ORDER BY   Inv_Part_#, Quo_Part_#
```

Inv_Part_#	Quo_Supp_#
106	
171	
172	
181	
124	51
125	51
134	51
135	51
221	51
231	51
105	52
205	52
206	52

```
124        53
125        53
134        53
135        53
222        53
232        53
241        53
```

A full outer join can be expressed using the Oracle-type syntax by including the "(+)" qualifier after each column name in the WHERE clause:

```
SELECT    Inv_Part_#, Quo_Supp_#
FROM      Inventory, Quotations,
WHERE     Inv_Part_#(+) = Quo_Part_#(+)
ORDER BY  Inv_Part_#, Quo_Part_#
```

UNION OPERATIONS

The SQL language includes a UNION operator that can be used to request Union relational operations. The Union operation can be used to combine tables in ways not possible by using conventional Join type operations. There are a variety of ways in which UNION can be used, and we will not discuss them all here. Note that not all relational database packages support the SQL UNION operator.

Combining SELECT Operation Results

The UNION keyword can be used in conjunction with multiple SELECT statements to perform a Union relational operation on the results of the individual SELECT statements. With a UNION operation, the rows produced by each SELECT statement are interleaved and duplicate rows are eliminated. For a UNION operation to be valid, the results of each SELECT statement must be similar. That is they must have the same number of columns, and corresponding columns must have compatible data types. For example, corresponding columns must contain either character or numeric data.

As an example, suppose that we have three different Quotations tables: one for parts in an "A" category, a second for parts in a "B" category, and a third for parts in a "C" category. Sample Quotations tables using this classification scheme are shown in Fig. 18.1.

Suppose we wish to select all parts, from all three Quotations tables, that are supplied by supplier 51. We can perform this selection as follows:

```
SELECT    Quo_Part_#, Price, 'A Part'
FROM      Quotations_A
WHERE     Quo_Supp_# = 51
    UNION
SELECT    Quo_Part_#, Price, 'B Part'
FROM      Quotations_B
WHERE     Quo_Supp_# = 51
    UNION
```

Table: Quotations_A				
Quo_Supp_#	Quo_Part_#	Price	Time	OnOrder
51	171	$21.00	15	12
54	106	$26.25	20	5
54	171	$22.50	12	15
61	106	$25.75	10	10
61	171	$30.00	15	20
61	172	$35.00	10	10

Record: 1

Table: Quotations_B				
Quo_Supp_#	Quo_Part_#	Price	Time	OnOrder
51	181	$12.50	10	25
57	181	$13.00	7	30
57	206	$15.75	15	50
61	206	$15.50	20	10
64	181	$12.75	10	15
64	206	$16.00	15	75

Record: 1

Table: Quotations_C				
Quo_Supp_#	Quo_Part_#	Price	Time	OnOrder
51	124	$1.25	5	400
51	125	$0.55	5	0
51	134	$0.40	5	500
51	135	$0.39	5	1000
51	221	$0.30	10	10000
51	231	$0.10	10	5000
52	105	$7.50	10	200
52	205	$0.15	20	0
52	206	$0.15	20	0
53	124	$1.35	3	500
53	125	$0.58	3	200
53	134	$0.38	3	200
53	135	$0.42	3	1000
53	222	$0.25	15	10000
53	232		15	0
53	241	$0.08	15	6000

Record: 1

Figure 18.1 Multiple Quotations tables.

```
SELECT    Quo_Part_#, Price, 'C Part'
FROM      Quotations_C
WHERE     Quo_Supp_# = 51
ORDER BY  1

Quo_Part_#    Price
        124    1.25    C Part
        125    0.55    C Part
        134    0.40    C Part
        135    0.39    C Part
        171   21.00    A Part
        181   12.50    B Part
        221    0.30    C Part
        231    0.10    C Part
```

Using a Descriptive Column

The above example illustrates the use of a *descriptive column*, in which a constant value is assigned to that column for each selected row. In this case, we are using the constant values to identify the table from which each result row came. A descriptive column can be used with any type of SELECT statement; however, it is most useful with a UNION operation, where the resulting column contains different data element values.

An ORDER BY clause can be used to determine the sequence of the final merged results table. If used, the ORDER BY clause should follow the last SELECT statement. Also, column numbers rather than column names should be used in the ORDER BY clause, since the corresponding columns in the different SELECT statements may not always have the same names.

Duplicate rows in the final results table are automatically removed by the UNION operation, so it is not necessary to specify DISTINCT. The ALL keyword can be specified in conjunction with UNION to prevent duplicate rows from being eliminated. With UNION ALL, duplicate rows are left in the resulting table. Since eliminating duplicate rows usually causes the database software to sort the results, UNION ALL can result in a more efficient query, even in cases where duplicate rows are not possible.

UNION cannot ordinarily be used to connect subqueries. All the SELECT statements must be main (outermost) queries, although any of the SELECT statements could invoke subqueries if required.

The results of SELECT statements that are joined by the UNION operator can be from different tables or from the same table. For example, the following two SELECT statements reference the same table, and their results are joined by a UNION operator in order to flag preferred customers on the resulting display:

```
SELECT    Sup_Supp_#, Name, 'Preferred' AS Type
FROM      Suppliers
WHERE     Code = 30
   UNION
SELECT    Sup_Supp_#, Name, '    '
FROM      Suppliers
WHERE     Code ¬= 30
ORDER BY  2
```

Sup_Supp_#	Name	Type
53	Atlantis Co.	
51	Defecto Parts	
57	Eagle Hardware	Preferred
64	Knight Ltd.	
61	Skylab Parts	
54	Titanic Parts	Preferred
52	Vesuvius Inc.	

Note that in the above example, we are using an AS specification to name the column containing the "Preferred" indications.

Left Outer Joins Using UNION

The SQL capabilities implemented by some database packages do not include facilities for directly expressing outer join operations. With some of these database products, it is possible to simulate an outer join by combining SELECT statements with the UNION operation.

Suppose we wish to list part numbers and the suppliers that supply them. If a part number has no supplier (i.e., has no entry in the Quotations table), we would like it listed with blanks in the Suppliers column. This is a left outer join of the Inventory and Quotations tables based on part number values. This left outer join operation can be simulated through the use of the UNION keyword as follows:

```
SELECT    Inv_Part_#, Quo_Supp_#
FROM      Inventory, Quotations
WHERE     Inv_Part_# = Quo_Part_#
     UNION
SELECT    Inv_Part_#, '     '
FROM      Inventory
WHERE     Inv_Part_# NOT IN (SELECT    Quo_Part_#
                             FROM      Quotations)
```

Inv_Part_#	Quo_Supp_#
124	51
125	51
134	51
135	51
221	51
231	51
105	52
205	52
206	52
124	53
125	53
134	53
135	53
222	53
232	53
241	53
106	
171	
172	
181	

In the above example, the first SELECT statement lists part numbers and suppliers for part numbers that appear in the Quotations table. The second SELECT statement lists part numbers and blanks for all part numbers that are in the Inventory table but are not in the Quotations table.

Full Outer Join Using UNION

If it were also possible for a part number to appear in the Quotations table without also being in the Inventory table, we could simulate a full outer join operation by including another UNION operator and a third SELECT statement to produce the full outer join:

```
SELECT    Inv_Part_#, Quo_Supp_#
FROM      Inventory, Quotations
WHERE     Inv_Part_# = Quo_Part_#
    UNION
SELECT    Inv_Part_#, '     '
FROM      Inventory
WHERE     Inv_Part_# NOT IN (SELECT   Quo_Part_#
                             FROM     Quotations)
    UNION
SELECT    Quo_Part_#, Quo_Supp_#
FROM      Quotations
WHERE     Quo_Part_# NOT IN (SELECT   Inv_Part_#
                             FROM     Inventory)
```

The third SELECT statement in the above example lists entries from the Quotations table for parts that have no corresponding entries in the Inventory table.

DUPLICATE COLUMN NAMES

In the sample tables we have been using, all the column names are unique. However, this may not always be true. There may be occasions when columns in different tables have the same name. As discussed in Chapter 11, this is often done to make clear the relationships that exist between tables. Suppose we named our columns using the same names for part numbers and supplier numbers in all three tables of the Order Entry database, as shown in Fig. 18.2.

Table Qualifiers

Now when we Join operations on these tables, we need a way to indicate to which table a column belongs. One way to do this is to prefix the column name with the name of the appropriate table:

```
SELECT    Inventory.Part_#, PartName, OnHand,
          Quotations.Supplier_#, Name, OnOrder
FROM      Inventory, Quotations, Suppliers,
          Inventory INNER JOIN Quotations
          ON Inventory.Part_# = Quotations.Part_#,
          Suppliers INNER JOIN Quotations
          ON Suppliers.Supplier_# = Quotations.Supplier_#,
ORDER BY  Inventory.Part_#, Quotations.Supplier_#
```

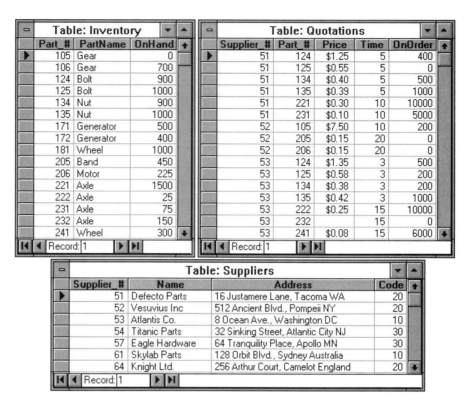

Figure 18.2 Column names need be unique only within the same table.

Correlation Variables

The use of table qualifiers can get cumbersome if table names are long. Another possibility is to assign a shorter name to each table, called a *correlation variable*, for the purposes of uniquely identifying columns in a SELECT statement. Correlation variables can be assigned in the FROM clause using the AS keyword:

```
SELECT    I.Part_#, PartName, OnHand,
          Q.Supplier_#, Name, OnOrder
FROM      Inventory AS I, Quotations AS Q, Suppliers AS S,
          Inventory INNER JOIN Quotations
          ON I.Part_# = Q.Part_#,
          Suppliers INNER JOIN Quotations
          ON S.Supplier_# = Q.Supplier_#,
ORDER BY  I.Part_#, Q.Supplier_#
```

In the above example, we are using AS keywords to assign the name I to the Inventory table, the name Q to the Quotations table and the name S to the Suppliers table. We are using these shorter names in place of the full table names to indicate the tables we are referencing.

Many database packages allow the AS keyword to be omitted in assigning correlation names, as in the following example:

```
SELECT    I.Part_#, PartName, OnHand,
          Q.Supplier_#, Name, OnOrder
FROM      Inventory I, Quotations Q, Suppliers S,
          Inventory INNER JOIN Quotations
          ON I.Part_# = Q.Part_#,
          Suppliers INNER JOIN Quotations
          ON S.Supplier_# = Q.Supplier_#,
ORDER BY  I.Part_#, Q.Supplier_#
```

SUMMARY

The SQL SELECT statement can be used to perform Join operations that combine data from multiple tables. Alternative methods of joining tables can be implemented using inner join, outer join, and Union operations.

A relational Join operation involves combining rows from two or more tables based on a comparison that is performed on column values in the tables being joined. An inner join operation can be specified using the INNER JOIN keywords in a FROM clause. Omitting the INNER keyword implies an inner join operation. With an inner join operation, only the rows that satisfy the join comparison appear in the result table. More than two tables can be joined by including additional join specifications in the FROM clause. Some SQL implementations employ alternative syntax for making inner join specifications. Joining tables without specifying a joining condition results in a Cartesian Product operation.

Outer join operations are used when the application requires that no rows be dropped from either or both of the tables being joined. When performing outer join operations on table A and table B, a left outer join operation includes in the result all the rows from table A, a right outer join operation includes in the result all the rows from table B, and a full outer join operation includes in the result all the rows from both table A and table B.

The SQL language includes a UNION operator that can be used to combine tables in ways not possible with Join operations. The UNION operator can be used to merge the results of two or more SELECT statements. Some types of outer join operations can be simulated using the Union operator for database software that does not support outer join syntax.

Column names need not be unique in the tables being joined. When joining tables with columns that have the same names, column names can be qualified with table names to ensure unique identification. Correlation variables can be assigned to column names to provide a shorthand method of referring to qualified column names in SELECT statements.

Chapter 19 shows how SQL statements can be used to create new tables, to load data into newly created tables, and to modify existing tables.

Creating and Updating Tables

In this chapter, we examine additional SQL statements that can be used to perform functions other than queries. We see how to create, alter, and drop table definitions, create indices, and create and drop views. We also discuss the SQL statements that are used to insert new data into existing tables, modify table data, and delete rows from tables.

Although the SQL language provides facilities that implement the data description language facilities needed to create, alter, and drop the definitions of SQL data objects, many relational database software products implement such facilities through user interface functions rather than explicitly using SQL facilities.

CREATING TABLES

The SQL statement used to create a new table definition is the CREATE TABLE statement. Figure 19.1 repeats the tables in the Order Entry database that we introduced in Chapter 15.

The following set of SQL statements might be used to create the three Order Entry database tables:

```
CREATE TABLE Inventory
      (
       Inv_Part_#      SMALLINT NOT NULL,
       PartName        CHARACTER(10),
       OnHand          INTEGER
      )

CREATE TABLE Quotations
      (
       Quo_Supp_#      SMALLINT NOT NULL,
       Quo_Part_#      SMALLINT NOT NULL,
       Price           DECIMAL(5,2),
       Time            SMALLINT,
       OnOrder         INTEGER
      )
```

```
╔═══════════════════════════════════════════════════════════════════╗
║                          Microsoft Access                           ║
╟─────────────────────────────────────────────────────────────────────╢
║  File   Edit   View   Records   Layout   Window   Help              ║
╚═══════════════════════════════════════════════════════════════════╝
```

Inv_Part_#	PartName	OnHand
105	Gear	0
106	Gear	700
124	Bolt	900
125	Bolt	1000
134	Nut	900
135	Nut	1000
171	Generator	500
172	Generator	400
181	Wheel	1000
205	Band	450
206	Motor	225
221	Axle	1500
222	Axle	25
231	Axle	75
232	Axle	150
241	Wheel	300

Table: Inventory — Record: 1

Quo_Supp_#	Quo_Part_#	Price	Time	OnOrder
51	124	$1.25	5	400
51	125	$0.55	5	0
51	134	$0.40	5	500
51	135	$0.39	5	1000
51	221	$0.30	10	10000
51	231	$0.10	10	5000
52	105	$7.50	10	200
52	205	$0.15	20	0
52	206	$0.15	20	0
53	124	$1.35	3	500
53	125	$0.58	3	200
53	134	$0.38	3	200
53	135	$0.42	3	1000
53	222	$0.25	15	10000
53	232		15	0
53	241	$0.08	15	6000

Table: Quotations — Record: 1

Sup_Supp_#	Name	Address	Code
51	Defecto Parts	16 Justamere Lane, Tacoma WA	20
52	Vesuvius Inc	512 Ancient Blvd., Pompeii NY	20
53	Atlantis Co.	8 Ocean Ave., Washington DC	10
54	Titanic Parts	32 Sinking Street, Atlantic City NJ	30
57	Eagle Hardware	64 Tranquility Place, Apollo MN	30
61	Skylab Parts	128 Orbit Blvd., Sydney Australia	10
64	Knight Ltd.	256 Arthur Court, Camelot England	20

Table: Suppliers — Record: 1

Figure 19.1   Order Entry database table contents.

```
CREATE TABLE Suppliers
        (
        Sup_Supp_#        SMALLINT NOT NULL,
        Name              CHARACTER(15),
        Address           VARCHAR(35),
        Code              SMALLINT
        )
```

Table Names

The table name must follow the keywords CREATE TABLE.

The table name given in the CREATE statement can be qualified by adding the *authorization ID* of the person creating the table. Each user, or group of users, that accesses the database software must typically have an authorization ID that identifies that user or group of users to the database software. If the user issuing the CREATE statement has an authorization ID of KKC01, the full table name for the first table would be KKC01.Inventory.

When you are accessing tables that you have created, it is not necessary to specify the authorization ID qualifier; the database software typically uses the current authorization ID as the default qualifier. However, if you are accessing tables created by another user, you may have to qualify the table name with the authorization ID of the person who created it in order to access the table. The SQL authorization scheme is described further in Chapter 20.

Column Definitions

Following the table name is a list of column definitions, separated with commas and enclosed in parentheses. The order in which the column names are listed in the CREATE TABLE statement determines the order in which data is stored in the table.

SQL Data Types

An *SQL data type* is typically specified for each column in a table definition. Each implementation of SQL, and each language with which SQL is used, may have its own set of defined data types. Each SQL implementation, and each supported language, must define its own mapping between host data types and SQL data types.

Box 19.1 describes the most commonly implemented data types that are defined in the SQL language. Box 19.1 also contains notes on how most SQL implementations treat the listed data types. Note that many SQL implementations define additional data types not defined by the SQL standard, and not all standard SQL data types may be supported by a particular implementation. The documentation for the database software in question should be consulted to see how data types are handled by that database software.

BOX 19.1   SQL data types.

Exact Numeric Data Types

- **INTEGER or INT.** Used to store integer data at an implementation-defined precision. The INTEGER data type is typically implemented in the form of 32-bit binary numbers that can be used to store decimal values in the range of ±2,147,483,647.

- **SMALLINT.** Used to store integer data at an implementation-defined precision. The INTEGER data type is typically implemented in the form of 16-bit binary numbers that can be used to store decimal values in the range of ±32,767.

- **NUMERIC, DECIMAL, or DEC.** Used for fixed-point decimal numbers having a fixed number of places after the decimal point. These data type definitions are followed by two numbers in parentheses, where the first number indicates the number of digits in the number and the second the number of decimal positions. For example, a column defined as DECIMAL (6,2) stores six-digit decimal numbers in the range of ±9999.99.

(Continued)

BOX 19.1 *(Continued)*

Approximate Numeric Data Types

- **FLOAT.** Used for floating-point binary numbers with a variable precision. The FLOAT keyword is followed by a number in parentheses that indicates the number of binary digits of precision that are to be used.

- **REAL.** Used for floating-point binary numbers with an implementation-defined precision. In a typical implementation, REAL specifies the use of single-precision floating point numbers that typically have a precision of approximately 23 bits.

- **DOUBLE.** Used for floating-point binary numbers with an implementation-defined precision. In a typical implementation, DOUBLE specifies the use of double-precision floating-point numbers that typically have a precision of approximately 52 bits.

String Data Types

- **CHARACTER or CHAR.** Used to define fixed-length character string data. The length, in characters, for the column is specified in parentheses following the CHAR keyword. For example, a column defined as CHAR (10) stores character strings that each contain 10 characters of alphanumeric data.

- **CHARACTER VARYING, CHAR VARYING, or VARCHAR.** Used to define variable-length character string data. The maximum number of characters for each data item in the column is specified in parentheses following the VARCHAR keyword.

- **BIT.** Used to define fixed-length bit string data. The length, in bits, for the column is specified in parentheses following the BIT keyword. For example, a column defined as BIT (32) stores bit strings that each contain 32 bits of binary data.

- **BIT VARYING.** Used to define variable-length bit string data. The maximum number of bits for the column is specified in parentheses following the BIT VARYING keywords.

Time and Date Data Types

- **DATE.** Used to store a calendar date value, the format of which depends on the SQL implementation.

- **TIME.** Used to store a time-of-day value, the format of which depends on the SQL implementation.

- **TIMESTAMP.** Used to store a value that combines a date and time-of-day value.

Not Null Specifications

In addition to specifying the data type, a column specification can also specify the way in which null data values are to be handled in that column. If we specify NOT NULL for a column, null values will not be allowed in that column. Trying to enter a null value in that column will result in an error condition.

DEFINING REFERENTIAL CONSTRAINTS

When defining tables, we can define any referential constraints that exist between them. This is done by defining primary keys and foreign keys for the tables. As we introduced in Chapter 12, when we define referential integrity constraints among a group of two or more tables, a table that contains a foreign key is called a *dependent table*; a table that contains a corresponding primary key is called a *parent table*.

Defining Primary Keys

The following example shows how we can define primary keys for the Inventory and Suppliers tables:

```
CREATE TABLE Inventory
        (
        Inv_Part_#      SMALLINT NOT NULL,
        PartName        CHAR(10),
        OnHand          INTEGER,
        PRIMARY KEY     (Inv_Part_#)
        )

CREATE TABLE Suppliers
        (
        Sup_Supp_#      SMALLINT NOT NULL,
        Name            CHAR(15),
        Address         VARCHAR(35),
        Code            SMALLINT,
        PRIMARY KEY     (Sup_Supp_#)
        )
```

In the above examples, each primary key consists of a single column. However, it is possible to define more than one column from a table as the primary key by listing all the column names in parentheses in the PRIMARY KEY clause, as with the Quotations table:

```
CREATE TABLE Quotations
        (
        Quo_Supp_#      SMALLINT NOT NULL,
        Quo_Part_#      SMALLINT NOT NULL,
        Price           DECIMAL(5,2),
        Time            SMALLINT,
        OnOrder         INTEGER,
        PRIMARY KEY     (Quo_Supp_#, Quo_Part_#)
        )
```

The column or columns that make up the primary key must have a unique value in each row, and cannot be null.

Defining Foreign Keys

When defining a table with one or more foreign keys, each foreign key must exactly match its corresponding primary key in the parent table; it must consist of the same number of columns and all the columns must be of the same data type and length as the columns that make up the primary key in the parent table. The following CREATE TABLE statement defines two foreign keys for the Quotations table, thus making it dependent on both the Suppliers and Inventory tables:

```
CREATE TABLE Quotations
       (
       Quo_Supp_#       SMALLINT NOT NULL,
       Quo_Part_#       SMALLINT NOT NULL,
       Price            DECIMAL(5,2),
       Time             SMALLINT,
       OnOrder          INTEGER,
       PRIMARY KEY      (Quo_Supp_#, Quo_Part_#),
       FOREIGN KEY      (Quo_Supp_#) REFERENCES Suppliers,
       FOREIGN KEY      (Quo_Part_#) REFERENCES Inventory
       )
```

As with a primary key definition, the FOREIGN KEY keywords are followed by the names of the columns that make up the foreign key. When a foreign key is defined, the database software will ensure that each foreign key value exactly matches an existing primary key value in the corresponding parent table.

With the previous table definitions, the database software will ensure that each supplier number value (Quo_Supp_#) in the Quotations table matches a corresponding supplier number value (Sup_Supp_#) in the Suppliers table and that each part number value (Quo_Part_#) in the Quotations table matches a part number value (Inv_Part_#) in the Inventory table. The database software ensures this correspondence by enforcing constraints on inserting, updating, and deleting rows in the tables. We discuss these constraints in the following sections, in which we show how data manipulation functions are performed.

DROPPING TABLE DEFINITIONS

To delete an entire table, we issue a DROP statement for it:

```
DROP TABLE Inventory
```

When a table is dropped, any data it contains is lost and any views or indices defined on the table are also dropped.

ALTERING TABLE DEFINITIONS

A table's definition can be modified after it has been created by issuing an ALTER TABLE statement. An ALTER statement allows new columns to be added and primary and foreign keys to be added or dropped. Other types of changes, such as changing the type or length of an existing column, must typically be made by first dropping the table and then recreating and reloading it.

The following ALTER TABLE statement adds a new column to the Inventory table:

```
ALTER TABLE Inventory
ADD Bin SMALLINT

SELECT * FROM Inventory
```

Inv_Part_#	PartName	OnHand	Bin
124	Bolt	900	—
125	Bolt	1000	—
105	Gear	0	—
106	Gear	700	—
171	Generator	500	—
172	Generator	400	—
134	Nut	900	—
135	Nut	1000	—
181	Wheel	1000	—
205	Band	450	—
206	Motor	225	—
221	Axle	1500	—
222	Axle	25	—
231	Axle	75	—
232	Axle	150	—
241	Wheel	300	—

When we add a column to a table, we must specify a data type for it in the same manner as when defining a new table. When a new column is added to a table, the database software inserts a null value for that column into each row in the table. Therefore, we cannot specify NOT NULL for a column that we are adding. After we have added a column, we can insert values into it by using INSERT statements, discussed later in this chapter.

We can also add referential constraints to tables by using ALTER to define a primary key or foreign key:

```
ALTER TABLE Inventory
        PRIMARY KEY (Inv_Part_#)

ALTER TABLE       Quotations
        FOREIGN KEY  Part_RC1 (Quo_Part_#)
        REFERENCES   Inventory
```

In the above example, we have explicitly assigned a name (Part_RC1) to this referential constraint. If we do not explicitly assign a name, as in the previous examples in this chapter, the database software typically assigns the name of the first column that makes up the foreign key as the name of the referential constraint.

A referential constraint can be dropped by using an ALTER statement:

```
ALTER TABLE Inventory
        DROP PRIMARY KEY

ALTER TABLE Quotations
        DROP FOREIGN KEY Part_RC1
```

When a primary or foreign key is dropped with ALTER, the key columns and their data values are not dropped; only the relational constraint is removed. A relational constraint is also automatically dropped when either the parent or dependent table is dropped.

DEFINING INDICES

Although they are not defined in the SQL standard, *index* objects are used with many relational database software products. An index contains pointers associated with different key values that are used to retrieve rows, to ensure their uniqueness, or to determine where new rows should be physically stored.

An index is typically created with a CREATE INDEX statement, as shown in the following example:

```
CREATE INDEX X_Quot
ON            Quotations  (Price)
```

The above statement gives the index a name (X_Quot), specifies the table upon which it is defined (Quotations), and specifies the names of the column or columns that make up the key (Price). In the above example, the X_Quot index does not reference a column that contains unique data item values; there may be several rows in the Quotations table that have the same value for price.

A unique index might be defined by including the keyword UNIQUE, as shown in the following example:

```
CREATE UNIQUE INDEX X_Quot_2
ON                  Quotations (Quo_Supp_#, Quo_Part_#)
```

The X_Quot_2 index causes the database software to ensure that there will not be two rows with the same values for supplier number and part number.

When a table is defined with a primary key, some relational database software products require that a unique index must be defined for the table using the primary key column or columns as the index key. Some database software products also recommend that an index be defined for a foreign key as well. A foreign key may or may not have unique values.

DEFINING VIEWS

We can use the CREATE VIEW statement to provide an alternative way of looking at data stored in tables. A view is a logical, or virtual, table that is derived from one or more base tables or other views. In general, views appear to the user as if they are real tables, and they can be operated on in the same manner as base tables. Views have several advantages:

- Views can reduce the perceived complexity of data by allowing simple versions of tables to be presented to users.

- Views can reduce the need for maintenance and can increase flexibility, eliminating much of the need for replication.
- Views can be individually protected, making it easy for authorized end users to make data available without compromising the security of sensitive data.

The following is an example of a single view, named Bolt_Nut, that incorporates data from all three of the sample tables:

```
CREATE VIEW Bolt_Nut
        (SupplierName, Part_#, PartName, LeadTime,
         OnHand, OnOrder, Price, TotalPrice)
    AS SELECT  Name, Quo_Part_#, PartName, Time, OnHand,
               OnOrder, Price, Price * OnOrder
       FROM    Inventory, Quotations, Suppliers,
               Inventory INNER JOIN Quotations
               ON Inv_Part_# = Quo_Part_#,
               Suppliers INNER JOIN Quotations
               ON Sup_Supp_# = Quo_Supp_#
       WHERE   PartName IN ('Nut', 'Bolt')
```

We could now list the contents of the view as if it were a physical table, as follows:

```
SELECT * FROM Bolt_Nut
```

SupplierName	Part_#	PartName	LeadTime	OnHand	OnOrder	Price	TotalPrice
Defecto Parts	124	Bolt	5	900	400	1.25	500
Defeclo Parts	125	Bolt	5	1000	0	0.55	0
Defecto Parts	134	Nut	5	900	500	0.40	200
Defecto Parts	135	Nut	5	1000	1000	0.39	390
Atlantis Co.	124	Bolt	3	900	500	1.35	675
Atlantis Co.	125	Dolt	3	1000	200	0.58	116
Atlantis Co.	134	Nut	3	900	200	0.38	76
Atlantis Co.	135	Nut	3	1000	1000	0.42	420

The above display assumes the original contents of the three tables. Any user who has the required authorization can now refer to Bolt_Nut in subsequent SQL statements as if it were an actual table structured as shown above.

In defining a view, we can use SELECT statements to select, rename, and rearrange columns. We can also use arithmetic expressions or built-in functions to create new columns. We can use any desired conditional expression in selecting rows that will appear in a view. We can use GROUP BY to provide summary data, and we can join tables in any desired manner.

A view is dependent on the underlying table on which it is defined. When we insert, change, or delete data from a view, those changes are applied to the underlying base table. If we drop a base table, views based on that table are also dropped.

The ALTER statement cannot be issued for a view; to change a view, it must be dropped and created again. Dropping a view affects only programs that use the view itself; dropping a view does not affect any of the tables on which the view is based.

INSERTING TABLE DATA

SQL statements are also available for adding, changing, and deleting data in tables. The statements for performing these functions are INSERT, UPDATE, and DELETE. We look first at examples of the INSERT statement for adding new rows to an existing table.

Inserting Individual Rows

We insert new rows into a table with the INSERT statement. The following INSERT statement could be used to add the first row to an empty Inventory table:

```
INSERT INTO Inventory
VALUES (126, 'Bolt', 0)
```

The VALUES clause is used to specify the data values to be inserted. The values must be listed in the same sequence in which the columns were defined in the CREATE TABLE statement. This sequence can be determined by issuing a SELECT * statement for the table. The data values must be consistent with the data types that were specified for the columns in the DEFINE TABLE statement; that is, they must be of the appropriate data types and lengths. If a column allows null values, the keyword NULL can be specified in place of a data value to insert a null value.

We could now issue a SELECT statement to see the results of the previous insertion:

```
SELECT *
FROM      Inventory
```

Inv_Part_#	PartName	OnHand
126	Bolt	0

We can insert data into only selected columns by listing the column names in parentheses following the table name:

```
INSERT INTO Inventory (Inv_Part_#, PartName)
VALUES (105, 'Gear')
```

Null values or default values are inserted in any columns not included in the list of column names, depending on how each column was defined in the CREATE TABLE statement. So in this case, a null value will be entered for OnHand:

```
SELECT * FROM Inventory
```

Inv_Part_#	PartName	OnHand
126	Bolt	0
105	Gear	—

Inserting Rows from Other Tables

Data can also be copied from one table to another by including a SELECT clause in an INSERT statement rather than a VALUES clause:

```
INSERT INTO Inventory (Inv_Part_#)
SELECT   DISTINCT Quo_Part_#
FROM     Quotations
WHERE    Price IS NOT NULL
```

The use of a SELECT statement rather than a VALUES clause allows us to add multiple rows to the table with a single INSERT statement. If we ran the above INSERT statement against an empty Inventory table, the result would be an Inventory table having only Inv_Part_# values in it:

```
SELECT * FROM Inventory
```

Inv_Part_#	PartName	OnHand
124	—	—
125	—	—
134	—	—
135	—	—
221	—	—
231	—	—
105	—	—
205	—	—
206	—	—
222	—	—
241	—	—

Inserting with Referential Integrity Constraints

If we are inserting rows into tables for which we have defined primary keys or foreign keys, the database software places constraints on the values of the primary keys and foreign keys that we can supply in the rows being inserted.

If we are inserting a new row into a table for which we have defined a primary key, the database software will reject the INSERT request if the row we are attempting to add has a primary key value that matches the key of a row already in the table. The database software will also reject the INSERT request if we are attempting to add a row that has a null value in any of the columns that make up the key.

If we are inserting a new row into a table for which we have defined a foreign key, the foreign key value must be either wholly or partially null, or the foreign key value must match the primary key value of a row in the parent table. If the foreign key value is partially null, the entire key is considered null and no part of the value is checked against primary key values in the parent table. The database software rejects the INSERT request if the defined integrity constraints are not satisfied.

UPDATING TABLE DATA

We can modify the data stored in a table by using the UPDATE statement. We can make changes that apply to all rows or only to selected rows, and we can specify new values directly or we can specify calculations to be performed in processing the update.

Updating Individual Rows

The following UPDATE statement modifies a single row in the Quotations table:

```
UPDATE  Quotations
SET     Price = 1.30, Time = 10
WHERE   Quo_Supp_# = 51
        AND
        Quo_Part_# = 124
```

To see the result of the update, we can use a SELECT statement:

```
SELECT  *
FROM    Quotations
WHERE   Quo_Supp_# = 51
        AND
        Quo_Part_# = 124
```

Quo_Supp_#	Quo_Part_#	Price	Time	OnOrder
51	124	1.30	10	400

Only those columns specified in the SET clause are affected by the UPDATE statement. The WHERE clause specifies the row or rows to which the change applies. In the previous example, only one row was updated.

Updating Multiple Rows

The following example increases by 10 percent the value of Price in all rows:

```
UPDATE Quotations
SET Price = Price * 1.10
```

Again, a SELECT statement shows the result of the update:

```
SELECT * FROM Quotations
```

Quo_Supp_#	Quo_Part_#	Price	Time	OnOrder
51	124	1.43	5	400
51	125	0.61	5	0
51	134	0.44	5	500
51	135	0.43	5	1000
51	221	0.33	10	10000
51	231	0.11	10	5000
52	105	8.25	10	200
52	205	0.17	20	0
52	206	0.17	20	0
53	124	1.49	3	500
53	125	0.64	3	200
53	134	0.42	3	200
53	135	0.46	3	1000
53	222	0.28	15	10000

```
53          232      —     15        0
53          241    0.09    15     6000
```

Updating Null Values

Notice that performing an arithmetic operation on a null value always results in a null value. The Price value for the next to the last row still contains a null Price value after the update operation.

Updating with Referential Integrity Constraints

If we have defined a primary key for the table, the database software typically enforces restrictions on the types of changes we can make to the values in columns that make up the primary key of the table. An UPDATE statement that changes any column in the primary key must update only one row. The uniqueness requirement of primary keys causes the database software to reject an UPDATE request that gives a primary key column a null value or attempts to change a primary key value so that it matches the primary key of some other row.

Referential constraints that we have specified by defining foreign keys further restrict the changes that we can make to primary key values. The database software will reject an UPDATE request that attempts to change a primary key value that has a matching foreign key value in a dependent table.

There are also restrictions to the types of changes that we can make to columns that make up a foreign key. If we attempt to change the value of a column that is part of a foreign key, the new foreign key value must be either wholly or partially null or it must match some other primary key value in the parent table.

DELETING TABLE DATA

We can delete rows from a table by issuing a DELETE statement.

Deleting Selected Rows

For example, the following example deletes all rows for supplier 53 from the Quotations table:

```
DELETE FROM Quotations
WHERE Quo_Supp_# = 53

SELECT * FROM Quotations
```

Quo_Supp_#	Quo_Part_#	Price	Time	OnOrder
51	124	1.43	5	400
51	125	0.61	5	0
51	134	0.44	5	500
51	135	0.43	5	1000

51	221	0.33	10	10000
51	231	0.11	10	5000
52	105	8.25	10	200
52	205	0.17	20	0
52	206	0.17	20	0

If we delete all the rows from a table, the table still exists in an empty state. We can later insert new rows into an empty table without having to create it over.

Deleting with Referential Integrity Constraints

Referential constraints on a group of tables for which we have defined primary keys and foreign keys have an impact on DELETE operations. There are no restrictions on deleting rows in a dependent table, but referential constraints can affect DELETE requests for a parent table.

When we define a foreign key, we can include an ON DELETE clause in the FOREIGN KEY specification that defines a *delete rule* for the foreign key. The delete rule determines the way in which the database software handles DELETE requests to ensure that referential constraints are enforced. Commonly implemented values for the ON clause are CASCADE, and SET NULL to specify the delete rules discussed in Chapter 12. With the DELETE CASCADE rule in effect, when we delete a row in a parent table, any rows in dependent tables that contain matching foreign key values are automatically deleted as well. With the DELETE SET NULL rule in effect, if we delete a row from a parent table, the database software changes to null values all matching foreign key values in dependent tables.

The following example shows the use of the ON clause in a FOREIGN KEY specification:

```
CREATE TABLE Quotations
      (
      Quo_Supp_#        SMALLINT NOT NULL,
      Quo_Part_#        SMALLINT NOT NULL,
      Price             DECIMAL(5,2),
      Time              SMALLINT,
      OnOrder           INTEGER,
      PRIMARY KEY       (Quo_Supp_#, Quo_Part_#),
      FOREIGN KEY       (Quo_Supp_#) REFERENCES Suppliers
                        ON DELETE CASCADE
      FOREIGN KEY       (Quo_Part_#) REFERENCES Inventory
                        ON DELETE SET NULL
      )
```

SUMMARY

The CREATE statement is used to add a new table definition to the database. In specifying definitions of the columns making up a table, each column specifies a data type. Possible data types include exact numeric data types, approximate numeric data types, string data types, and time and date data types. Referential constraints are specified for tables by defining primary keys and foreign keys. The DROP statement can be used to delete existing table definitions, and the ALTER statement can be used to modify existing table definitions. The functions of the CREATE, DROP, and ALTER SQL statements are performed in some relational database implementations through user interface functions. The CREATE and DROP statements can be used to create and drop views, and some relational database software products allow the use of the CREATE, DROP, and ALTER statement for working with indices.

The INSERT statement can be used to insert rows of data into a table that has already been defined using the CREATE statement. A VALUES clause is used to specify the data item values to insert into a row. A SELECT clause can be included in an INSERT statement to copy data item values from some other table. The UPDATE statement can be used to update data item values in existing rows. A WHERE clause can be included to specify specific rows, or the UPDATE statement can operate on all rows in the table. The DELETE statement can be used to delete existing rows from a table.

Chapter 20 describes the authorization functions that the ANSI standard version of the SQL language defines.

Authorization Facilities

No query system would be complete without security provisions to prevent unauthorized access to data. Given the potential importance of the data that is maintained by client/server database software, providing security mechanisms can be a key issue. There are several different ways in which access to database resources can be controlled. This chapter examines the authorization system defined by the SQL language. It also briefly discusses additional security facilities that may be provided by external authorization and authentication mechanisms.

Note that the security facilities discussed in this chapter pertain mainly to client/server database software products that manage data that may be accessed by a variety of users. A user may choose not to implement security facilities if the database software is being used to manage data that is accessed by a single user.

AUTHORIZATION FACILITIES

The approach that SQL defines for security is that all users must be *authorized* to perform the functions they request. For example, in order to access database tables and to modify tables or the data they contain, we must have first been granted the proper authorization to do so. Authorization applies to processing performed by application programs as well as processing performed interactively through a query system supported by the database software. Some database software products may allow an application program to be precompiled and compiled without any privileges having been granted. However, it may be necessary to have proper authorization to execute the program.

AUTHORIZATION IDENTIFIERS

Authorization is typically granted by the person or group responsible for administering the database software and is granted on the basis of the *authorization identifiers* that are assigned to users. The database software system administration staff grants and revokes authorization based on the authorization IDs that are assigned to database users.

The primary authorization ID of a user may be supplied through some mechanism that is external to the database software. For example, a user's authorization ID may be the same as the logon identifier that user employs to logon to a network in order to connect to a database server.

PRIVILEGES

Authorization is provided through one or more *privileges* that a user must be granted. A privilege authorizes a user to perform a certain category of actions that can be applied to one or more SQL data objects.

Objects

The SQL data objects on which privileges can be granted include:

- Base tables
- Views
- Columns
- Domains

A particular database software system may define additional classes of objects for which privileges can be granted, such as indices.

Action Categories

The categories of actions associated with privileges refer to the types of SQL statements that can be issued against the object in question. The actions that are associated with privileges vary from one database software to another, but allowable action categories generally carry the names of SQL statements and typically include the following:

- SELECT
- INSERT
- UPDATE
- DELETE

IMPLICIT AUTHORIZATION

Some privileges do not have to be granted explicitly; a user possesses some privileges implicitly, as a result of having been granted other privileges. For example, a user that has SELECT privileges on certain base tables is also allowed to create views based on those tables.

A user that has been granted the privilege to create tables is implicitly authorized to also perform certain operations on the tables that user creates. For example, the user can select, insert, update, and delete data in those tables. Generally, a user that is able to create an SQL data object is also allowed to access, alter, or drop it.

EXPLICIT AUTHORIZATION

Authorization to access SQL objects is explicitly controlled through the use of the GRANT and REVOKE statements. We use the GRANT statement to grant users the privilege to perform certain operations on an SQL object, such as a table or view. We use the REVOKE statement to remove privileges that were previously granted.

Table Privileges

One way to grant privileges is based on *table privileges* in which privileges apply to all the columns in a table. When using the GRANT statement to grant table privileges, we specify the particular type of privilege being granted, the name of the table or tables to which that privilege applies, and the authorization identifiers of one or more users. For example, the following GRANT statement grants the users whose authorization IDs are KKC01 and CLW01 the privilege to issue SELECT statements that reference any of the columns in the Suppliers table:

```
GRANT SELECT
      ON Suppliers
      TO KKC01, CLW01
```

We can also use the keyword ALL to grant privileges for all operations on an object.

```
GRANT ALL
      ON Suppliers
      TO KKC01, CLW01
```

We can use the TO PUBLIC clause to grant privileges to all users:

```
GRANT SELECT ON Geninfo
      TO PUBLIC
```

The above statement allows all users to retrieve data from the Geninfo table.

Column Privileges

As an alternative to granting table privileges, we can grant *column privileges* based on selected columns in a specified table. To do this, we follow the action keyword with a list of column names. The following GRANT statement allows user DEL17PUR to update only the PartName and OnHand columns in the Inventory table:

```
GRANT UPDATE (PartName, OnHand)
      ON Inventory
      TO DEL17PUR
```

Passing Authorization to Other Users

We can add the clause WITH GRANT OPTION to a GRANT statement to give the specified users the privilege to pass on authorization to other users. With the following GRANT statement, we are allowing user DEL17PUR to select data from the Inventory table, to update its part name and on-hand values, and also to grant those privileges to other users:

```
GRANT SELECT, UPDATE (PartName, OnHand)
      ON Inventory
      TO DEL17PUR
      WITH GRANT OPTION
```

REMOVING PRIVILEGES

We can remove privileges that we previously granted by issuing a REVOKE statement:

```
REVOKE SELECT ON Suppliers
       FROM KKC01
```

It is not necessary to revoke all the privileges that were granted, nor is it necessary to revoke privileges from all the users to whom they were granted. The REVOKE statement specifies the operations, tables, and users to which the REVOKE applies.

OTHER SECURITY MECHANISMS

In addition to the SQL authorization system discussed in this chapter, additional security mechanisms that can be used with client/server database software products include the use of views and external security facilities provided by the underlying operating system.

Views

SQL views can be used to control access to sensitive data. We might define a view in such a way that users of the view are restricted to accessing only selected columns or selected rows of the underlying tables. For example, one view might allow users to access general personnel information, but not salaries. Another view might allow a department manager to access salary information for one department but not for others.

External Security Facilities

With some operating systems, passwords can be used to protect the underlying files that are used to implement relational databases. Passwords can be used to protect system files as well as the data sets containing application databases.

Some operating systems implement more elaborate security facilities. For example in the IBM mainframe environment, the *Resource Access Control Facility* (RACF) is a powerful authorization and authentication system that can be used to prevent unauthorized users or applications from accessing databases. RACF can be used to protect specific data sets, direct access storage device volumes, or other system resources.

SUMMARY

The approach to security used by most implementations of SQL is based on granting users authorization to perform required functions. Authorization applies to the processing performed by application programs as well as processing performed interactively through a query system. Authorization is provided by granting users specific privileges based on their authorization identifiers. The SQL objects on which privileges can be granted include base tables, views, columns, and domains. The categories of actions that can be associated with privileges include SELECT, INSERT, UPDATE, and DELETE. Privileges are granted using the GRANT statement and revoked using the REVOKE statement. In addition to granting specific privileges to a user, a user can be given authorization to pass on his or her own privileges to other users.

Additional security mechanisms that SQL implementations may employ include the use of views to control access to sensitive data and external security facilities, including the use of passwords to protect sensitive resources.

Chapter 21 begins our investigation of SQL capabilities for use with conventional programming languages.

Programming with Embedded SQL

In the previous chapters in Part IV, we looked at examples of SQL statements that were invoked interactively using a database software facility that executes SQL statements directly. Most database software products also allow SQL statements to be executed as part of application programs written in some host programming language. SQL statements that are included as part of an application program written in a conventional programming language are referred to as *embedded SQL*. This chapter and the next examine the use of embedded SQL in application programs.

In this chapter, we look at the syntax of embedded SQL statements, discuss the general processing requirements associated with the use of relational data in an application program, and walk through a sample program that illustrates how we can retrieve data from a database by issuing SELECT statements in an application program.

SQL APPLICATION PROGRAMS

The SQL language standard defines bindings for seven different programming languages:

- C
- COBOL
- FORTRAN
- PL/I
- ADA
- Pascal
- MUMPS

Each implementation of SQL defines the host languages it supports and defines specific binding requirements.

A number of approaches are taken with respect to including SQL functions in application programs written in conventional host languages. With one approach, the application program uses host language facilities to make procedure calls to modules that invoke SQL functions. With such an approach, the SQL statement to be executed may be passed to the appropriate procedure in the form of a character string.

An alternative is to allow SQL statements to be intermixed with host language programming statements. With such an approach, a *precompiler* is used that translates the SQL statements into appropriate subroutine calls and parameter lists. The program examples in this book assume that the precompiler approach is used by the database software.

FOURTH-GENERATION LANGUAGES

SQL capabilities have been incorporated into a number of fourth-generation languages that include database capabilities. Many relational database software products are supplied with such fourth-generation languages that have integrated SQL support. For example Microsoft's Access supports a programming language called Access Basic that includes a subset of SQL.

SYNTAX FOR EMBEDDED SQL STATEMENTS

SQL statements that are embedded in an application program typically follow the same general syntax rules as the SQL statements we saw in the previous chapters. In COBOL, PL/I, C, and FORTRAN programs, most database software products require that an SQL statement begin with the keywords "EXEC SQL." Each language may also require that SQL statements be terminated in a particular way. The ending terminators typically used with four commonly used programming languages are shown in Box 21.1. Box 21.2 shows examples of SELECT statements coded in COBOL, PL/I, C, and FORTRAN.

BOX 21.1 SQL statement terminators.	
Language	**Terminator**
COBOL	"END-EXEC."
PL/I	";"
C	";"
FORTRAN	no continuation character in column 6 of the next line

HOST IDENTIFIERS

The names to which SQL statements refer can either be SQL data names known to the database software, such as the names of database tables and columns, or they can be names known only to the application program, such as the names of data elements defined by the program. SQL data names are coded in the normal manner, such as the table column names Quo_Supp_# and OnOrder and the table name Quotations.

```
┌─────────────────────────────────────────────────────┐
│  BOX 21.2   Embedded SELECT statements in             │
│             four programming languages.               │
├─────────────────────────────────────────────────────┤
│                                                       │
│  COBOL                                                │
│        EXEC SQL SELECT    QUO_PART_#, SUM(ONORDER)    │
│                 FROM      QUOTATIONS                   │
│                 GROUP BY QUO_PART_#                    │
│                 ORDER BY QUO_PART_#                    │
│             END-EXEC.                                  │
│                                                       │
│  PL/I                                                 │
│        EXEC SQL SELECT    QUO_PART_#, SUM(ONORDER)    │
│                 FROM      QUOTATIONS                   │
│                 GROUP BY QUO_PART_#                    │
│                 ORDER BY QUO_PART_#;                   │
│                                                       │
│  C                                                    │
│        EXEC SQL SELECT    QUO_PART_#, SUM(ONORDER)    │
│                 FROM      QUOTATIONS                   │
│                 GROUP BY QUO_PART_#                    │
│                 ORDER BY QUO_PART_#;                   │
│                                                       │
│  FORTRAN                                              │
│          EXEC SQL SELECT  QUO_PART_#, SUM(ONORDER)    │
│          C        FROM    QUOTATIONS                   │
│          C        GROUP BY QUO_PART_#                  │
│          C        ORDER BY QUO_PART_#                  │
│                                                       │
└─────────────────────────────────────────────────────┘
```

Names that are known to the application program and not to the database software are called *host identifiers*. A host identifier is generally a data element that is defined in the normal way in the application program. A host identifier is distinguished from an SQL name in an embedded SQL statement by preceding the host identifier with a colon (:). A host identifier is coded without the colon outside of SQL statements.

The following SQL SELECT statement includes both SQL data names and host variable names:

```
SELECT    Quo_Supp_#, Quo_Part_#, OnOrder
FROM      Quotations
INTO      :quo_supp, :quo_part, :onOrder
WHERE     Quo_Supp_# = :save_supp;
```

Host identifiers can be used to provide input to an SQL statement. For example, the :save_supp host identifier in the above example supplies the value for the Quo_Supp_# column of the Quotations table to be used in evaluating the WHERE clause conditional expression. In an application program that issues the above query, the program must store an appropriate value into the field identified by the :save_supp host identifier before executing the query.

Fields named by host identifiers can be used to receive the results of an SQL statement's processing, such as the :quo_supp, :quo_part, and :onOrder host identifiers in the previous example. When the SQL statement is executed, the database software performs the processing specified by the SQL statement and places the results of the query into the :quo_supp, :quo_part, and :onOrder fields. The program can then use the results of the query for any desired processing.

PROCESSING QUERY RESULTS

When we execute an SQL query interactively, the results of the query are normally displayed on the screen of the user interface device. When a query is embedded in an application program, the query results are normally passed to the program for processing. For example, when an SQL SELECT statement returns a single value for each specified column, the values can be placed directly into host variables using an INTO clause, as shown in the examples in Box 21.2. The SELECT statement returns a single supplier number value and a single code value, so the INTO clause causes the returned values to be stored directly into the :supp_no and :supp_code host variables.

However, application programs often issue SQL queries that return multiple rows. The sample retrieval program that we will look at in this chapter is an example of such a program.

SQL RETRIEVAL PROGRAM

Figure 21.1 contains the partial coding for an application program, written in the COBOL language, that issues embedded SQL statements. We have included only the coding that is specifically related to database processing.

This program, although simple in nature, demonstrates the basic coding requirements for an application program that accesses SQL data. We will next examine the sample program, one piece at a time.

The program shown in Fig. 21.1 uses the following SQL SELECT statement query to produce a listing of the part information stored in the Inventory and Quotations tables:

```
SELECT     INV_PART_#, PARTNAME, QUO_SUPP_#, PRICE, ONHAND, ONORD
FROM       INVENTORY, QUOTATIONS,
           INVENTORY INNER JOIN QUOTATIONS
           ON INV_PART_# = QUO_PART_#
WHERE      PRICE > :MINPRICE
ORDER BY   INV_PART_#, QUO_SUPP_#
```

If we processed a similar query as the above using an interactive facility against the table contents shown in Fig. 21.2 and a value of .50 substituted for :MINPRICE, we would receive the results shown at the top of page 276.

```
DATA DIVISION.

WORKING-STORAGE SECTION.

    EXEC SQL DECLARE PARTROW CURSOR FOR
        SELECT   INV_PART_#, PARTNAME, QUO_SUPP_#, PRICE, ONHAND, ONORD
        FROM     INVENTORY, QUOTATIONS,
                 INVENTORY INNER JOIN QUOTATIONS
                 ON INV_PART_# = QUO_PART_#
        WHERE    PRICE >:MINPRICE
        ORDER BY INV_PART_#, QUO_SUPP_#
        END-EXEC.

77  MINPRICE     PIC S999V99 COMP-3.

01  PARTINFO.
    05 PARTNO    PIC S9(4)   COMP.
    05 PARTNAME  PIC X(15).
    05 SUPPNO    PIC S9(4)   COMP.
    05 PRICE     PIC S999V99 COMP-3.
    05 ONHAND    PIC S9(4)   COMP.
    05 ONORD     PIC S9(4)   COMP.

PROCEDURE DIVISION.

    [Initialize processing and store minimum price in MINPRICE.]

PROCESS-PART.
    EXEC SQL OPEN PARTROW END-EXEC.
    EXEC SQL FETCH PARTROW INTO :PARTINFO END-EXEC.
               [Test for no-data condition.]
    IF   NO-DATA
         PERFORM NOINFO-MSG
    ELSE
         PERFORM PROCESS-PARTLINE UNTIL NO-DATA.

    EXEC SQL CLOSE PARTROW END-EXEC.

    STOP RUN.

PROCESS-PARTLINE.
    PERFORM PRINT-PARTLINE.
    EXEC SQL FETCH PARTROW INTO :PARTINFO END-EXEC.
               [Test for no-data condition.]

PRINT-PARTLINE.
    [Print Part Report.]

NOINFO-MESSAGE.
    [Print no-data-found message.]
```

Figure 21.1 Partial COBOL SQL program.

Inv_Part_#	PartName	Quo_Supp_#	Price	OnHand	OnOrder
105	Gear	52	7.50	0	200
124	Bolt	51	1.25	900	400
124	Bolt	53	1.35	900	500
125	Bolt	51	0.55	1000	0
125	Bolt	53	0.58	1000	200

USING A CURSOR

When an SQL query is expected to return multiple rows, we cannot simply assign the values it returns to host variables. Instead, we must declare a *cursor* to be used in conjunction with an associated SQL query. We then use the cursor to successively access the individual rows that the query returns. The following code, taken from our sample program, declares a cursor and its associated query:

```
EXEC SQL DECLARE PARTROW CURSOR FOR
     SELECT     INV_PART_#, PARTNAME, QUO_SUPP_#, PRICE, ONHAND, ONORD
     FROM       INVENTORY, QUOTATIONS,
                INVENTORY INNER JOIN QUOTATIONS
                ON INV_PART_# = QUO_PART_#
     WHERE      PRICE > :MINPRICE
     ORDER BY   INV_PART_#, QUO_SUPP_#
     END-EXEC.
```

The above code associates a cursor named PARTROW with the results that will be returned by the SELECT statement included in the cursor declaration.

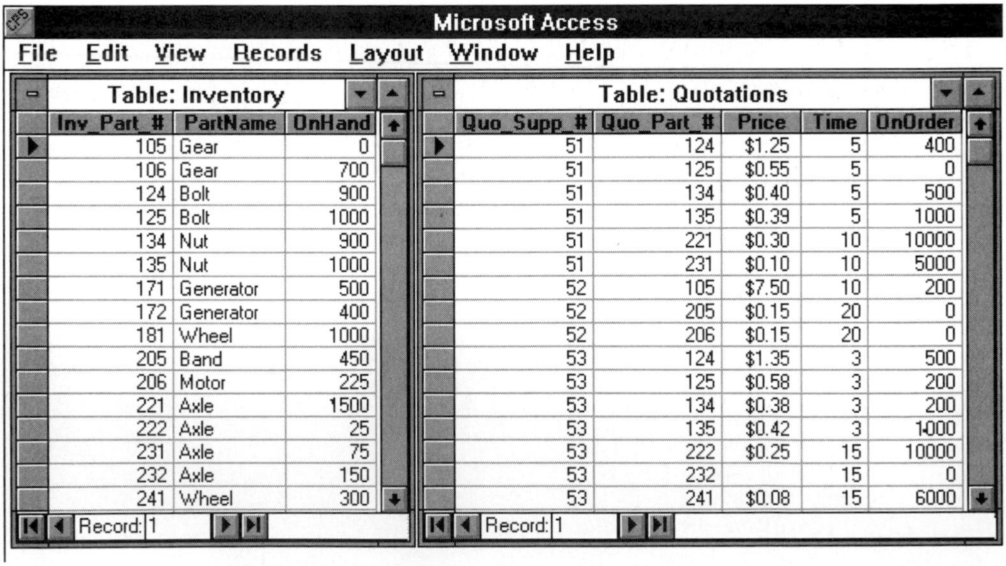

Inv_Part_#	PartName	OnHand
105	Gear	0
106	Gear	700
124	Bolt	900
125	Bolt	1000
134	Nut	900
135	Nut	1000
171	Generator	500
172	Generator	400
181	Wheel	1000
205	Band	450
206	Motor	225
221	Axle	1500
222	Axle	25
231	Axle	75
232	Axle	150
241	Wheel	300

Quo_Supp_#	Quo_Part_#	Price	Time	OnOrder
51	124	$1.25	5	400
51	125	$0.55	5	0
51	134	$0.40	5	500
51	135	$0.39	5	1000
51	221	$0.30	10	10000
51	231	$0.10	10	5000
52	105	$7.50	10	200
52	205	$0.15	20	0
52	206	$0.15	20	0
53	124	$1.35	3	500
53	125	$0.58	3	200
53	134	$0.38	3	200
53	135	$0.42	3	1000
53	222	$0.25	15	10000
53	232		15	0
53	241	$0.08	15	6000

Figure 21.2 Inventory and Quotations table contents.

To initially process the query and to prepare the cursor for processing, we issue an OPEN statement:

```
EXEC SQL OPEN PARTROW END-EXEC.
```

After the OPEN has been executed, we process the first row of the results, by issuing a FETCH statement:

```
EXEC SQL FETCH PARTROW
         INTO :PARTINFO
         END-EXEC.
```

The FETCH statement causes a single row from the query results to be placed into the specified data area. In this case, the specified data area is a data structure whose data element types and lengths match the six data elements that are returned by the SELECT statement:

```
01 PARTINFO.
   05 PARTNO      PIC S9(4)   COMP.
   05 PARTNAME    PIC X(15).
   05 SUPPNO      PIC S9(4)   COMP.
   05 PRICE       PIC S999V99 COMP-3.
   05 ONHAND      PIC S9(4)   COMP.
   05 ONORD       PIC S9(4)   COMP.
```

After accessing the first row, the program performs the necessary processing to determine if it has executed successfully or if it has reached the end of the data in the result table. Each database software implementation specifies details concerning how such conditions are tested. The SQL standard current at the time of writing defines a parameter named SQLSTATE that contains a 5-character code indicating the results of the SQL statement previously executed. An SQLSTATE parameter value of "02000" indicates that there is no more data available in the table being processed. Some SQL implementations that implement earlier versions of the SQL standard use a parameter named SQLCODE for the same purpose. An SQLCODE value of 100 also indicates an end-of-data condition.

If there is no data available after the first FETCH statement is executed, the program assumes that there is no data in the table that satisfies the condition of the SELECT statement, issues a message, and then terminates the program's execution. If the first FETCH does return a row, the program prints the values returned for the first row and then attempts to fetch and print the next row of the results:

```
PROCESS-PARTLINE.
    PERFORM PRINT-PARTLINE.
    EXEC SQL FETCH PARTROW INTO :PARTINFO END-EXEC.
    [Test for no-data condition.]

PRINT-PARTLINE.
    [Print Part Report.]
```

The UNTIL clause in the PERFORM statement that executes PROCESS-PARTLINE causes the program to repeatedly execute PROCESS-PARTLINE, testing for an end-of-data condition after each execution of the FETCH statement. After the program has processed the last row of the results, the program executes a CLOSE statement for the cursor:

```
EXEC SQL CLOSE PARTROW END-EXEC.
```

By closing the cursor, the program can later open the cursor again, if desired, to use the SQL query to produce a new set of results.

THE WHENEVER STATEMENT

As an alternative to explicitly testing the SQLSTATE or SQLCODE parameters, an application program can use a WHENEVER statement to process SQL return codes. A WHENEVER statement is different in scope from an IF statement. An IF statement test is applied only when the IF statement is executed; a WHENEVER statement specifies processing that is to be performed whenever a particular type of condition occurs and applies to *all* SQL statements that follow it in the source code. The SQL standard defines two conditions that can be specified in a WHENEVER statement:

- WHENEVER SQLERROR. Causes the database software to test for any negative return code value.
- WHENEVER NOT FOUND. Causes the database software to test for a condition indicating that no row was found that satisfied the specified operation.

A WHENEVER statement can specify either of the following two actions:

```
WHENEVER condition CONTINUE.
WHENEVER condition GO TO label.
```

CONTINUE causes the program to continue execution with the next program statement when the condition occurs. GO TO passes control to the statement having the specified label.

The processing specified in a WHENEVER statement applies to all SQL statements that follow it *in the source code*, not in the execution path. If we include a single WHENEVER statement at the beginning of the source code, it applies to all the other SQL statements that are executed by the program. If we include a second WHENEVER statement later in the program, the first WHENEVER statement would apply to all SQL statements between the first WHENEVER statement and the second WHENEVER statement; the second WHENEVER statement would apply to all the SQL statements that follow it in the source code.

Figure 21.3 shows a version of the sample program from Fig. 21.1, in which a WHENEVER statement handles the end-of-data condition. In this version of the program, we do not print a message when the initial FETCH returns no values. We simply terminate the program when end of data is reached.

LOADING DATA INTO TABLES

Individual relational database software products provide various facilities for loading data into newly defined tables. These may include various types of utility programs as well as

```
DATA DIVISION.

WORKING-STORAGE SECTION.

    EXEC SQL DECLARE PARTROW CURSOR FOR
        SELECT   INV_PART_#, PARTNAME, QUO_SUPP_#, PRICE, ONHAND, ONORD
        FROM     INVENTORY, QUOTATIONS,
                 INVENTORY INNER JOIN QUOTATIONS
                 ON INV_PART_# = QUO_PART_#
        WHERE    PRICE > :MINPRICE
        ORDER BY INV_PART_#, QUO_SUPP_#
        END-EXEC.

    EXEC SQL INCLUDE SQLCA END-EXEC.

77 MINPRICE        PIC S999V99 COMP-3.

01 PARTINFO.
    05 PARTNO      PIC S9(4)   COMP.
    05 PARTNAME    PIC X(15).
    05 SUPPNO      PIC S9(4)   COMP.
    05 PRICE       PIC S999V99 COMP-3.
    05 ONHAND      PIC S9(4)   COMP.
    05 ONORD       PIC S9(4)   COMP.

PROCEDURE DIVISION.

        [Initialize processing and store minimum price in MINPRICE.]

PROCESS-PART.

WHENEVER NOT FOUND GO TO END-JOB.
    EXEC SQL OPEN PARTROW END-EXEC.

GET-ROW.

    EXEC SQL FETCH PARTROW INTO :PARTINFO END-EXEC.
    PERFORM PRINT-PARTLINE.
    GO TO GET-ROW.

END-JOB.

    EXEC SQL CLOSE PARTROW END-EXEC.

    STOP RUN.

PRINT-PARTLINE.
        [Print Part Report.]
```

Figure 21.3   Using a WHENEVER statement to test a condition.

support for the SQL INSERT statement for inserting new rows into tables. The INSERT statement can be used to insert rows one at a time or to copy data from one table to another, processing multiple rows with a single statement.

When we load data into a table using INSERT statements embedded in an application program, we can insert data into the table one row at a time, as in the following embedded SQL INSERT statement example:

```
EXEC SQL INSERT INTO Inventory
            VALUES (:trpart, :trname, :tronhand);
```

The above statement inserts one row of data at a time into the Inventory table, using host variables to specify data element values for the three table columns.

We can also insert data only into selected columns by naming the columns:

```
EXEC SQL INSERT INTO Inventory (Inv_Part_#, PartName)
            VALUES (:trpart, :trname);
```

Null values are inserted in any columns not included in the list of column names; in the above example, a null value is entered for the OnHand column.

INSERTING MULTIPLE ROWS

We can also issue INSERT statements that copy data from one table to another by including a SELECT statement rather than a VALUES clause in the INSERT statement:

```
EXEC SQL INSERT INTO Inventory (Inv_Part_#)
            SELECT DISTINCT Quo_Part_#
            FROM            Quotations
            WHERE           Price IS NOT NULL;
```

With the above type of INSERT statement, data is inserted into multiple rows with a single execution of the INSERT statement. Copying from one table to another is often done to create test tables that contain data that is extracted from a production database.

MODIFYING DATA

Application programs with embedded SQL can include SQL statements that perform all the traditional update operations of row insertion, row modification, and row deletion. Figure 21.4 contains the partial coding for a program that updates the Quotations table.

The first procedure in the program, ADD-QUOT, adds a new row to the table with an INSERT statement. The data element values for the row being added are supplied using host variables. Following the INSERT statement, the program tests for a duplicate key value to determine if an attempt is being made to add a row for which that key value already exists. The program might test an SQLSTATE or SQLCODE parameter value for this purpose.

The second procedure, CHANGE-QUOT, uses an UPDATE statement to modify the data in an existing row. Again, the values used for the update are supplied using host variables. Following the UPDATE statement, the program tests for a no-data condition, again possibly using SQLSTATE or SQLCODE. A no-data condition indicates that no Quotations table row was found with the values indicated in the WHERE clause.

```
DATA DIVISION.

WORKING-STORAGE SECTION.

01 QUOT-TRANS
   02  QUOSUPP-TRANS   PIC S9(4)    COMP.
   02  QUOPART-TRANS   PIC S9(4)    COMP.
   02  PRICE-TRANS     PIC S999V99 COMP.
   02  TIME-TRANS      PIC S9(4)    COMP.
   02  ONORDER-TRANS   PIC S9(4)    COMP.
   02  TYPE-TRANS      PIC X.
   .
   .
   .
PROCEDURE DIVISION.

   [Initialize processing, get transaction, edit, determine type,
   and perform appropriate processing routine.]
```

Routine to add a row to the Quotations table.

```
ADD-QUOT.
   EXEC SQL INSERT INTO QUOTATIONS
              (QUO_SUPP_#, QUO_PART_#, PRICE, TIME, ONORDER)
          VALUES
              (:QUOSUPP-TRANS, :QUOPART-TRANS, :PRICE-TRANS,
               :TIME-TRANS, :ONORDER-TRANS)
       END-EXEC.
   [Test for duplicate.]
       IF DUPLICATE-DATA PERFORM DUPLICATE-ADD.
```

Routine to update a row in the Quotations table.

```
CHANGE-QUOT.
   EXEC SQL UPDATE QUOTATIONS
          SET PRICE          = :PRICE-TRANS,
              TIME           = :TIME-TRANS
              ONORDER        = :ONORDER-TRANS
          WHERE QUO_SUPP_#   = :QUOSUPP-TRANS
            AND QUO_PART_#   = :QUOPART-TRANS
       END-EXEC.
   [Test for no data.]
       IF NO-DATA PERFORM TRANS-NOT-FOUND.
```

Routine to delete a row from the Quotations table.

```
DELETE-QUOT.
   EXEC SQL DELETE FROM QUOTATIONS
          WHERE QUO_SUPP_#   = :QUOSUPP-TRANS
            AND QUO_PART_#   = :QUOPART-TRANS
       END-EXEC.
   [Test for no data.]
       IF NO-DATA PERFORM TRANS-NOT-FOUND.
```

Figure 21.4 Partial program that modifies Quotations table data.

   The third routine, DELETE-QUOT, issues a DELETE statement to delete a row. Host variables are used to identify the row to be deleted. As with the UPDATE statement, the program tests for a no-data condition, which indicates that the row to be deleted does not exist in the table.

MODIFYING MULTIPLE ROWS

The partial program in Fig. 21.4 uses INSERT, UPDATE, and DELETE statements that affect one row of the table at a time. However, just as with interactive SQL, a program can issue SQL statements that update multiple rows. For example, the following embedded SQL statement could be used to update all the Quotations table rows for a given supplier:

```
EXEC SQL UPDATE Quotations
            SET Price = Price * 1.10
            WHERE Quo_Supp_# = :quosupp_trans;
```

Similarly, we could issue a single statement that deletes multiple rows:

```
EXEC SQL DELETE FROM Quotations
            WHERE Quo_Supp_# = :quosupp_trans;
```

And we can add multiple rows to a table, in the same way that we load data into a new table, by selecting data from some other table:

```
EXEC SQL INSERT INTO Quotations
                (Quo_Supp_#, Quo_Part_#, Price)
                SELECT Supp_#, Part_#, QuotPrice
                FROM   Newsupp;
```

In the above example, we are assuming that there is a table named Newsupp that contains the supplier number, part numbers, and prices for a new supplier that we are adding to the Quotations table.

UPDATING USING A CURSOR

As an alternative to the types of statements discussed above, a program can use a cursor to handle multiple updates one row at a time. The partial program in Fig. 21.5 shows an example of updating the Quotations table using a cursor. In the program in Fig 21.5, we are using a cursor and its associated SELECT statement to process all the rows from the Quotations table for a particular supplier number. We retrieve each row using a FETCH statement and perform the CHECK_PRICE_CHANGE procedure to determine if the price should be increased. If so, we issue an UPDATE statement, referencing the row currently pointed to by the cursor, to change the Price value in that row.

The UPDATE statement clause that refers to the row currently referenced by the cursor is:

```
WHERE CURRENT OF QUOT_CURSOR
```

In order to update a column using a WHERE CURRENT OF *cursor* clause, the DECLARE statement for the cursor must specify that the column is eligible for updating. The pertinent clause in the DECLARE statement for QUOT_CURSOR is:

```
FOR UPDATE OF PRICE
```

```
DATA DIVISION.
WORKING-STORAGE SECTION.

        EXEC SQL DECLARE QUOT-CURSOR FOR
                    SELECT * FROM QUOTATIONS
                       WHERE QUO_SUPP_# = :SUPPNO-IN
                       FOR UPDATE OF PRICE
            END-EXEC.

77   SUPPNO-IN       PIC 999.
77   CALC-PRICE      PIC S999V99     COMP-3.

01   QUOT-INFO
        02   SUPPNO    PIC S9(4)      COMP.
        02   PARTNO    PIC S9(4)      COMP.
        02   PRICE     PIC S999V99    COMP-3.
        02   TIME      PIC S9(4)      COMP.
        02   ONORDER   PIC S9(4)      COMP.

PROCEDURE DIVISION.

        [Initialize processing.]

    EXEC SQL WHENEVER SQLERROR
            GO TO SQL-PROBLEM
        END-EXEC.

        [Get supplier number.]

    PERFORM CHANGE-SUPP.
        .
        .

CHANGE-SUPP.
    EXEC SQL OPEN QUOT-CURSOR
        END-EXEC.
    EXEC SQL FETCH QUOT-CURSOR INTO :QUOT-INFO
        END-EXEC.
        [Test for no data.]
    IF NO-DATA PERFORM SUPP-NOT-FOUND
    ELSE
        PERFORM PROCESS-SUPP UNTIL NO-DATA.
    EXEC SQL CLOSE QUOT-CURSOR
        END-EXEC.

PROCESS-SUPP.
    PERFORM CHECK-PRICE-CHANGE.
    IF CHANGE-OK
        EXEC SQL UPDATE QUOTATIONS
                    SET PRICE = :CALC-PRICE
                    WHERE CURRENT OF QUOT-CURSOR
            END-EXEC.
    EXEC SQL FETCH QUOT-CURSOR INTO :QUOT-INFO
        END-EXEC.

SQL-PROBLEM.
        [Print message.]
    STOP RUN.
```

This statement updates the row to which the cursor currently points.

Figure 21.5   Partial program that uses a cursor to update Quotations table data.

Our example specifies that a single column is eligible for updating; however, multiple columns can be specified in the FOR UPDATE clause if desired. They can then be included in the SET clause of the UPDATE statement.

There is one restriction concerning updating table columns with a cursor. A column that is part of a primary key cannot be updated using a cursor.

DELETING DATA USING A CURSOR

Rows can also be deleted a row at a time when results are being processed using a cursor. The following is an example of a DELETE statement that could be used to delete the row currently referenced by the cursor:

```
EXEC SQL DELETE FROM      Quotations
              WHERE CURRENT OF quot_cursor;
```

It is not necessary to specify column names in a FOR UPDATE clause in the DECLARE CURSOR statement in order to delete rows.

SYNCHRONIZATION PROCESSING

When data is updated in an environment that allows concurrent access to data by multiple users, precautions must be taken to ensure that data integrity problems do not occur. For example, if two programs were permitted to change the same row of a table at the same time, these changes might be recorded incorrectly. For example, the DB2 database software uses a system of resource locks to prevent problems associated with concurrent access. Many other client/server database software products implement similar mechanisms.

Before a program is allowed to make a change to data in a table, locks must be placed on any resources needed to make the change. The program then releases the locks when the change processing is completed. No other user can access the resources until the locks are released.

Most client/server database software products handle the placing and releasing of locks automatically. However, many database software products also allow an application program to affect how long locks are held by allowing it to explicitly establish synchronization points during update processing. When a program establishes a synchronization point, it specifies either that changes made up to that point are to be considered committed, or permanent, or that the changes should be rolled back, or undone. When a program establishes a synchronization point, any locks being held on resources are released.

Establishing Synchronization Points

A program implicitly establishes a synchronization point by terminating either normally or abnormally. If a program terminates normally, all changes made to that point are committed; if the program terminates abnormally, changes are rolled back.

Database software that allows programs to establish additional synchronization points to control recovery processing typically implements the SQL COMMIT and ROLLBACK statements. Figure 21.6 shows a portion of a program that explicitly establishes synchronization points by issuing the COMMIT and ROLLBACK statements. The partial program in Fig 21.6 updates the Quotations table. If the update is successful, the change is committed. If it is not successful, the WHENEVER statement causes the ROLLBACK statement to be executed, causing the database software to undo any changes the program made to the database up to that point.

Units of Recovery

The processing that is performed from one synchronization point to the next is often called a *unit of recovery*. A unit of recovery always begins at the start of a program's execution and ends when the program establishes a synchronization point. As we stated previously, a program can explicitly establish a synchronization point by executing a statement such as COMMIT or ROLLBACK, or it can implicitly define a synchronization point by terminating normally or abnormally.

```
            .
            .
CHANGE-QUOT.
    EXEC SQL WHENEVER SQLERROR
            GO TO UNDO
        END-EXEC.
    EXEC SQL UPDATE QUOTATIONS
            SET PRICE        = :PRICE-TRANS,
                TIME         = :TIME-TRANS,
                ONORDER      = :ONORDER-TRANS
            WHERE QUO_SUPP_#  = :QUOSUPP-TRANS
              AND QUO_PART_#  = :QUOPART-TRANS
        END-EXEC.
    IF SQL-CODE = NO-DATA
        PERFORM TRANS-NOT-FOUND
    ELSE
        EXEC SQL COMMIT END-EXEC.   ◄──── The COMMIT statement commits all
                                          changes that have been made since
                                          the previous synchronization point.
CHANGE-QUOT-EXIT.
    EXIT.

UNDO.
    EXEC SQL ROLLBACK END-EXEC.  ◄──── The ROLLBACK statements cause
    EXIT.                              the DBMS to undo any changes
                                       that were made since the previous
TRANS-NOT-FOUND.                       synchronization point.
    EXEC SQL ROLLBACK END-EXEC.  ◄────
            .
            .
```

Figure 21.6   Partial program that establishes synchronization points.

When a unit of recovery ends, all changes are either committed or rolled back. If a system failure occurs during a unit of recovery, all changes made during that unit are rolled back so the database is restored to the condition that existed at the beginning of the unit of recovery.

When a program does not explicitly define synchronization points, the unit of recovery encompasses the entire execution of the program. This type of processing might be appropriate for a program that executes quickly, possibly processing a single transaction each time it executes. Program termination automatically generates the necessary synchronization point.

If a program executes for a longer period of time, perhaps processing a series of transactions where each transaction is independent of the others, it is often better to define a separate synchronization point after processing each transaction. With this approach, the program may create a separate unit of recovery for each transaction. If a long-running program does not explicitly define synchronization points during its execution, it may interfere with other programs that may require concurrent access to the same databases.

Processing Related Transactions

It is not always appropriate to create a separate unit of recovery for each transaction processed. For example, suppose we were processing the Suppliers and Quotations tables, shown in Fig. 21.7, and we wanted to change a supplier number value in both tables. We would probably not want to commit the changes until we know that both tables have been successfully changed, otherwise it might be possible for the following sequence of events to occur:

1. Update the Suppliers table.
2. Commit the change to the Suppliers table.
3. Update the Inventory table.
4. An error occurs.
5. The change to the Inventory table is backed out.

At this point, we have a situation in which the Suppliers table has been updated but the Inventory table has not.

A possible approach for processing multiple updates in a single unit of recovery is illustrated in Fig. 21.8. If an error occurs during processing of either table, the WHENEVER statement will cause the ROLLBACK to be executed, and any changes made up to that point will be rolled back. If both tables are updated successfully, the COMMIT statement causes all changes to be committed.

SUMMARY

SQL application programs can be written in a variety of conventional programming languages and in a number of fourth-generation languages as well. Host identifiers defined within an application program can be used in an SQL statement to provide input to an SQL

Table: Quotations

Quo_Supp #	Quo_Part #	Price	Time	OnOrder
51	124	$1.25	5	400
51	125	$0.55	5	0
51	134	$0.40	5	500
51	135	$0.39	5	1000
51	221	$0.30	10	10000
51	231	$0.10	10	5000
52	105	$7.50	10	200
52	205	$0.15	20	0
52	206	$0.15	20	0
53	124	$1.35	3	500
53	125	$0.58	3	200
53	134	$0.38	3	200
53	135	$0.42	3	1000
53	222	$0.25	15	10000
53	232		15	0
53	241	$0.08	15	6000

Record: 1

Table: Suppliers

Sup_Supp #	Name	Address	Code
51	Defecto Parts	16 Justamere Lane, Tacoma WA	20
52	Vesuvius Inc	512 Ancient Blvd., Pompeii NY	20
53	Atlantis Co.	8 Ocean Ave., Washington DC	10
54	Titanic Parts	32 Sinking Street, Atlantic City NJ	30
57	Eagle Hardware	64 Tranquility Place, Apollo MN	30
61	Skylab Parts	128 Orbit Blvd., Sydney Australia	10
64	Knight Ltd.	256 Arthur Court, Camelot England	20

Record: 1

Figure 21.7   Quotations and Suppliers table contents.

statement or to receive the results of the processing of an SQL statement. A host identifier name is preceded by a colon when used in an SQL statement.

The results of SQL statements typically consist of a table containing multiple rows. When a SELECT statement may return multiple rows, an application program can use a cursor to process the resulting rows individually. The cursor is defined for a particular SELECT statement and is processed by the program using OPEN, FETCH, and CLOSE statements.

Database software implementations use a variety of methods for determining whether an SQL statement has executed successfully and for testing for various conditions, such as reaching the end of the available data in a result table. The current SQL standard defines an SQLSTATE parameter that contains a 5-character code indicating SQL statement results. Some SQL implementations use an SQLCODE parameter for a similar purpose. As an alternative to explicitly testing SQLSTATE or SQLCODE parameter values, a WHENEVER statement can be used to specify the processing to be performed when various conditions occur.

Individual relational database software products provide various means for loading data into newly defined tables. The SQL standard defines an INSERT statement that can be used for this purpose. The INSERT statement can be used to insert rows one at a time, and to copy tables from one table to another.

```
        .
        .
        .
CHANGE-SUPPNO.
    EXEC SQL WHENEVER SQLERROR GO TO UNDO
        END-EXEC.
    EXEC SQL UPDATE SUPPLIERS
            SET SUPPNO = :NEW-SUPP
            WHERE SUPPNO = :CURR-SUPP
        END-EXEC.
      [Test for no data.]
    IF NO-DATA PERFORM SUPP-NOT-FOUND
    ELSE
        PERFORM CHANGE-QUOT.
CHANGE-SUPPNO-EXIT.
    EXIT.


UNDO.
    EXEC SQL ROLLBACK END-EXEC.  ◄────
    GO TO CHANGE-SUPPNO-EXIT
```

> This statement rolls back all changes if an error occurs during the execution of any SQL statement.

```
CHANGE-QUOT.
    EXEC SQL OPEN QUOT-CURSOR END-EXEC.
    EXEC SQL FETCH QUOT-CURSOR INTO :QUOT-INFO
        END-EXEC.
      [Test for no data.]
    IF NO-DATA GO TO CHANGE-QUOT-EXIT.


PERFORM PROC-QUOT UNTIL NO-DATA.
    EXEC SQL COMMIT END-EXEC.   ◄────
    EXEC SQL CLOSE QUOT-CURSOR END-EXEC.
CHANGE-QUOT-EXIT.
    EXIT.
```

> This statement commits changes after all updates have been successfully completed.

```
PROC-QUOT.
    EXEC SQL UPDATE QUOTATIONS
            SET QUO_SUPP_# = :NEW-SUPP
            WHERE CURRENT OF QUOT-CURSOR
        END-EXEC.
    EXEC SQL FETCH QUOT-CURSOR INTO :QUOT-INFO
        END-EXEC.
      [Test for no data.]
        .
        .
```

Figure 21.8 A partial program in which a single unit of recovery is used to process a group of related updates.

Individual database software products also provide various means for updating existing tables, including inserting new rows, modifying existing rows, and deleting rows. The SQL INSERT, UPDATE, and DELETE statements are defined by the SQL standard for performing table updating operations.

The SQL language includes the COMMIT and ROLLBACK statements that can be employed with a system of locks for controlling concurrent access to a database by multiple users. The COMMIT and ROLLBACK statements establish synchronization points that define units of recovery to control recovery processing. At the end of each unit of recovery, all changes that have been made to the database are either all considered permanent or all removed from the database.

Chapter 22 concludes this book with a look at dynamic SQL statements that can be modified at execution time by the application program.

Programming with Dynamic SQL

All the examples of embedded SQL statements we looked at in Chapter 21 are examples of *static SQL statements*. In those examples, we knew the statement type and general structure of each statement ahead of time, and we coded the SQL statements directly into the program. Many SQL implementations also support *dynamic SQL*. With dynamic SQL, an application program can construct SQL statements as it executes rather than compiling the SQL statements directly into the source code. The SQL standard includes a dynamic SQL specification. In this chapter, we examine the processing required to construct and execute SQL statements dynamically.

STATIC SQL STATEMENT EXECUTION

With static SQL statements, each SQL statement is fixed before the program executes. With static SQL statements, we generally use host variables to change the way a statement executes, as illustrated in the following SQL statement example:

```
EXEC SQL UPDATE Quotations
         SET    Price = :price_trans,
                Time = :time_trans,
                OnOrder = :onorder_trans
         WHERE  Quo_Supp_# = :quosupp_trans
                AND
                Quo_Part_# = :quopart_trans;
```

DYNAMIC SQL STATEMENT EXECUTION

With dynamic SQL, the application program can construct SQL statements in data areas at run time, based on inputs available to the program, and then execute the generated statements. The SQL statements can be modified as necessary by the application program, and the actual SQL statements that are executed may vary from one execution of the program to another.

Not all SQL statements can be constructed and executed dynamically. Box 22.1 lists some of the statements that cannot execute dynamically. Also, the process used for preparing and executing a dynamic SQL statement varies with the type of statement.

> ## BOX 22.1   SQL statements that cannot be executed dynamically.
>
> - CLOSE
> - DECLARE
> - DESCRIBE
> - EXECUTE
> - EXECUTE IMMEDIATE
> - FETCH
> - OPEN
> - PREPARE
> - WHENEVER

STATEMENTS OTHER THAN SELECT

The process used for dynamically executing an SQL statement is simplest if we know that the generated statement will not be a SELECT statement. For this type of dynamic SQL statement, the following steps are involved:

1. Construct an image of the SQL statement in a data area and verify that it is of an appropriate type to execute dynamically.
2. Execute the statement by issuing an EXECUTE IMMEDIATE statement that refers to the data area containing the image of the SQL statement to be executed.
3. Handle any error conditions that may occur.

The EXECUTE IMMEDIATE statement performs the same functions that are performed when an application program executes a similar static SQL statement.

FIXED-LIST SELECT STATEMENTS

A dynamic SELECT statement that always returns the same number and type of data elements is known as a *fixed-list SELECT statement*. Since the number and types of the data elements to be returned is known ahead of time, appropriate host variables can be defined in the application program's source code.

A program typically executes a dynamic SELECT statement of the fixed-list variety in the following manner:

1. Construct an image of the SELECT statement in a data area.
2. Issue a PREPARE statement that refers to the data area containing the SELECT statement image. The PREPARE statement translates the image of the SELECT statement into executable form.
3. Declare a cursor that references the name of the data area that contains the SELECT statement image.

4. Use the cursor to process the SELECT statement by opening the cursor, fetching rows, and closing the cursor.

5. Handle any error conditions that may occur.

The number, type, and size of the data elements returned by a fixed-list dynamic SELECT statement cannot be changed at execution time. A fixed-list SELECT statement is often useful when the SELECT statement must be able to refer to different tables of the same type or when the program wishes to vary the selection conditions that are specified in the SELECT statement's WHERE clause.

VARYING-LIST SELECT STATEMENTS

If the definition of the variables to be returned by a SELECT statement is to be modified dynamically, the process of executing a dynamic SELECT statement becomes more complex. Since the number and types of the data elements to be returned are not known in advance, and cannot be compiled into the source code, appropriate host variables cannot be defined. This means that storage for the data elements returned must be allocated dynamically by the application program. Address pointers to the values returned must also be established at execution time.

The typical process used for executing a varying-list SELECT statements is as follows:

1. Construct an image of the SELECT statement in a data area.

2. Declare a cursor for the SELECT statement naming the data area that contains the image of the SELECT statement.

3. Issue a PREPARE statement to translate the SELECT statement into executable form.

4. Issue a DESCRIBE statement, which returns information about the type and size of each of the data times that will be returned.

5. Determine the amount of storage that will be required for a row of retrieved data, based on the information returned by the DESCRIBE statement. Allocate the storage required.

6. Determine an address for each item of retrieved data that will be returned by the SELECT statement and insert these addresses in the appropriate variables to tell the database software where to store each retrieved item.

7. Open the cursor, fetch rows, and close the cursor.

8. Free the storage allocated for the retrieved data elements.

9. Handle any error conditions that may occur.

LANGUAGE REQUIREMENTS

Generally, dynamic SQL applications can be coded using any of the conventional programming languages that the database software supports. However, the addressing and storage allocation requirements associated with varying-list SELECT statements generally limit their use to applications coded in languages like PL/I, Assembler, and C, that permit easy access to underlying operating system facilities. For example, it is difficult in a fourth-generation language or in a COBOL or FORTRAN program to handle storage allocation and the storing of the data element addresses without resorting to Assembler subroutines.

SUMMARY

With dynamic SQL, the application program can construct SQL statements in data areas at run time, based on inputs available to the program. The generated statements are then executed. The SQL statements can be modified as necessary by the application program, and the actual SQL statements that are executed may vary from one execution of the program to another.

Dynamic SQL statements are handled somewhat differently depending on whether the SQL statements are other than SELECT statements, fixed-list SELECT statements, or varying-list SELECT statements.

Dynamic SQL statements can be executed using any programming language that supports SQL but are best handled using languages that permit easy access to low-level operating system facilities.

PART VI

APPENDICES

Appendix A

Query by Example

Many relational database software systems that support SQL for implementing a client/server environment support additional query languages that are meant to be employed by end users. Many of these end-user query languages are based on a particularly successful and easy-to-use query language called *Query by Example* (QBE). This appendix shows how QBE can be used to perform many of the same functions that were shown in Part IV using SQL.

QBE uses a very different syntax than SQL. Rather than using English-like statements, QBE displays table structures on the display of a user interface device and allows the user to manipulate the display directly to define the operations to be performed. The user can see the tables on the screen, fill them in, and request various types of operations—such as display, update, insert, and delete—by making appropriate entries on the display.

Each vendor of a relational database product that has developed a query language based on QBE has implemented the language in a slightly different way. Most use the rich facilities provided by modern graphical user interfaces to make the basic QBE language particularly easy for end users to employ in formulating queries.

For ease of presentation of QBE examples, we use the implementation of QBE that is part of the Query Management Facility (QMF) used in conjunction with IBM's DB2 for mainframes. The QMF implementation of QBE is a character-oriented implementation of the language that is designed to be used in conjunction with 3270-type terminals and has a syntax that is close to the original version of the QBE language. If a user understands the basic characteristics of the QBE language, it is a simple matter to apply those principles to a particular, possibly graphically-oriented, implementation of the language.

DISPLAYING TABLE STRUCTURES

QBE is used to manipulate the rows and columns of the tables making up a relational database. Figure A.1 shows the tables of the Order Entry database to which the QBE examples in this appendix refer.

Table: Inventory		
Inv_Part_#	PartName	OnHand
105	Gear	0
106	Gear	700
124	Bolt	900
125	Bolt	1000
134	Nut	900
135	Nut	1000
171	Generator	500
172	Generator	400
181	Wheel	1000
205	Band	450
206	Motor	225
221	Axle	1500
222	Axle	25
231	Axle	75
232	Axle	150
241	Wheel	300

Record: 1

Table: Quotations				
Quo_Supp_#	Quo_Part_#	Price	Time	OnOrder
51	124	$1.25	5	400
51	125	$0.55	5	0
51	134	$0.40	5	500
51	135	$0.39	5	1000
51	221	$0.30	10	10000
51	231	$0.10	10	5000
52	105	$7.50	10	200
52	205	$0.15	20	0
52	206	$0.15	20	0
53	124	$1.35	3	500
53	125	$0.58	3	200
53	134	$0.38	3	200
53	135	$0.42	3	1000
53	222	$0.25	15	10000
53	232		15	0
53	241	$0.08	15	6000

Record: 1

Table: Suppliers			
Sup_Supp_#	Name	Address	Code
51	Defecto Parts	16 Justamere Lane, Tacoma WA	20
52	Vesuvius Inc	512 Ancient Blvd., Pompeii NY	20
53	Atlantis Co.	8 Ocean Ave., Washington DC	10
54	Titanic Parts	32 Sinking Street, Atlantic City NJ	30
57	Eagle Hardware	64 Tranquility Place, Apollo MN	30
61	Skylab Parts	128 Orbit Blvd., Sydney Australia	10
64	Knight Ltd.	256 Arthur Court, Camelot England	20

Record: 1

Figure A.1   Order Entry database table contents.

A user typically begins interacting with QBE by displaying an outline of the table to be manipulated. The following shows a QBE outline of the Quotations table as it might be presented on a character-oriented user-interface device:

Quotations	Quo_Supp_#	Quo_Part_#	Price	Time	OnOrder

The table name appears on the left, followed by the table's column names, in the order in which the column names were defined when the table was created.

There may be times when not all the columns will fit on the screen. For large tables, keys on the user-interface device or graphical elements on the display may be provided that allow the display to be scrolled to the left and right. Once we have displayed a table's columns, we can typically tell QBE that we will not be working with certain columns. QBE then eliminates that column from the display. This has no effect on the underlying table, just on the display.

ENTERING A QBE QUERY

In the character-oriented version of QBE that we are using to present examples, we define a query by entering operators and values in the table structure. For example, suppose we wanted to perform the following query, expressed in the form of an SQL SELECT statement:

```
SELECT    *
FROM      Quotations
WHERE     Quo_Part_# = 124
```

If we are using the QMF implementation of QBE, and the table structure shown previously, we could perform the above query by entering a "P." operator (meaning print) under the table name and the value "124" under the Quo_Part_# column:

Quotations	Quo_Supp_#	Quo_Part_#	Price	Time	OnOrder
P.		124			

Entering a "P." operator under a specific column indicates that we want values displayed for that column; entering the "P." operator under the table name indicates that we want all columns displayed. Entering the value "124" in the Quo_Part_# column indicates that we want only rows that have a Quo_Part_# value of 124 displayed.

After we have entered our query, we indicate that the query is to be run, and QBE then displays a screen that contains the results of the query:

Quo_Supp_#	Quo_Part_#	Price	Time	OnOrder
51	124	1.25	5	400
53	124	1.35	3	500

The following is another example:

SQL Query

```
SELECT    Inv_Part_#, PartName
FROM      Inventory
WHERE     PartName = 'Bolt'
```

Equivalent QBE Query

Inventory	Inv_Part_#	PartName	OnHand
	P.	P. Bolt	

Results

Inv_Part_#	PartName
124	Bolt
125	Bolt

In this example, we are specifying the "P." operator only for selected columns. Note that this particular QBE implementation does not require that we use quotation marks with the value "Bolt." Quotation marks are not necessary with the QMF implementation of QBE unless the value contains blanks or special characters.

If we specify no Boolean operator with the value, QBE assumes that we want an equal operator to be used in selecting the rows to display. We can explicitly supply the operator if we want some other type of comparison to be performed:

SQL Query

```
SELECT    Quo_Supp_#, Quo_Part_#, Price
FROM      Quotations
WHERE     Price > 1.00
```

Equivalent QBE Query

Quotations	Quo_Supp_#	Quo_Part_#	Price	Time	OnOrder
	P.	P.	P. >1.00		

Results

Quo_Supp_#	Quo_Part_#	Price
51	124	1.25
52	105	7.50
53	124	1.35

We might also be able to use the NULL keyword in order to select only rows that contain null values:

SQL Query

```
SELECT    *
FROM      Quotations
WHERE     Price IS NULL
```

Equivalent QBE Query

Quotations	Quo_Supp_#	Quo_Part_#	Price	Time	OnOrder
P.			NULL		

Results

Quo_Supp_#	Quo_Part_#	Price	Time	OnOrder
53	232	—	15	0

USE OF IN, BETWEEN, AND LIKE

Many QBE implementations support the use of IN and BETWEEN for multiple values in a condition, and LIKE for partial values. (See Chapter 16 for a discussion of IN, BETWEEN, and LIKE operations.) Several SQL queries from earlier chapters are repeated here, followed by their QMF QBE equivalents:

SQL Query

```
SELECT     Quo_Supp_#, Quo_Part_#, Price
FROM       Quotations
WHERE      Quo_Part_# IN (105, 135, 205)
```

Equivalent QBE Query

Quotations	Quo_Supp_#	Quo_Part_#	Price	Time
	P.	P. IN (105, 135, 205)	P.	

Results

Quo_Supp_#	Quo_Part_#	Price
51	135	0.39
52	105	7.50
52	205	0.15
53	135	0.42

SQL Query

```
SELECT     Sup_Supp_#, Name, Address
FROM       Suppliers
WHERE      Address LIKE '% MN%'
```

Equivalent QBE Query

Suppliers	Sup_Supp_#	Name	Address	Code
	P.	P.	P. LIKE '% MN%'	

Results

Sup_Supp_#	Name	Address
57	Eagle Hardware	64 Tranquility Place, Apollo, MN

SQL Query

```
SELECT     *
FROM       Inventory
WHERE      PartName LIKE '_O%'
```

Equivalent QBE Query

Inventory	Inv_Part_#	PartName	OnHand
P.		—	LIKE '_O%'	

Results

Inv_Part_#	PartName	OnHand
124	Bolt	900
125	Bolt	1000
206	Motor	225

UNIQUE ROWS

It is possible to eliminate duplicate rows from the displayed results. We specify this by including the "UNQ." operator under the table name:

SQL Query

```
SELECT    DISTINCT Quo_Supp_#
FROM      Quotations
WHERE     OnOrder > 200
```

Equivalent QBE Query

Quotations	Quo_Supp_#	Quo_Part_#	Price	Time	OnOrder
UNQ.	P.				>200

Results

Quo_Supp_#
51
53

MULTIPLE CONDITIONS

We can specify multiple conditions by entering conditional expressions under more than one column. If we enter all the conditions on the same line, QBE typically assumes that we mean them to be connected by AND:

SQL Query

```
SELECT    Quo_Supp_#, Quo_Part_#, Price
FROM      Quotations
WHERE     Quo_Part_# = 124
          AND
          Price > 1.30
```

Equivalent QBE Query

Quotations	Quo_Supp_#	Quo_Part_#	Price	Time	OnOrder
	P.	P. 124	P. >1.30		

Results

Quo_Supp_#	Quo_Part_#	Price
53	124	1.35

If we want the conditions to be connected by OR, then we must enter them on separate lines in the table structure.

To expand the skeleton table to allow more than one line of input, we might employ a user-interface function to enlarge the display, causing a line to be added to the skeleton table. The following example shows an example of using the OR operator:

SQL Query

```
SELECT     Quo_Supp_#, Quo_Part_#, Price, Time
FROM       Quotations
WHERE      Price > 1.30
       OR
           Time > 10
```

Equivalent QBE Query

Quotations	Quo_Supp_#	Quo_Part_#	Price	Time	OnOrder
	P.	P.	P. >1.30	P.	
	P.	P.	P.	P. >10	

Results

Quo_Supp_#	Quo_Part_#	Price	Time
52	105	7.50	10
52	205	0.15	20
52	206	0.15	20
53	124	1.35	3
53	222	0.25	15
53	232	–	15
53	241	0.08	15

Here QBE selects a row if it meets the conditions specified in either line. We must include the "P." operators in both lines, and we must include them in the same set of columns on both lines.

EXAMPLE ELEMENTS

In some cases, it is necessary to connect two or more tables that are displayed on the screen. To do this, we can enter *example elements* in the table structure. An example element is a name we assign to a column so that we can refer to that column elsewhere in the query. In the character-oriented form of QBE implemented by QMF, an example element name begins with an underscore (_) and consists of up to 18 alphabetic or numeric characters.

One use for example elements is to specify selection conditions using a *condition box*.

CONDITION BOXES

In some cases, it is easier to specify selection conditions by using SQL-style conditional expressions that explicitly state the AND and OR operators. To do this, we create a condition box by invoking the appropriate user-interface function. QBE then adds a special table structure to the screen in which we can enter selection conditions. We then define a selection condition in the condition box and connect it to our table by using example elements, as in the following query:

SQL Query

```
SELECT     *
FROM       Quotations
WHERE      Quo_Part_# < 200
           AND
           (Price > 1.00 OR Time < 10)
```

Equivalent QBE Query

Quotations	Quo_Supp_#	Quo_Part_#	Price	Time	OnOrder
P.		_QP	_Part	_Time	

	CONDITIONS	
	_QP < 200 AND (_Part > 1.00 OR _Time < 10)	

Results

Quo_Supp_#	Quo_Part_#	Price	Time	OnOrder
51	124	1.25	5	400
51	125	0.55	5	0
51	134	0.40	5	500
51	135	0.39	5	1000
52	105	7.50	10	200
53	124	1.35	3	500
53	125	0.58	3	200
53	134	0.38	3	200
53	135	0.42	3	1000

EXPRESSIONS IN CONDITIONS

We can use arithmetic expressions in defining selection conditions. If the arithmetic expression involves multiple columns, then we must use a condition box to specify the selection condition:

SQL Query

```
SELECT     Quo_Supp_#, Quo_Part_#
FROM       Quotations
WHERE      Price * OnOrder > 500.00
```

Equivalent QBE Query

Quotations	Quo_Supp_#	Quo_Part_#	Price	Time	OnOrder
	P.	P.	_Prce		_Ord

```
|                        CONDITIONS                     |
| _Prce * _Ord > 500.00                                 |
```

Results

Quo_Supp_#	Quo_Part_#
51	221
52	105
53	124
53	222

NEGATIVE CONDITIONS

The QMF implementation of QBE allows us to use negative conditions in much the same way as SQL does. The NOT operator can be used in conjunction with NULL, IN, BETWEEN, and LIKE; it can also be used preceding any type of condition in a condition box. The comparison operator = can be preceded by either NOT or we can use ¬=. Operators involving > or < cannot be immediately preceded by either NOT or ¬; instead, the entire condition must be preceded by NOT. For example:

```
Quotations | Quo_Supp_# | Quo_Part_# | Price | Time | OnOrder |
           | P.         | P.         | _Prce |      | _Ord    |

|                        CONDITIONS                     |
| NOT _Prce * _Ord > 500.00                             |
```

COMPLEX QBE OPERATIONS

The Query by Example language can be used to formulate more complex queries than those described thus far. It can also be used to perform manipulations on relational databases other than queries, such as inserting, updating, and deleting rows. The remainder of this appendix introduces some additional types of database manipulations that can be performed using QBE. Keep in mind that not all versions of QBE support the same range of capabilities.

COLUMNS OF CALCULATED VALUES

We can add columns to the skeleton table that QBE displays in order to display values that are calculated from other columns. In the following example, we are displaying the results of multiplying Price values by OnOrder values. To do this, we make room in the skeleton table by deleting the Time column. We then invoke an enlarge function to add an empty column to the table and enter an arithmetic expression into the new column:

SQL Query

```
SELECT     Quo_Supp_#, Quo_Part_#, Price * OnOrder
FROM       Quotations
WHERE      Price > 1.00
```

Equivalent QBE Query

```
Quotations | Quo_Supp_# | Quo_Part_# | Price | OnOrder |                    |
           | P.         | P.         | _Prce | _Ord    | P._Prce * _Ord |

|    CONDITIONS    |
|   _Prce > 1.00   |
```

Results

Quo_Supp_#	Quo_Part_#	Price*OnOrder
51	124	500.00
52	105	1500.00
53	124	675.00

Notice that we have used example elements in defining the column that contains the calculated values. We can use example elements anywhere that we need to refer to a column value.

SPECIFYING ROW SEQUENCE

The QMF version of QBE provides the "AO." and "DO." operators to specify columns to be used in sorting the resulting display into a desired sequence. The "AO." operator indicates ascending sequence and "DO." descending sequence. If we specify multiple columns, we can include a number in parentheses following the operator to indicate which column is most significant, which is second, and so on. For example:

SQL Query

```
SELECT    Quo_Part_#, Quo_Supp_#, Price
FROM      Quotations
ORDER BY  Quo_Part_#, Price DESC
```

Equivalent QBE Query

```
Quotations | Quo_Supp_# | Quo_Part_# | Price      | Time | OnOrder |
           | P.         | P.AO(1).   | P.DO(2).   |      |         |
```

Results

Quo_Supp_#	Quo_Part_#	Price
52	105	7.50
53	124	1.35
51	124	1.25
53	125	0.58
51	125	0.55
51	134	0.40
53	134	0.38
53	135	0.42
51	135	0.39

```
52        205    0.15
52        206    0.15
51        221    0.30
53        222    0.25
51        231    0.10
53        232     —
53        241    0.08
```

We can also use a column of calculated values for sequencing the display by including the appropriate operator in the calculated column:

SQL Query

```
SELECT    Quo_Supp_#, Quo_Part_#, Price * OnOrder
FROM      Quotations
WHERE     Price > 1.00
ORDER BY  Quo_Part_#, 3 DESC
```

Equivalent QBE Query

```
Quotations | Quo_Supp_# | Quo_Part_# | Price| OnOrder |                     |
           | P.         | P. AO(1).  | _Prce| _Ord    | P.DO(2)._Prce * _Ord |

|    CONDITIONS   |
|   _Prce > 1.00  |
```

Results

```
Quo_Supp_#    Quo_Part_#    Price*OnOrder
       52           105          1500
       53           124           075
       51           124           500
```

JOINING TABLES

We can define QBE queries that use relational Join operations to combine data from two or more tables. We begin by displaying all the tables that we are joining by issuing multiple DRAW commands, one for each table. We then specify the manner in which we want to join the tables by using example elements:

SQL Query

```
SELECT    Inv_Part_#, PartName, OnHand, Quo_Supp_#, OnOrder
FROM      Inventory, Quotations
          Inventory JOIN Quotations
          ON Inv_Part_# = Quo_Part_#
```

Equivalent QBE Query

```
Inventory | Inv_Part_# | PartName | OnHand |      |      |      |
P.        | _Part      |          |        | Supp | _OO  |      |
```

Quotations	Quo_Supp_#	Quo_Part_#	Price	Time	OnOrder
	_Supp	_Part			_OO

Results

Inv_Part_#	PartName	OnHand	Quo_Supp_#	OnOrder
105	Gear	0	52	200
124	Bolt	900	51	400
124	Bolt	900	53	500
125	Bolt	1000	51	0
125	Bolt	1000	53	200
134	Nut	900	51	500
134	Nut	900	53	200
135	Nut	1000	51	1000
135	Nut	1000	53	1000
205	Band	450	52	0
206	Motor	225	52	0
221	Axle	1500	51	10000
222	Axle	25	53	10000
231	Axle	75	51	5000
232	Axle	150	53	0
241	Wheel	300	53	6000

In the above example, we are using the example element "_Part" to join the two tables together based on part number values. QBE selects data only where a row in Inventory and a row in Quotations have the same value for part number. In QBE, the comparison used for joining is assumed to be an equal comparison (Equijoin) between any columns in which we have entered the same example element name.

The results of a QBE query always take the form of a single table. Therefore, we can specify "P." operators in only one of the tables displayed on the screen. In the above example we are using the Inventory table to specify the columns that we want displayed. Since we want data displayed from both the Inventory and the Quotations tables, we have added two empty columns in the Inventory table, and we have used example elements ("_Supp" and "_OO") to identify the columns from the Quotations table that we want displayed in addition to columns that come directly from the Inventory table.

BUILT-IN FUNCTIONS AND GROUP BY

Many implementations of QBE support the use of the same built-in functions as SQL, both for the entire table and for subsets of rows based on grouping by a specified column or columns. The following example shows how we can use built-in functions for an entire table. Notice that we show the table in two parts, but on the user-interface device, the entire table is displayed horizontally. We might use a horizontal scroll function to display a portion of the table if it is too wide to fit on the screen.

SQL Query

```
SELECT    SUM(OnOrder), SUM(Price * OnOrder), MAX(Price), AVG(Price)
FROM      Quotations
```

Equivalent QBE Query

```
Quotations | Price | OnOrder |                   |                           |
+...
           | _Prce | _Ord    | P.SUM._Ord | P.SUM.(_Prce * _Ord) |

..._____|_____|
        P.MAX._Prce | P.AVG._Prce |
```

Results

SUM(OnOrder)	SUM(Price*OnOrder)	MAX(Price)	AVG(Price)
35000	10357.00	7.50	0.92333333

In the above example, we are using the example elements _Prce and _Ord to specify the columns that will be used with the built-in functions. The built-in functions are then specified in unnamed columns. The first unnamed column, for example, uses the SUM built-in function to total on-order quantities.

With QMF, we use the "G." operator to specify grouping, as in the following example:

SQL Query

```
SELECT     PartName, SUM(OnHand)
FROM       Inventory
GROUP      BY PartName
```

Equivalent QBE Query

```
Inventory | Inv_Part_# | PartName | OnHand |              |
          |            | G.P.     | _OH    | P.SUM.(_OH) |
```

Results

PartName	SUM(OnHand)
Axle	1750
Band	450
Bolt	1900
Gear	700
Generator	900
Motor	225
Nut	1900
Wheel	1300

In the above example, we are grouping on the contents of the PartName column and thus are calculating total OnHand amounts for groups of parts having the same name. When we do grouping, we must not specify "P." for a column unless it has a single value for the group of rows we are specifying. For example, specifying "P." for the Inv_Part_# column would be invalid, since there can be multiple values of part number for each part name value.

LINKED QUERIES

Most implementations of QBE do not support subqueries in the same manner as SQL; however, by linking tables with example elements, it is possible to perform some of the types of queries that can be requested using SQL subqueries. Generally, the linking is done to determine a condition value.

CONDITION VALUE IN A DIFFERENT TABLE

The condition value may be in a different table than that being used to display data:

SQL Query

```
SELECT    Quo_Part_#, Price
FROM      Quotations
WHERE     Quo_Supp_# IN (SELECT  Sup_Supp_#
                         FROM     Suppliers
                         WHERE    Code = 20)
```

Equivalent QBE Query

Quotations	Quo_Supp_#	Quo_Part_#	Price	Time	OnOrder
	_Supp	P.	P.		

Suppliers	Sup_Supp_#	Name	Address	Code
	_Supp			20

Results

Quo_Part_#	Price
124	1.25
125	0.55
134	0.40
135	0.39
221	0.30
231	0.10
105	7.50
205	0.15
206	0.15

Here the query in the Suppliers table finds all the supplier numbers for which the code is 20. We are then using these supplier numbers to select rows from the Quotations table.

We can often use built-in functions and grouping when linking tables:

SQL Query

```
SELECT    Inv_Part_#, PartName, OnHand
FROM      Inventory
WHERE     Inv_Part_# IN (SELECT    Quo_Part_#
```

```
FROM       Quotations
GROUP BY Quo_Part_#
HAVING     SUM(OnOrder) > 500)
```

Equivalent QBE Query

Inventory	Inv_Part_#	PartName	OnHand	
P.	_Part			

Quotations	Quo_Supp_#	Quo_Part_#	Price	Time	OnOrder
		G._Part			_Ord

CONDITIONS	
SUM._Ord > 500	

Results

Inv_Part_#	PartName	OnHand
124	Bolt	900
134	Nut	900
135	Nut	1000
221	Axle	1500
222	Axle	25
231	Axle	75
241	Wheel	300

In the above example, we are summarizing on-order quantity by part number. We are selecting part numbers where the on-order sum is greater than 500. We are then displaying information from the Inventory table for the selected part numbers.

CONDITION VALUE IN THE SAME TABLE

It is also possible to link a table to itself. We can do this by using two copies of the same table structure, or we can enter two queries in the same table structure. Here is an example using two separate table structures:

SQL Query

```
SELECT     DISTINCT Quo_Supp_#, Quo_Part_#, Price
FROM       Quotations
WHERE      Price > ANY (SELECT  Price
                        FROM    Quotations
                        WHERE   OnOrder > 0)
```

Equivalent QBE Query

Quotations	Quo_Supp_#	Quo_Part_#	Price	OnOrder
			_Prce	>0

Quotations	Quo_Supp_#	Quo_Part_#	Price	OnOrder
UNQ.	P.	P.	P. >MIN._Prce	

Results

Quo_Supp_#	Quo_Part_#	Price
51	124	1.25
51	125	0.55
51	134	0.40
51	135	0.39
51	221	0.30
51	231	0.10
52	105	7.50
52	205	0.15
52	206	0.15
53	124	1.35
53	125	0.58
53	134	0.38
53	135	0.42
53	222	0.25

The first query selects all values for price where the on-order quantity is greater than 0. The second query determines the minimum value selected by the first query and selects distinct rows with a price greater than the minimum.

The following example shows how we can use grouped data by linking a table to itself:

SQL Query

```
SELECT     Quo_Supp_#, Quo_Part_#, Price
FROM       Quotations Row_Q
WHERE      Price = (SELECT  MIN(Price)
                    FROM    Quotations
                    WHERE   Quo_Part_# = Row_Q.Quo_Part_#)
```

Equivalent QBE Query

Quotations	Quo_Supp_#	Quo_Part_#	Price	OnOrder
		G._QP	_Prce	
	P.	P._QP	P.MIN._Prce	

Results

Quo_Supp_#	Quo_Part_#	Price
51	124	1.25
51	125	0.55
51	135	0.39
51	221	0.30
51	231	0.10
52	105	7.50
52	205	0.15
52	206	0.15
53	134	0.38
53	222	0.25
53	241	0.08

Here the first query groups prices by part number. The second query then determines the minimum price for each part number and selects the row or rows for that part number with a price equal to the minimum price.

COMBINING QUERY RESULTS

Some implementations of QBE allow us to perform Union relational operations by combining the results from two or more queries. With QMF, we can do this by specifying multiple query lines, where each line contains a P. operator. The following is an example of a Union operation:

SQL Query

```
SELECT      Sup_Supp_#, Name, 'Preferred'
FROM        Suppliers
WHERE       Code = 30
        UNION
SELECT      Sup_Supp_#, Name, '     '
FROM        Suppliers
WHERE       Code ¬= 30
```

Equivalent QBE Query

Suppliers	Sup_Supp_#	Name	Code	
	P.	P.	30	P. 'Preferred'
	P.	P.	¬= 30	P. ' '

Results

Sup_Supp_#	Name	
51	Defecto Parts	
52	Vesuvius Inc.	
53	Atlantis Co.	
54	Titanic Parts	Preferred
57	Eagle Hardware	Preferred
61	Skylab Parts	
64	Knight Ltd.	

To combine queries in the above manner, the two queries must select the same number of columns and the columns must be of the same data type. The columns selected can be from different tables as long as they meet the number and type restrictions.

UPDATING TABLES

As we introduced earlier, in addition to allowing us to formulate query requests, many implementations of QBE also allow us to add, change, or delete data from tables. In the QMF implementation of QBE, these functions are performed using the "I.", "U." and "D." operators. We can insert data directly by entering it in the table structure, or we can copy data from another table. When we insert data directly, we can enter multiple rows on the screen if we like:

```
Inventory | Inv_Part_# | PartName | OnHand |
I.        | 126        | Bolt     | 0      |
I.        | 107        | Gear     | 25     |
```

We can also update data values by using the "U." operator:

SQL Query

```
UPDATE    Quotations
SET       Price = 1.30, Time = 10
WHERE     Quo_Supp_# = 51
          AND
          Quo_Part_# = 124
```

Equivalent QBE Query

```
Quotations | Quo_Supp_# | Quo_Part_# | Price     | Time     | OnOrder |
           | 51         | 124        | U. 1.30   | U. 10    |         |
```

In the above example, the values we have entered for supplier and part identify the row to be updated. The values for price and time, which we have preceded with a "U." operator, represent the new values for the row.

We can delete rows from a table by using the "D." operator:

```
Quotations | Quo_Supp_# | Quo_Part_# | Price     | Time     | OnOrder |
D.         | 52         |            |           |          |         |
```

This deletes all rows for supplier 52.

Keep in mind that if the tables we are accessing have referential constraints defined for them through the use of primary keys and foreign keys, the same inserting, updating, and deleting restrictions apply as for the SQL updating that we discussed in Chapter 19.

Appendix **B**

Codd's Relational Rules

In the 1980s the relational approach to database became extremely popular. Because of this popularity, vendors of all types of database software proclaimed the latest releases of their database offerings to now include relational facilities. E. F. Codd, the first to describe the relational approach, became concerned that it was becoming difficult to determine just how "relational" a particular database software product actually was.

To help clarify the situation, Codd published two articles in Computerworld [1, 2] that described clearly what features a database management system should have to be considered "fully relational." These features are described by means of twelve rules that are preceded by a general principle called Rule Zero. Individual vendors will continually debate whether all of these principles are, in fact, valid, and authorities will disagree over just how closely a particular offering conforms to Codd's principles. However, we feel that the reader will find it interesting to read a list of Codd's rules, written using informal language. The list can serve as a useful checklist for evaluating relational database packages.

RULE 0—RELATIONAL DATABASE MANAGEMENT

A relational database software package must use only its relational capabilities to manage the information stored in the database.

RULE 1—INFORMATION REPRESENTATION

All information stored in a relational database must be represented only by data element values that are stored in the tables that make up the database. Associations between data elements must not be logically represented in any other way, such as by using pointers from one table to another.

RULE 2—LOGICAL ACCESSIBILITY

Every data element value stored in a relational database must be accessible by stating the name of the table it is stored in, the name of the column under which it is stored, and the value of the primary key that defines the row in which it is stored.

RULE 3—REPRESENTATION OF NULL VALUES

The database software must have a consistent method for representing null values. For example, null values for numeric values must be distinct from zero or any other numeric value, and null character strings must be distinct from strings of blanks or any other character values.

RULE 4—CATALOG FACILITIES

The logical description of a relational database must be represented in the same manner as ordinary data so that the facilities of the relational database software can be used to maintain database descriptions.

RULE 5—DATA LANGUAGES

A relational software product may support many different types of languages for describing data and accessing the database. However, there must be at least one language that uses ordinary character strings to support the definition of data, the definition of views, the manipulation of data, constraints on data integrity, information concerning authorization, and the boundaries of recovery units.

RULE 6—VIEW UPDATABILITY

Any view that can be defined using combinations of base tables that are, in theory, updatable must be capable of being updated by the database software.

RULE 7—INSERT, UPDATE, AND DELETE

Any operand that describes the results of a single retrieval operation must also be capable of being applied to a single insert, update, or delete operation as well.

RULE 8—PHYSICAL DATA INDEPENDENCE

Changes that are made to physical storage representations or access methods must not require changes to be made to application programs.

RULE 9—LOGICAL DATA INDEPENDENCE

Changes that are made to tables that do not modify any of the data already stored in the tables must not require changes to be made to application programs.

RULE 10—INTEGRITY CONSTRAINTS

Constraints that apply to entity integrity and referential integrity must be specifiable by the data language implemented by the database software and not by statements coded into application programs.

RULE 11—DATABASE DISTRIBUTION

The data language implemented by the database software must support the ability to distribute the database without requiring changes to be made to application programs. This facility must be provided in the data language whether or not the database software itself supports distributed databases.

RULE 12—NONSUBVERSION

If the database software supports facilities that allow an application program to operate on tables a row at a time, an application program using this type of database access must be prevented from bypassing entity integrity or referential integrity constraints that are defined for the database.

REFERENCES

1. Codd, E. F. "Is your DBMS Really Relational?" *Computerworld,* Oct. 14, 1985.
2. Codd, E. F. "Does your DBMS Run by the Rules?" *Computerworld,* Oct. 21, 1985.

Appendix **C**

Object-Oriented Databases

A traditional database stores just data—with no procedures. As we have seen throughout this book, a traditional relational database does not store procedures, but in addition, it attempts to make the data it stores *completely independent* from the procedures that access it. The data is made accessible by diverse users for diverse purposes through the use of relational database software.

In contrast, an *object-oriented database* (OODB) stores *objects*. An object consists of data accompanied by *methods* which implement the actual procedures that process the data. For those unfamiliar with the terminology associated with object oriented computing, a few of the terms associated with object technology are defined in Box C.1.

After relational databases had been in use for some time, a need arose to associate certain procedures with the data and to activate those procedures automatically when the data was accessed. This allows database software to compute values for certain data elements rather than simply retrieving them from the database—a process referred to as putting *intelligence* into the database. Intelligent database techniques are useful for controlling data integrity and security in a client/server environment because it is quite difficult to validate the identity of a client accessing a database server in a highly distributed environment.

Object-oriented databases take the idea of intelligent databases to its logical conclusion. No data is accessed except through the methods stored in the database. These methods are ready to take action the moment they receive a request. The data of all objects is thus encapsulated. The data is generally active rather than passive.

Object-oriented databases will become a very important type of database technology. Complex questions arise about how such databases should be structured. Should they be extensions of today's relational databases, or should they have entirely different structures?

ACTIVE DATABASES

The classic relational database is *passive*. It merely stores data in a data-independent way. An *active* database will take certain actions automatically when an attempt is made to read or update the data. As we discussed above, this is an example of putting intelligence into the database.

> ### BOX C.1   Object-oriented computing terminology.
>
> - **Object Type.** An *object type* is a type of entity in the real world, either real or abstract, about which we store data. The definition of an object type includes a specification of the types of operations that can be performed to manipulate the data stored about that object type.
>
> - **Operation.** An *operation* is an activity that is performed to access or manipulate the data associated with an object type. An important notion associated with object-oriented computing is that the operations associated with an object type reference only the data associated with that object type and do not reference data associated with any other object type.
>
> - **Method.** A *method* specifies the way in which an operation that is performed on the data associated with an object type is encoded in computer software. A method consists of procedures that can be executed in a computer to access or manipulate the data associated with an object type.
>
> - **Class.** A *class* is a computer implementation of an object type. It includes a data structure that defines the data associated with the object type and a set of methods specifying all the operations that can be performed on the data associated with that class.
>
> - **Object.** An *object* is an instance of an object type. It consists of a description of the set of data items associated with the object instance and a description of the computer code that implements the methods associated with the object's type.
>
> - **Encapsulation.** *Encapsulation* refers to the way in which an object's data, and the operations that can be performed on that data, are packaged together. In effect, encapsulation hides the implementation details of an object from its users.
>
> - **Inheritance.** An object type can be made up of lower-level object types which, in turn, can also be made up of still lower-level object types. *Inheritance* refers to the characteristic of an object type that allows it to take on (inherit) the properties of its parent class, including the data structures and methods used by the parent class. An object type can override an inherited property with data structures and methods of its own.

With an active database, the basic structure of the relational database could be the same as that of an equivalent passive database. But with an active database, the *database software* must be different. For example, the database software may apply security safeguards, implement integrity controls, or perform other types of computations automatically. Active database features are particularly useful in a highly distributed, client/server environment.

Some database software vendors have already implemented some active features in traditional client/server relational database software products. An example of this is Sybase, which implements features in the database server component that performs authentication procedures for client components that are attempting to access the server. However, active databases are best implemented with object-oriented techniques.

KNOWLEDGEBASES

The so-called *artificial intelligence* world conceived another form of active database. The artificial intelligence community is based on the assumption that it would be desirable to store *knowledge* in a computer system. Knowledge is regarded as being active, whereas data or information is passive. Knowledge can be considered to consist of a set of *facts* and *rules* that a computer might be able to act upon. Knowledgebases became *frame-oriented*, where a *frame* is an object having a collection of rules associated with it.

Computer systems called *expert systems* have been developed by organizations that specialize in artificial intelligence technology. An expert system uses a special form of database that is sometimes called a *knowledgebase*. A knowledgebase stores a set of data together with a set of rules that can be applied to the data. The expert system software implements an *inference engine* that is capable of using the knowledgebase to search for applicable rules and to perform automatic reasoning. The inference engine chains rules together. It might use forward chaining or backward chaining, or both. The expert system concept has been successfully applied to some highly complex problems.

OBJECT-ORIENTED DATABASES

The technology behind object-oriented databases evolved in parallel with the work that was being done on knowledgebases and expert systems. However, object-oriented database technology was developed for a different purpose.

Object-oriented databases first evolved from a need to support object-oriented programming. Smalltalk and C++ programmers needed a store for what they called *persistent data*, that is, data that remains after a process terminates. Object-oriented databases become important for certain types of applications with complex data, such as computer-aided design and computer-aided engineering (CAD/CAE).

Object-oriented databases tended to be used to support diverse data types rather than only the simple tables, columns, and rows of relational databases. Richly diverse abstract, user-defined data types needed support, including objects storing speech, images, and full motion video. A particularly important type of data often stored in object-oriented databases has come to be called the *binary large object (blob)*. Blobs are large, relatively unformatted data objects containing such components as images, sound clips, video clips, and unformatted text. Applications such as newspaper layout and video retrieval in advertising agencies began to make use of object-oriented databases with blobs. All of these needs have converged to create the technology surrounding object-oriented databases (see Fig. C.1).

A UNIFIED CONCEPTUAL MODEL

In traditional computing, the conceptual models for analysis, the concrete procedural models for design, and the logical data models for database definition and access are all different. Traditional analysis uses entity-relationship models and functional decomposition. During the analysis and design process, analysts typically develop matrices mapping functions and entity types. Traditional design uses a different view of the world—data flow diagrams and structure charts. Programming uses still another different conceptual model; programmers do not think in terms of data flow diagrams. Relational database technology uses yet another conceptual model employing tables, with the need to apply

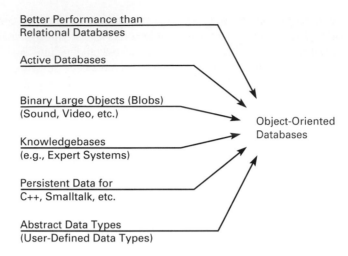

Figure C.1 A number of needs are converging to create the technology of object-oriented databases.

relational operations to the tables. The conceptual model of SQL is quite different from the conceptual models of entity-relationship diagrams, functional decomposition, data flow diagrams, structure charts, or Visual Basic code.

In contrast, object-oriented techniques use the same conceptual models for analysis, design, and construction. The object-oriented database conceptual model uses the same symbology as the rest of the object-oriented world, rather than using separate relational tables and data manipulation operations. Using the same conceptual model for all aspects of application development simplifies the construction of systems, especially when object-oriented CASE tools can be used. This improves communication among users, analysts, and programmers, and lessens the likelihood of errors.

Object-oriented databases were designed from the start to be well integrated with object-oriented programming languages, such as C++ and Smalltalk. They use the same object model. A database language that is handled as an extension to a traditional programming language is unnecessary. For example, with some object-oriented database products, C++ is used for all database definitions and manipulation. The same object model is also used for analysis and design. The analyst may determine high-level objects and high-level behavior. The designer pushes this down to low-level objects that inherit properties and behavior from the higher-level objects. With good object-oriented CASE tools, as soon as the objects are specified on the screen, code can be interpretively generated for them.

Design techniques for object-oriented database are also better integrated into the overall application design process. Relational database design is quite separate from program design. The database is a separate space from the program space. The programmer has to figure out how to extract data from the tables and load data into the tables. With object-oriented databases, the programmer deals with transient and persistent objects in a uniform way. The persistent objects are in the object-oriented database, and thus the conceptual walls between programming and database are removed. Analysis, design, code generation, and database generation can be done iteratively by one person using a unified conceptual model. This can greatly increase the rate at which a creative person can invent and refine a new information system.

To summarize, the ability to employ a unified conceptual model throughout all the phases of analysis, design, programming, and database implementation results in:

- Higher productivity. The work of translating between paradigms is avoided.
- Fewer errors. Errors in translation between the paradigms are avoided.
- Better communication among users, analysts, and implementors.
- Better quality.
- More flexibility.

OBJECT-ORIENTED DATABASE ARCHITECTURE

In the late 1980s, the first object-oriented databases appeared. Some of the early object-oriented database products and their vendors are listed in Box C.2. The early products were designed as extensions to object-oriented programming languages, such as Smalltalk and C++. The design of current object-oriented databases should take full advantage of CASE techniques and incorporate methods created in a variety of ways, including declarative statements, code generators, and rule-based inferencing.

BOX C.2 Some object-oriented database software.	
Product	**Vendor**
Gemstone	Servio Corporation, Alameda, CA
Itasca	Itasca Systems Inc., Minneapolis, MN
Objectivity	Objectivity, Menlo Park, CA
Object Store	Object Design Inc., Burlington, MA
Ontos	Ontos Inc., Sellerica, MA
Versant	Versant Object Technology, Menlo Park, CA

Many facilities provided by conventional database software continue to be important in object-oriented databases. These include locking mechanisms for implementing concurrency controls, recovery facilities, two-phase commit protocols, security safeguards, data integrity controls, data distribution techniques, and database maintenance tools.

Some features of object-oriented database software are independent of the fundamental architecture of an object-oriented database but are common to most object-oriented databases. These include the following:

- **Versions.** Most database systems allow only one representation of a particular database entity to exist in the database. The provision for multiple *versions* allow alternative representations to exist simultaneously. This capability is useful in many application areas where a design is evolving and where different strategies are being explored concurrently. For example, designers of an integrated circuit may want to try different component layouts to maximize chip density; or software developers may maintain several versions of a particular software subsystem, perhaps using different algorithms, in order to examine the effect of each on overall system performance.

- **Shared Transactions.** Transactions typically isolate an individual's actions from the database until the changes made by the transaction are either all committed or all rolled back. Only after the changes made by a transaction have been committed do the changes become globally visible. *Shared transactions* support groups of users who want to coordinate their efforts in real time. The concept of the shared transaction allows several end users to participate in the processing performed in a single transaction. Shared transactions allow users to share intermediate database results. This is useful in such applications as electronic conferences and document editing where several parties may work on a document concurrently.

DEVELOPMENT WITH OBJECT-ORIENTED DATABASES

Object-oriented databases are developed by first describing the object types that are important in the application realm. The behaviors associated with those objects are then identified. The object types that are identified determine the classes that will form the definition of the object-oriented database.

For example, a database designed to store the geometry of mechanical parts might include classes such as Cylinder, Sphere, and Cube. The behavior of a Cylinder might include information about its dimensions, volume, and surface area, resulting in a class definition for the Cylinder class that might look something like this:

```
class Cylinder {
                float height ();
                float radius ();
                float volume ();
                float surfaceArea ();
                {
```

In the above definition, height (), radius (), volume (), and surfaceArea () represent the messages that can be sent to a Cylinder object. Similar definitions would be developed for Cube and Sphere.

Note the absence of implementation details, including whether the information is stored or computed. The implementation is accomplished in the same language by writing functions corresponding to the object-oriented requests, such as in the following procedure definition:

```
Cylinder::height () {return CylinderHeight }
Cylinder::volume () {return Pl * radius () * radius ()* height () }
```

In this case, the height of the Cylinder is stored as a data element, while the volume is computed by the appropriate formula. Note that the internal implementation of volume uses requests to get height and radius. However, the most important aspect is the simplicity and uniformity that users of the Cylinder class experience. They just need to know what types of requests they can make and how to make them. The entire application can be written in one uniform style.

This approach also gives the object-oriented database flexibility. Since the entire application is written by sending requests, implementations can be altered to any degree without affecting applications. Consequently, the application is simpler and much easier to maintain and enhance. In this sense, object-oriented databases provide even greater separation between system specification and its implementation.

THREE APPROACHES TO BUILDING OBJECT-ORIENTED DATABASES

Three approaches have proven useful for software developers in building object-oriented database software.

Approach 1. Using Conventional Database Software

With this approach, existing conventional database software is used. The developer adds a layer for processing object-oriented requests and for storing methods. This approach has one merit: the highly complex code of today's database software can be used without change. This may make it possible to implement an object-oriented database much more quickly than starting from scratch.

Approach 2. Adding Capabilities to Existing Database Software

With the second approach, object-oriented capabilities are added to traditional, existing relational database software. With this approach, the tools, techniques, and vast experience associated with relational database technology can be used to build a new object-oriented database software product. Pointers may be added to relational tables linking them to large binary objects. Several existing relational database vendors advocate this approach.

Approach 3. Rethinking the Database Software Architecture

With the third, the software developer rethinks the architecture of database systems and produces a new architecture optimized to meet the needs of object-oriented technology. The object-oriented database companies listed in Box C.2 have all taken this approach, largely because they can achieve much better performance than by extending relational technology.

Vendors taking this approach claim that relational technology is a subset of a more generalized database capability. Relational data structures might be used where appropriate, but other types of data structures are sometimes better for complex objects. Structures other than relational structures may make it possible to access the data associated with a complex object without needing to move the disk drive access mechanism.

The object-oriented database vendors quote cases involving complex objects in which nonrelational object-oriented databases are roughly two orders of magnitude faster than relational databases for storing and retrieving complex information. They claim that these nonrelational structures are essential in applications such as computer-aided design and engineering.

DATA INDEPENDENCE VERSUS ENCAPSULATION

As we have seen, a major goal of traditional database technology is data independence. Data structures should be independent of the processes that use the data. The data can be employed in any way the end user requires. In contrast, a major goal of object-oriented technology is *encapsulation*. Encapsulation means that the data associated with an object can only be employed with the methods that are part of the class.

Object-oriented classes are intended to be reusable. Therefore, another goal of object-oriented technology is achieving maximum reusability. Because of this, classes should be bug free and should be modified only when absolutely necessary. Traditional database technology is designed to support processes that are subject to endless modification. Therefore, data independence is necessary. The object-oriented database supports classes, some of which rarely change. Change comes from interlinking classes in diverse ways. The data structures in an object-oriented database should be tightly optimized to support the class in which they are encapsulated.

The goals in relational database technology and object-oriented database technology, then, are fundamentally different. The goal of relational databases, that of making the data independent of the application, will remain important for much data. We will always need databases that can be used in unpredictable ways. In contrast, object-oriented databases establish data that are used only with defined methods.

Relational databases and object-oriented databases, meet different needs, both of which are important. In the foreseeable future, object-oriented database technology will not replace relational database technology but will coexist with it.

COMPLEXITY OF DATA STRUCTURES

Objects are composed of objects that, in turn, are composed of objects, and so on. Because of this, the data structures for a high-level object sometimes become extremely complex. The data for each object should be clustered together. When an object is used, its data should be readable without having to move the disk access mechanism. It may be difficult to do this with a relational database. An object may employ data from multiple relations and hence require multiple movements of the access mechanism.

Object-oriented database systems have deliberately avoided the relational data model in order to improve machine performance. They allow the data for one class to be interlinked efficiently, often resorting to the pointer structures that relational databases avoid.

PERFORMANCE

Object-oriented databases often outperform relational databases by a wide margin for applications having much data connectivity. This is one of the primary reasons that applications sharing this characteristic often benefit greatly from using object-oriented database techniques.

Soft Pointers

Object-oriented databases allow objects to refer directly to one another using soft pointers. This makes it possible for an object-oriented database to be much faster in getting from object A to object B than a relational database, which may have to use relational join operations to accomplish this. Even an optimized join is typically much slower than a simple traversal from one object to another. Thus, even without any special tuning, an object-oriented database is usually faster at these pointer-chasing mechanics.

Physical Clustering

Object-oriented databases make physical clustering more effective. Most database systems allow the developer to place related structures close to each other in disk storage. This dramatically reduces retrieval time for the related data, since all data are read with one, instead of several, disk reads. However, in a relational database system, objects get translated into tabular representations and typically get spread out over multiple tables. Thus, in a relational database, these related rows must be clustered together, so that the whole object can be retrieved with one disk read. In an object-oriented database, this is automatic. Furthermore, clustering related objects, such as all subparts of an assembly, can dramatically affect the overall performance of an application. This is relatively straightforward in an object-oriented database, since this represents the first level of clustering. In contrast, physical clustering is typically impossible in a relational database, because it requires a second level of clustering—one level to cluster the rows representing individual objects and a second for the groups of rows that represent related objects.

Storage Structures

Object-oriented databases use diverse storage structures. In a relational database, data that cannot be expressed easily in tabular form is difficult to store and access efficiently. For example, multimedia applications require the storage of large data streams representing digitized video and audio data. CAD applications often require the storage of large numbers of very small objects, such as the points defining the geometry of a mechanical part. Neither is well suited to representation in a table. Therefore, relational databases cannot provide efficient storage management for these application areas. The storage model for object-oriented databases is unlimited, since the system is by nature extensible. Object-oriented databases can provide different storage mechanisms for different kinds of data. As a result, they have proven very effective in supporting both multimedia and CAD applications.

AVOIDING REDUNDANCY

With relational databases, data is normalized to help avoid redundancy and the anomalies caused by data redundancy. Normalization effectively addresses redundancy in data but does not address redundancy in application code.

Object-oriented technology uses inheritance to lessen redundant development of methods. It also allows classes to be designed for reuse in many applications. Encapsulation and inheritance thus lower the amount of redundant code, as well as redundant data, in two ways—by inheritance and by reuse of classes. Such facilities for enhancing reusability can lower the cost of both development and maintenance.

Recently, capabilities in relational databases have been introduced for implementing triggers or procedures that can be executed by the database. Using these capabilities to place common processing into the database itself is an improvement over traditional relational technology. However, relational technology still deliberately separates the processing from those entities naturally associated with the processing. For instance, one could write a trigger enforcing the behavior that a terminated employee's salary must be $0. However, the relational data model does not permit the termination process to be directly associated with the Employee table. In an object-oriented database, this process is straightforward. The Employee class would simply define the terminate request and enforce the $0 salary constraint.

DIFFERENCES BETWEEN RELATIONAL DATABASE
AND OBJECT-ORIENTED DATABASE

As we have now shown, relational database technology and object-oriented database technology have fundamentally different goals and different characteristics. In some computing environments, the goals of classic relational databases predominate. In other computing environments, relational databases do not adequately meet the needs, and object-oriented databases have major advantages. It is not likely that one database software product will ever meet all types of computing needs.

Insight into the advantages of one database technology over another requires an understanding of the application development process. The development process is not completely general. One database technology cannot satisfy all application domains, and the requirements of applications must be considered when analyzing the advantages of one database technology over another. Box C.3 summarizes the major differences between relational database technology and object-oriented database technology.

Relational Databases

Primary Goal. Data independence. Data can be physically reorganized without affecting how it is used.

Data Only. The database generally stores only data and not procedures.

Data Sharing. Data can be accessed by any process. Data is designed for any type of use.

Passive Data. Data is passive. Certain limited operations may be automatically triggered when the data is used.

Constant Change. Processes using data constantly change.

Simplicity. Users perceive the data as columns, rows, and tables.

Separate Tables. Each table is separate. Join operations can be used to relate data in separate tables.

Nonredundant Data. Normalization of data is done to help eliminate redundancy in data. It does nothing to help redundancy in application development.

Data Language. The SQL language is typically used for the manipulation of tables.

Performance. Performance is a concern with highly complex data structures.

Object-Oriented Databases

Primary Goals. Encapsulation and class independence. Classes can be reorganized without affecting how they are used.

Data Plus Methods. The database stores data plus methods.

Encapsulation. Data can be used only by the methods of classes. Data is designed for use by specific methods only.

Active Objects. Objects are active. Requests cause objects to execute their methods. Some methods may be highly complex, for example those using rules and an inference engine.

Classes and Reusability. Objects are designed for high reusability and rarely change.

Complexity. Data structures may be complex. Users are unaware of the complexity because of encapsulation.

Interlinked Data. Data may be interlinked so that class methods achieve good performance. Tables are one of many data structures that may be used. Binary large objects (blobs) are used for sound, images, video, and large unstructured bit streams.

Nonredundant Methods. Nonredundant data and methods are achieved with encapsulation and inheritance. Inheritance helps to lower redundancy in methods, and class reuse helps to lower overall redundancy in development.

Object-Oriented Requests. Requests cause the execution of methods. Diverse methods can be used.

Class Optimization. The data for one object can be interlinked and stored together so that it can be accessed from one position of the access mechanism. Object-oriented databases give much higher performance than relational databases for certain applications with complex data.

(Continued)

BOX C.3   *(Continued)*

Different Conceptual Model. The model of data structure and access represented by tables and Join operations is different from that in analysis, design, and programming. Design must be translated into relational tables and SQL-style access.

Consistent Conceptual Model. The models used for analysis, design, programming, and database access and structure are similar. Application concepts are directly represented by classes in the object-oriented database. The more complex the application and its data structures, the more this saves time and money in application development.

A primary goal of relational databases is *data independence*. Data is normalized and completely separated from the processing that is performed on it. Thus, the data can be used for different applications, many of which may be unanticipated when the database is first designed.

A primary goal of the object-oriented database is *encapsulation*. The data is associated with a specific class that uses specific methods. The database stores that data plus the methods. The data and methods are inseparable. The data is not designed for any type of use but for use by the class. The class will be used in many different applications, many of which are not yet anticipated. We have class independence, not merely data independence.

With a relational database, the data can be physically reorganized without changing application programs that use the data. With an object-oriented database, the data and the methods associated with the class can be reorganized without disrupting systems that use the class.

Object-oriented databases support active objects, whereas traditional databases store passive data. As the world of computing progresses, more and more systems will be built that require the use of active objects.

The object-oriented database supports complex data structures and does not break them down into tables. Complex data structures are encapsulated in the classes, just as DNA is encapsulated in biological cells. To take highly complex data structures and decompose them into tables every time you store them has been likened to decomposing your car into its components every time you put it in the garage. The more complex the data structure, the greater the advantage of the object-oriented database. The cells in your body would be very inefficient if their DNA was stored in relational form and accessed with SQL.

Appendix D

Glossary

ACCESS. The operation of seeking, reading, or writing data on a storage unit.

ACCESS MECHANISM. A device for moving one or more reading and writing heads to the position over a data recording medium at which certain data is to be read or written. Alternatively, the storage medium may be moved to the access mechanism.

ACCESS METHOD. A technique for moving data between a computer and its peripheral devices: for example, serial access, random access, virtual sequential access method (VSAM), hierarchical indexed sequential access method (HISAM), access via *secondary indices*, and *relational* accesses such as joins, projects, or other relational algebra operations.

ACCESS TIME. The time that elapses between an instruction being given to access some data and that data becoming available for use.

ACTION. Something accomplished by a single program access command when using the database. A *simple action* is a command that creates, reads, updates, or deletes an instance of a single record. A *compound action* is a command that requires multiple instances of records because it performs a sort, search, join, projection, or other relational operation.

ACTIVITY RATIO. The fraction of records in a file or data set which have activity (are updated or inspected) in a given period or during a given run.

ADDRESS. An identification (number, name, label) for a location in which data is stored.

ADDRESSING. The means of assigning data to storage locations, and subsequently retrieving them, on the basis of the key of the data.

ALGORITHM. A computational procedure containing a finite sequence of steps.

ALL-KEY TABLE. A relational table where all columns (data elements) comprise the tables primary key. See also *Primary key.*

ALTERNATE KEY. In a situation in which two or more data elements can serve as primary keys, one data element is designated the primary key, and the remaining candidate keys are called alternate keys. See also *Primary key* and *Candidate key.*

ALTERNATE TRACK. A track that is automatically substituted for a damaged track on a disk or other storage device.

ALTER STATEMENT (SQL). A statement that can be issued to modify the characteristics of a table.

ANSI/SPARC. A study group within the American National Standards Institute (ANSI), called ANSI/Systems Planning and Requirements Committee (ANSI/SPARC), that was formed in 1975 to investigate database technology.

ANSI/SPARC DATABASE ARCHITECTURE. Database architecture, defined by the ANSI/SPARC Committee, defining three views of data: external schema, conceptual schema, and internal schema. Each of the data views is described separately, and ideally, a database management system should be capable of making the necessary transformations from one data view to another. See also *External schema, Conceptual schema,* and *Internal schema.*

ANTICIPATORY STAGING. Blocks of data are moved from one storage device to another device with a shorter access time, in anticipation of their being needed by the computer programs. This is to be contrasted with demand staging, in which the blocks of data are moved *when* programs require them, not *before.*

ASSOCIATION. A relationship between entities or data elements in a logical data model. See also *One-to-one association, One-to-many association, and Many-to-many association.*

ASSOCIATIVE STORAGE (MEMORY). Storage that is addressed by content rather than by location, thus providing a fast way to search for data with certain contents. (Conventional storage has addresses related to the physical location of the data.)

ATTRIBUTE. A piece of information that represents a single property of an entity. Sometimes called a nonprime attribute to distinguish data elements that are not part of a primary key from data elements that are part of a primary key. In a bubble chart, an attribute is a data element whose bubble has no one-to-one links leading to any other bubble.

AUTHENTICATION MECHANISM. Database software function that allows an information system to determine the identity of a user who is requesting access to a database. Systems of user IDs and passwords are often used to implement an authentication mechanism. See also *Authorization mechanism.*

AUTHORIZATION MECHANISM. Database software function that permits different users to be allowed or denied access to different parts of a database, and controls the operations a user can perform on data that can be accessed. The authorization mechanism can also be used by one user to control the authorizations given to other users. See also *Authentication mechanism.*

AVAILABILITY. A measure of the reliability of a system, showing the fraction of time when one performs a function as intended. Availability is calculated by dividing the time the function is performed as intended by the total time during which the function should have been performed.

BACHMAN NOTATION. User view and logical data model diagramming notation in which a single-head arrow indicates a "one" cardinality and a double-head arrow indicates a "many" cardinality. See also *Crow's-foot notation.*

BASE TABLE. In a relational database, a table that is not derived from other tables. See also *View.*

BINARY SEARCH. A method of searching a sequenced table or file. The procedure involves selecting the upper and lower half based on an examination of its midpoint value. The selected portion is then similarly halved, and so on until the required item is found.

BLOCKING. The combining of two or more physical records so that they are jointly read or written by one machine instruction.

BUBBLE CHART. A data modeling diagram, using crow's-foot notation, that consists of interconnected ellipses to show data elements and their associations. See also *Crow's-foot notation.*

BUCKET. An area of storage that may contain more than one physical record and that is referred to as whole by some addressing techniques.

BUFFER. An area of storage that holds data temporarily while it is being received, transmitted, read, or written. It is often used to compensate for differences in the speed or timing of devices. Buffers are used in terminals, peripheral devices, storage units, and in the CPU.

BUILT-IN FUNCTION (SQL). SQL includes a set of built-in functions that can be used with the SELECT statement to perform operations on a table or on sets of rows from a table.

BUSINESS AREA. Functional area of an enterprise that performs one or more business functions for which detailed logical data modeling can be performed.

BUSINESS ENTITY. See *Entity.*

CANDIDATE KEY. Two or more data elements, or groups of data elements, that can all serve as the primary key in a bubble chart, record diagram, or relational table.

CARTESIAN PRODUCT OPERATION. Operation defined by the relation in which each row of the first table is concatenated with each row of the second table and produces a result table with a number of rows that is the product of the number of rows in the first table and the number of rows in the second table. See also *Relational algebra.*

CATALOG. A directory of all files available to the computer.

CELL. Contiguous storage locations referred to as a group in an addressing or file-searching scheme. The cell may be such that it does not cross mechanical boundaries in the storage unit; for example, it could be a track or a cylinder.

CELLULAR CHAINS. Chains that are not permitted to cross cell boundaries.

CELLULAR MULTILIST. A form of multilist organization in which the chains cannot extend across cell boundaries.

CELLULAR SPLITTING. A technique for handling records added to a file. The records are organized into cells, and a cell is split into two cells when it becomes full.

CHAIN. An organization in which records or other items of data are strung together by means of pointers.

CHANNEL. In a mainframe computer, a subsystem handling input to an output from the central processing unit (CPU). Data from storage units, for example, flow into the CPU via a channel.

CHAR DATA TYPE (SQL). Used to define fixed-length character data. The length of the column is specified in parentheses following CHAR.

CHECKPOINT/RESTART. A means of restarting a program at some point other than the beginning, used after a failure or interruption has occurred. Checkpoints may be used at intervals throughout an application program; at these points records are written giving enough information about the status of the program to permit its being restarted at that point.

CIRCULAR FILE. An organization of a file of high volatility, in which new records being added replace the oldest records.

CLIENT. See *Client system.*

CLIENT PROCESS. In client/server computing, a process that makes a request for a service. See also *Client/server computing.*

CLIENT/SERVER. See *Client/server computing.*

CLIENT/SERVER COMPUTING. A broad computing paradigm in which an application's processing load can be distributed among a variety of processors, with each machine being assigned the tasks for which it is best suited. Some processors operate in the role of clients and make requests for services; other processors operate in the role of servers and accept requests from clients and pass results back.

CLIENT/SERVER DATABASE. A form of database that is implemented on one or more computing systems that play the role of server systems and that can be accessed by application programs running on other computing systems that play the role of client systems. See also *Client/server computing.*

CLIENT/SERVER SYSTEM. See *Client/server computing.*

CLIENT SYSTEM. In client/server computing, a computing system that makes a request for services that are provided by other computing systems that play the role of server systems.

CODASYL. Conference on Data System Languages. The organization that specified the programming language COBOL and has also specified a set of machine-independent and application-independent languages designed for database management operations on a database that implements a network database model. See also *Network database model.*

COMMIT STATEMENT (SQL). Statement used to establish a synchronization point indicating that all changes that have been made to resources up to that point are to be made permanent.

COMPACTION. A technique for reducing the number of bits in data without destroying any information content.

CONCATENATE. To link together. A concatenated key is composed of more than one data element. See also *Concatenated key.*

CONCATENATED KEY. Two or more data elements in a bubble chart, record diagram, or relational table that are combined to serve as a primary key.

CONCEPTUAL SCHEMA. Defined by the ANSI/SPARC database architecture as a computerized representation of a logical data model. See also *ANSI/SPARC database architecture, Logical data model, External schema,* and *Internal schema.*

CONDITION BOX (QBE). We create a condition box by issuing the DRAW COND command. QBE then adds a special table structure to the screen in which we can enter selection conditions.

CREATE VIEW STATEMENT (SQL). A statement used to create a view that provides an alternative way of looking at data stored in base tables. See also *View, Base table.*

CROW'S-FOOT NOTATION. Data modeling notation in which the following symbology is used to indicate cardinalities in associations:

　　　One cardinality:　　　————|——

　　　Many cardinality:　　　————< 　　See also *Bachman notation, Bubble chart.*

CURSOR. An SQL data object, supported by most relational database software, that allows an application program to operate on table data a row at a time.

CYLINDER. That area of a storage unit that can be read without the movement of an access mechanism. The term is typically used to describe disk drives, in which a cylinder consists of one track on each disk surface, such that all the tracks could have a read/write head positioned over them simultaneously.

DASD. Direct-access storage device.

DATA ADMINISTRATOR. An individual with an overview of an organization's data. The data administrator is responsible for designing the data model and obtaining agreement about the descriptions of data that are maintained in the data dictionary. The function is responsible for the most cost-effective organization and best use of an enterprise's data resources.

DATA AGGREGATE (CODASYL). A named collection of data elements within a record. There are two types: vectors and repeating groups. A vector is a one-dimensional, ordered collection of data elements, all of which have identical characteristics. A repeating group is a collection of data that occurs an arbitrary number of times within a record occurrence. The collection may consist of data elements, vectors, and repeating groups.

DATABASE. A stored collection of interrelated data elements that can be accessed in a shared manner by any number of computer applications.

DATABASE ADMINISTRATION. Personnel function or activity concerning the overall control of some or all of an organization's data and the policy-oriented tasks regarding data strategy and overall data planning. The database administrator is responsible for determining what in the business environment needs to be represented in the database. The database administrator may also work with end users and information systems staff members to document the data that will be stored in database form.

DATABASE CLIENT. In client/server computing, a computing system that sends requests for data access services to one or more other computing systems that play the role of database servers.

DATABASE DESIGN. Personnel function or activity concerning designing, controlling, and coordinating the data that is stored in an individual database. In many cases, the database designer may work closely with the database administrator to ensure that database design work is carefully coordinated throughout the organization.

DATABASE MANAGEMENT SYSTEM (DBMS). Software system used to access the data stored in a database and to present multiple different user views of the data to end users and application programmers. See also *Database, User view*.

DATABASE SERVER. In client/server computing, a computing system that runs database software, that accesses a database or a portion of a distributed database, and that provides services to other computing systems that play the role of database clients.

DATABASE SOFTWARE. Specialized software that serves as an intermediary between users or application programs and the files that implement a database.

DATABASE SYSTEM. Information system that uses a database as a repository for the data used by the system. See also *Database*.

DATABASE TRIGGER. A stored procedure, containing conditional statements and procedural code, that causes the database software to execute the procedural code when the specified condition is satisfied. See also *Stored procedure*.

DATA CONTROL LANGUAGE (DCL). A database language that allows people to perform administrative procedures relating to database objects, such as granting authorization to users for their access and requesting commitment or rollback functions.

DATA DEFINITION LANGUAGE. See *Data description language*.

DATA DESCRIPTION LANGUAGE (DDL). A database language that allows people to create, alter, and delete the various objects that implement the database, such as the tables, user views, domains, and indices of a relational database. Sometimes called a data definition language.

DATA DICTIONARY SOFTWARE. Database software implementing functions that help the organization to organize the names and descriptions of data elements. Advanced data dictionaries have functions that enable them to represent and report on the cross-references between components of data and business models. The data dictionary provides a central place to store data about data (meta-data).

DATA DIVISION (COBOL). That division of a COBOL program that consists of entries used to define the nature and characteristics of the data to be processed by the object program.

DATA ELEMENT. A single, atomic, piece of data that cannot be subdivided and still retain any meaning. The terms *data item* and *field* are often used synonymously with data element.

DATA INDEPENDENCE. Property of being able to change the overall logical or physical structure of the data without changing the application program's view of the data.

DATA MANAGEMENT. A general term that collectively describes those functions of an information system that provide creation of and access to stored data, enforce data storage conventions, and regulate the use of input/output devices.

DATA MANIPULATION LANGUAGE. The language which the programmer uses to cause data to be transferred between his program and the database. The data manipulation language is not a complete language by itself. It relies on a host programming language to provide a framework for it and to provide the procedural capabilities required to manipulate data.

DATA MODEL. See *Logical data model.*

DATA SET. A named collection of logically related data elements, arranged in a prescribed manner, and described by control information to which the programming system has access.

DBMS. Database management system.

DCL. Data Control Language.

DDL. Data Description Language.

DECIMAL DATA TYPE (SQL). Used for numbers with a fixed number of places after the decimal point. It is followed by two numbers in parentheses, where the first number indicates the number of digits in the number and the second the number of decimal positions.

DELETE STATEMENT (SQL). A statement used to delete rows from tables or views.

DEVICE INDEPENDENCE. Data organization that is independent of the device on which the data are stored.

DICTIONARY. See *Data dictionary software.*

DIFFERENCE OPERATION. Operation defined by relational algebra that combines two source tables to produce a result table containing only those rows that are in the first table and are not also in the second table. See also *Relational algebra.*

DIRECT ACCESS. Retrieval or storage of data by a reference to its location on a volume, rather than relative to the previously retrieved or stored data. The access mechanism goes directly to the data in question, as is normally required with online use of data.

DIRECT-ACCESS STORAGE DEVICE (DASD). Mainframe term referring to a data storage unit on which data can be accessed directly without having to progress through a serial file such as tape. A disk drive is a direct-access storage device.

DISTRIBUTED FREE SPACE. Space left empty at intervals in a data layout to permit the possible insertion of new data.

DISTRIBUTED RELATIONAL DATABASE ARCHITECTURE (DRDA). An IBM architecture describing an overall plan and strategy for the implementation of hardware and software to provide access to databases that are stored on more than one computing system.

DIVIDE OPERATION. An operation defined by relational algebra that produces a result table containing only columns from the dividend table that are not in the divisor table. See also *Relational algebra.*

DML. Data manipulation language.

DOMAIN. The set of values allowed for the data elements in a given column, or group of columns, of a relational database.

DRDA. Distributed Relational Database Architecture.

DROP STATEMENT (SQL). A statement that deletes a base table or view from a relational database.

DYNAMIC SQL. Type of SQL statements that an application program constructs as it executes rather than being compiled directly into the source code. See also *Static SQL.*

DYNAMIC STORAGE ALLOCATION. The allocation of storage space to a procedure based on the instantaneous or actual demand for storage space by that procedure, rather than allocating storage space to a procedure based on its anticipated or predicted demand.

EMBEDDED POINTERS. Pointers contained in the data records rather than in a directory or catalog.

ENTITY. Something about which information is stored. An entity might be a tangible object, such as an employee, a part, or a place. An entity can also be intangible, such as an event, a job title, a customer account, a profit center, or some abstract concept.

ENTITY INTEGRITY. A rule or constraint, defined by the relational data model, stating that a column (data element) that is part of a primary key can have a null value. This rule is necessary if the primary key is to fulfill its role of uniquely identifying the rows in a table.

ENTITY RECORD. A record containing the attributes pertaining to a given entity.

ENTITY-RELATIONSHIP DIAGRAM. Database analysis diagram that documents a map of the business entities about which information must be stored and shows the relationships that exist among them.

EQUIJOIN OPERATION. A Join operation in which an equal comparison in performing the Join. See also *Join operation.*

EXCLUSIVE-ACCESS LOCK. A lock that allows the lock owner to read and change the locked data in any desired way. No other user can access the locked data or acquire a lock on it while an exclusive-access lock is in effect. See also *Locking mechanism.*

EXTENDED ENTERPRISE. A view of an enterprise that includes the internal functions of the enterprise and also the functions of the organizations with which the enterprise interacts, including customers and suppliers.

EXTENT. A contiguous area of data storage.

EXTERNAL SCHEMA. Defined by the ANSI/SPARC database architecture as a computerized representation of a user view. See also *ANSI/SPARC database architecture, Conceptual schema,* and *Internal schema.*

FIFTH NORMAL FORM. A data structure is said to be in fifth normal form if it is in fourth normal form and if it also contains no join dependencies. See also *Normalization, Join dependency,* and *Fourth normal form.*

FIRST NORMAL FORM. A data structure is said to be in first normal form if it is in tabular form and contains no repeating data elements or repeating groups of data elements. A data structure in first normal form is often called a table or a flat file. See also *Normalization* and *Flat file.*

FLAT FILE. A two-dimensional array of data elements that constitutes a table in a relational database.

FLOAT DATA TYPE (SQL). Used for floating-point numbers.

FOREIGN KEY. A column (data element) in a relational database containing data element values drawn from the same domain as the column or columns that form the primary key in some other table.

FOURTH NORMAL FORM. A table is said to be in fourth normal form if it is in third normal form and also has a concatenated key such that no part of the concatenated key is unrelated to any of the other data elements making up the key. Fourth normal form involves the idea of multivalued dependencies, in which a given value for a single column identifies multiple values of another column. See also *Normalization, Concatenated key,* and *Third normal form.*

FULL OUTER JOIN OPERATION. See *Outer join operation.*

FUNCTIONAL DECOMPOSITION. Breaking the operations of an enterprise into a hierarchy of functions which are represented on a *function chart.*

FUNCTION CHART. A chart showing the *logical* operations carried out in an enterprise. A hierarchical breakdown of these operations is usually drawn. The lowest-level function in the hierarchy is called an *activity* and is the basis for the design of *physical* procedures.

GATEWAY. A computing system or software function that performs a protocol or API translation function and serves as an intermediary between computing systems or between communications networks.

GRANT STATEMENT (SQL). A statement used to give users authorization to perform certain operations on tables or views.

HIERARCHICAL DATABASE MODEL. A database architecture in which data elements are arranged in the form of an inverted tree structure in which no data element has more than one parent.

HIERARCHICAL FILE. A file in which some records are subordinate to others in a tree structure.

HOMONYM. A data element in a logical data model that has exactly the same name as some other data element but has a different meaning.

HOST LANGUAGE DATABASE SOFTWARE. Obsolete term characterizing a database software product that provides application programming support and that requires database applications to be written in a conventional programming language.

HOST VARIABLE (SQL). Names in an application program that are known to the application program but not to the database software. A host variable is generally a data element that is defined in the normal way in the application program.

HUFFMAN CODE. A code for data compaction in which frequently used characters are encoded with a smaller number of bits than infrequently used characters.

INDEX. Object implemented by some relational database software that controls the order in which a table is accessed or stored.

INDIRECT ADDRESSING. Any method of specifying or locating a storage location whereby the key (of itself or through calculation) does not represent an address: for example, locating an address through indices.

INFORMATION STRATEGY PLANNING (ISP). A function related to the high-level planning of an organization's information resources.

INNER JOIN OPERATION. A Join operation in which the result table consists only of those rows that satisfy the comparison operation on which the Join operation is based. With an inner join operation, there is a possibility that some of the rows from the source tables being joined will not be represented in the result table. See also *Join operation* and *Outer join operation.*

INSERT STATEMENT (SQL). A statement used to add new rows to tables or views.

INTELLIGENT DATABASE. A database that contains shared logic as well as shared data, and automatically invokes that logic when the data is accessed. Logic, constraints, and controls relating to the usage of the data are represented in an intelligent data model.

INTERNAL SCHEMA. Defined by the ANSI/SPARC database architecture as a computerized representation of the physical data structures. See also *ANSI/SPARC database architecture, Physical data structure, External schema,* and *Conceptual schema.*

INTERSECTING ATTRIBUTE. An attribute in a logical data model bubble chart with more than a single "one" link entering it.

INTERSECTION DATA. One or more data elements that are associated with the many-to-many association between two individual primary keys.

INTERSECTION OPERATION. An operation defined by relational algebra. The Intersection operator combines the rows from two tables to form a third table that contains only those rows that are in both of the original tables. See also *Relational algebra.*

INVERTED FILE. A file structure that permits fast spontaneous searching for previous unspecified information. Independent lists or indices are maintained in records keys which are accessible according to the values of specific fields.

ISAM. Indexed sequential access method.

ISOLATED ATTRIBUTE. An attribute in a logical data model bubble chart with no "one" links entering or leaving it (only "many" links).

ISP. Information strategy planning.

JOIN DEPENDENCY. A constraint in a relational database that determines which projections of a table can be validly rejoined. See also *Join operation, Normalization,* and *Fifth normal form.*

JOIN OPERATION. Operation, defined by relational algebra, that combines the rows from two or more source tables and results in a single result table. The Join operation must be based on one or more columns from each of the two tables whose data values share a common domain. The resulting table is formed in such a way that in each row, the data values from the two columns (or sets of columns) on which the join is based satisfy a comparison operator. The comparison operator specifies an equal comparison in most Join operations. See also *Inner join operation, Outer join operation.*

KEY. A data element or combination of data elements used to identify or locate a record occurrence (or other data grouping).

LATENCY. The time taken for a storage location to reach the read/write heads on a rotating surface. For general timing purposes, average latency is used; this is the time taken by one half-revolution of the surface.

LEFT OUTER JOIN OPERATION. See *Outer join operation.*

LOCKING MECHANISM. A software mechanism that controls whether some other user can access a resource, and if so, in what way. *See also Shared-access lock, Update-access lock,* and *Exclusive-access lock.*

LOGICAL DATA MODEL. A data structure documenting the entire collection of data elements, and their associations, that will be stored in database form to support a business function. The logical data model documents the organization's overall view of a database. It is a logical map that identifies all the data stored in a database and combines all the individual user views into one integrated structure. See also *User view* and *Physical data structure.*

MAINFRAME. Computer system typically costing in the millions of dollars and requiring a specialized room with raised flooring to hide interconnections between components.

MANY-TO-MANY ASSOCIATION. A relationship between two entities or data elements in which zero, one, or multiple occurrences of the first entity or data element are related to zero, one, or multiple occurrences of the second entity or data element. See also *One-to-one association* and *One-to-many association.*

META-DATA. Data about data.

MINICOMPUTER. Computer system, typically costing in the tens to hundreds of thousands of dollars, serving multiple users; or a system serving a single user for specialized applications, such as engineering design or advanced computer graphics.

MULTILIST ORGANIZATION. A *chained* file organization in which the chains are divided into fragments and each fragment is indexed, to permit faster searching.

MULTIVALUED DEPENDENCY. A dependency defined in terms of the set of values from one column that is associated with a given pair of values from two other columns.

NATURAL JOIN OPERATION. An Equijoin operation with one of the identical columns eliminated. See also *Equijoin operation* and *Join operation.*

NESTED QUERY (SQL). A query in which one SELECT statement is nested within an outer SELECT statement. The nested SELECT is called a subselect or subquery.

NETWORK. Collection of computer systems interconnected by data communications facilities. See also *Network database model.*

NETWORK DATABASE MODEL. A database architecture that permits data elements to be associated in an arbitrary graph structure, instead of in a strict hierarchy.

NONPRIME ATTRIBUTE. An attribute that has no one-to-one association with any other attribute and so is not part of the primary key of a record or data element grouping. Same as attribute.

NORMALIZATION. Procedure used to place data elements into tables, according to a set of dependency rules, in such a way as to create stable data structures that minimize data redundancy and maximize data independence. See also *First normal form, Second normal form, Third normal form, Fourth normal form,* and *Fifth normal form.*

NORMALIZED DATA STRUCTURE. A data structure from which repeating groups have been removed in order to place the data into the tables of a relational database. This level of normalization, in which the data has been placed into first normal form, is the only level of normalization that is addressed by the relational data model itself. Further normalization is possible and desirable. See also *First normal form, Second normal form, Third normal form, Fourth normal form,* and *Fifth normal form.*

OBJECT-ORIENTED DATABASE (OODB). A database (used to store the objects that form the basis of object-oriented computing) that consists of data as well as references to the procedures that are used to perform operations on that data.

ODBC. Open Database Connectivity.

ONE-TO-MANY ASSOCIATION. A relationship between two entities or data elements in which each occurrence of one entity or data element is related to zero, one, or multiple occurrences of the second entity or data element. See also *One-to-one association* and *Many-to-many association.*

ONE-TO-ONE ASSOCIATION. A relationship between two entities or data elements in which each occurrence of one entity or data element is related to a single occurrence of the second entity or data element. See also *One-to-many association* and *Many-to-many association.*

ONLINE STORAGE. Storage devices, especially the storage media they contain, under the direct control of a computing system, not offline or in a volume library.

OODB. Object-oriented database.

OPEN DATABASE CONNECTIVITY (ODBC). A database application programming interface (API) standard published by Microsoft Corporation.

OPEN SYSTEMS COMPUTING. A form of computing, relying heavily on international standards, that is designed to allow computing equipment and software from many different vendors to be used cooperatively to solve business problems.

OUTER JOIN OPERATION. A Join operation in which all rows in one or both of two tables being joined are represented in the result table, even if values that satisfy the comparison operation are not found for one or more rows. A left outer join operation consists of the results of an inner join operation plus the information from the rows in the source table on the left that were excluded from the result of the inner join. A right outer join operation consists of the results of an inner join operation plus the information from the rows in the source table on the right that were excluded from the result of the inner join. A full outer join operation consists of the results of an inner join operation plus the information from the rows in both source tables that were excluded from the result of the inner join. See also *Join operation* and *Inner join operation.*

PARTITIONING. A method of dividing a database into multiple segments such that each segment can be stored in a different location. See also *Replication.*

PERSONAL COMPUTER. Inexpensive computer system that serves the needs of a single user, typically for business or productivity applications.

PHYSICAL DATA STRUCTURE. The actual files, data element occurrences, indices, pointers, and other data structures that are used to physically implement a logical data model in a computer system. See also *User view* and *Logical data model.*

POINTER. The address of a record (or other data groupings) that can be used to locate the record in a database or file. The address can be absolute, relative, or symbolic.

PRIMARY KEY. A data element or group of data elements that relate in a one-to-one association with one or more other data elements. A primary key is said to identify one or more other data elements. See also *One-to-one association.*

PROJECT OPERATION. An operation defined by relational algebra that accepts a source table and produces a result table containing all the rows from the source table, but only specified columns. See also *Relational algebra.*

PROTOCOL. Term referring to a specification defining the formats of messages that are exchanged between two communicating machines or processes and the rules that govern how those messages are exchanged.

QBE. Query by Example.

QUERY BY EXAMPLE (QBE). An easy-to-use database language that allows the user to formulate queries and manipulate data using a tabular data format that is ideally suited to working with a relational database. Many modern database software products provide an end-user-oriented query and data manipulation.

RDA. Relational Database Access.

RECORD DIAGRAM. A database diagram in which a primary key and the attributes it identifies are placed in adjacent boxes making up record groupings. Only the associations between primary keys are explicitly shown in a record diagram.

REFERENTIAL INTEGRITY. A rule or constraint, defined by the relational data model, stating that every foreign key value in one table must either match a primary key value in some other table, or it must be wholly null.

RELATION. A flat file. One of the tables making up a relational database.

RELATIONAL ALGEBRA. A set of relational operators that can be applied to one or more source tables to produce one or more result tables. See also *Restrict operation, Project operation, Divide operation, Join operation, Union operation, Cartesian Product operation, Intersection operation,* and *Difference operation.*

RELATIONAL DATABASE. A database made up of tabular data structures that conforms to the relational database model. See also *Relational database model.*

RELATIONAL DATABASE ACCESS (RDA). A database access protocol standard defined by X/Open, an international standards organization.

RELATIONAL DATABASE MODEL. A database architecture that presents a generalized way of thinking about data that is described in terms of objects, operators that can be applied to those objects, and a set of integrity rules. Data in the relational database model is represented in the form of one or more tabular data structures consisting of rows and columns.

RELATIONAL OPERATION. See *Relational algebra.*

REPLICATION. A method of physically implementing a database in which certain data element values from the database are stored in multiple locations, possibly to make the database more available and resistant to failures. Entire databases can be replicated, or, if partitioning is also used, selected sections of the database that have been split up using partitioning can be replicated. See also *Partitioning.*

RESTRICT OPERATION. Operation defined by relational algebra that accepts a source table and produces a result table containing all the columns from the source table but only specified rows. See also *Relational algebra.*

REVOKE STATEMENT (SQL). A statement used to remove an authorization previously granted with a GRANT statement. See also *GRANT statement.*

RIGHT OUTER JOIN OPERATION. See *Outer join operation.*

ROLLBACK STATEMENT (SQL). A statement used to indicate that changes made to the database up to the most recent synchronization point are to be reversed, thus restoring the database to the condition in which it existed prior to the establishment of that synchronization point.

ROOT KEY. A primary key in a logical data model that has no "one" link leaving it to another key. A logical data model diagram should be drawn so that the root keys are at the top, with "one" links between keys pointing upward where possible.

ROW. A row in a relational database represents a particular entity occurrence. A particular row contains a set of data elements, one for each column in the table.

SCHEMA. In the ANSI/SPARC database architecture, a computerized representation of a view of the data represented in a database. See also *External schema, Conceptual schema,* and *Internal schema.*

SEARCH KEY. Synonymous with *secondary key.*

SECONDARY KEY. A data element in a logical data model that has no one-to-one associations with any other data elements but has one or more one-to-many associations with other data elements.

SECOND NORMAL FORM. A data structure is said to be in second normal form if it is in first normal form and each attribute in the data structure is dependent on all the data elements making up the primary key and not on any subset of them. See also *Normalization* and *First normal form.*

SELECT STATEMENT (SQL). A statement used to specify database retrievals and to create alternative views of the data contained in one or more base tables.

SELF-CONTAINED DATABASE SOFTWARE. Obsolete term characterizing a database software product that provides its own built-in language and other facilities for accessing a database and for creating database applications.

SEQUENTIAL PROCESSING. Accessing records in ascending sequence by key; the next record accessed will have the next higher key, regardless of its physical position in the file.

SERIAL PROCESSING. Accessing records in their physical sequence. The next record accessed will be the record in the next physical position/location in the field.

SERVER PROCESS. In client/server computing, a process that performs a service for some other process. See also *Client/server computing* and *Client process.*

SERVER SYSTEM. In client/server computing, a computing system that provides services to application programs that run on other computing systems and that play the role of client systems.

SHARED-ACCESS LOCK. A lock that allows the lock owner and other concurrent users to read the locked data but not to change it. Other users can also acquire a shared-access or update-access lock on the data after the first user has acquired a shared access lock on it. See also *Locking mechanism* and *Update-access lock.*

SQL. Structured Query Language.

SQL SCHEMA. In the Structured Query Language (SQL) international standard, a computerized representation of the data in a relational database on which a set of SQL statements operates.

STATIC SQL. SQL statements that are compiled directly into an application program and that cannot be modified at execution time. See also *Dynamic SQL.*

STORED PROCEDURE. A set of procedural code stored in the database that is executed by the database software either on demand by an application program or when an associated database trigger is activated.

STRUCTURED QUERY LANGUAGE (SQL). A database language, containing statements making up a data description language (DDL), data manipulation language (DML) and data control language (DCL) that can be used to perform operations on the data in a relational database. SQL has become an accepted standard that most relational database products implement.

SYNONYM. A data element that has a different name from some other data element, but has an identical meaning as that data element.

THIRD NORMAL FORM. A data structure is said to be in third normal form if it is in second normal form and every nonkey column is nontransitively dependent on the primary key. See also *Normalization* and *Second normal form.*

THREE-SCHEMA ARCHITECTURE. Database architecture that permits user views, the logical data model, and physical data structures to be specified independently. The database software then performs the transformations that are necessary to convert from one form of representation to the others. See also *ANSI/SPARC database architecture, External schema, Internal schema, User view, Logical data model,* and *Physical data structure.*

TRIGGER. See *Database trigger.*

UNION OPERATION. An operation defined by relational algebra in which the rows from two source tables are combined to form a result table containing those rows that are in either or both of the source tables. See also *Relational algebra.*

UPDATE-ACCESS LOCK. A lock that allows the lock owner to read the locked data with an intent to change it. When the owner finally does change the data, the lock is typically changed to an exclusive-access lock. Other users can acquire shared-access locks and read the data while the lock remains an update-access lock. See also *Locking mechanism* and *Exclusive-access lock.*

UPDATE STATEMENT (SQL). A statement used to change the values in existing rows in base tables or views.

USER VIEW. Collection of data elements and their associations that is perceived by one or more end users or by an individual application program or group of related application programs. A user view generally encompasses only a subset of the data elements that are stored in a database. See also *Logical data model* and *Physical data structure.*

VIEW. A virtual table that is produced by performing one or more relational operations on one or more base tables. See also *Base table.*

WHENEVER STATEMENT (SQL). A statement that specifies processing to be performed whenever a particular type of condition occurs and applies to *all* SQL statements that follow it in the source listing.

Index

The Conceptual Prism of Information Technology:

THE JAMES MARTIN BOOKS

Information Technology Management and Strategy

AN INFORMATION SYSTEMS MANIFESTO

INFORMATION ENGINEERING (Book I: Introduction)

INFORMATION ENGINEERING (Book II: Planning and Analysis)

STRATEGIC INFORMATION PLANNING METHODOLOGIES (second edition)

SOFTWARE MAINTENANCE: THE PROBLEM AND ITS SOLUTIONS

DESIGN AND STRATEGY FOR DISTRIBUTED DATA PROCESSING

Expert Systems

BUILDING EXPERT SYSTEMS: A TUTORIAL

Methodologies for Building Systems

STRATEGIC INFORMATION PLANNING METHODOLOGIES (second edition)

INFORMATION ENGINEERING (Book I: Introduction)

INFORMATION ENGINEERING (Book II: Planning and Analysis)

INFORMATION ENGINEERING (Book III: Design and Construction)

STRUCTURED TECHNIQUES: THE BASIS FOR CASE (revised edition)

Object-Oriented Programming

OBJECT-ORIENTED ANALYSIS AND DESIGN

PRINCIPLES OF OBJECT-ORIENTED ANALYSIS AND DESIGN

OBJECT-ORIENTED METHODS: A FOUNDATION

OBJECT-ORIENTED METHODS: THE PRAGMATICS

OBJECT-ORIENTED TOOLS

Analysis and Design

STRUCTURED TECHNIQUES: THE BASIS FOR CASE (revised edition)

DATABASE ANALYSIS AND DESIGN

DESIGN OF MAN-COMPUTER DIALOGUES

DESIGN OF REAL-TIME COMPUTER SYSTEMS

DATA COMMUNICATIONS DESIGN TECHNIQUES

DESIGN AND STRATEGY FOR DISTRIBUTED DATA PROCESSING

SOFTWARE MAINTENANCE: THE PROBLEM AND ITS SOLUTIONS

SYSTEM DESIGN FROM PROVABLY CORRECT CONSTRUCTS

INFORMATION ENGINEERING (Book II: Planning and Analysis)

INFORMATION ENGINEERING (Book III: Design and Construction)

CASE

STRUCTURED TECHNIQUES: THE BASIS FOR CASE (revised edition)

INFORMATION ENGINEERING (Book I: Introduction)

Languages and Programming

APPLICATION DEVELOPMENT WITHOUT PROGRAMMERS

FOURTH-GENERATION LANGUAGES (Volume I: Principles)

FOURTH-GENERATION LANGUAGES (Volume II: Representative 4GLs)

FOURTH-GENERATION LANGUAGES (Volume III: 4GLs from IBM)

Diagramming Techniques

DIAGRAMMING TECHNIQUES FOR ANALYSTS AND PROGRAMMERS

RECOMMENDED DIAGRAMMING STANDARDS FOR ANALYSTS AND PROGRAMMERS

ACTION DIAGRAMS: CLEARLY STRUCTURED SPECIFICATIONS, PROGRAMS, AND PROCEDURES (second edition)